T0400133

Interpreting Music Video

Interpreting Music Video introduces students to the musical, visual, and sociological aspects of music videos, enabling them to critically analyze a multimedia form with a central place in popular culture.

With highly relevant examples drawn from recent music videos across many different genres, this concise and accessible book brings together tools from musical analysis, film and media studies, gender and sexuality studies, and critical race studies, requiring no previous knowledge in any of these fields.

Exploring the multiple dimensions of music videos, this book is the perfect introduction to critical analysis for students of music, media studies, communications, and popular culture.

Brad Osborn is associate professor of music theory and affiliated faculty in American studies at the University of Kansas. His monograph *Everything in its Right Place: Analyzing Radiohead* was published in 2017. Along with Larry Starr and Christopher Waterman, he is the co-author of the textbook *American Popular Music* (6th edition ff.).

Interpreting Music Video

Popular Music in the Post-MTV Era

Brad Osborn

Routledge
Taylor & Francis Group

NEW YORK AND LONDON

First published 2021
by Routledge
52 Vanderbilt Avenue, New York, NY 10017

and by Routledge
2 Park Square, Milton Park, Abingdon, Oxon, OX14 4RN

Routledge is an imprint of the Taylor & Francis Group, an informa business

© 2021 Brad Osborn

The right of Brad Osborn to be identified as author of this work has
been asserted by him in accordance with sections 77 and 78 of the
Copyright, Designs and Patents Act 1988.

All rights reserved. No part of this book may be reprinted or
reproduced or utilised in any form or by any electronic, mechanical,
or other means, now known or hereafter invented, including
photocopying and recording, or in any information storage or
retrieval system, without permission in writing from the publishers.

Trademark notice: Product or corporate names may be trademarks
or registered trademarks, and are used only for identification and
explanation without intent to infringe.

Library of Congress Cataloging-in-Publication Data
Names: Osborn, Brad, author.
Title: Interpreting music video: popular music in the
post-MTV era / Brad Osborn.
Description: New York: Routledge, 2021. | Includes bibliographical
references and index.
Identifiers: LCCN 2020045350 (print) | LCCN 2020045351 (ebook) |
ISBN 9780367479985 (paperback) | ISBN 9780367479992 (hardback) |
ISBN 9781003037576 (ebook)
Subjects: LCSH: Music videos—History and criticism. |
Music videos—Social aspects.
Classification: LCC PN1992.8.M87 O85 2021 (print) |
LCC PN1992.8.M87 (ebook) | DDC 302.23/1—dc23
LC record available at https://lccn.loc.gov/2020045350
LC ebook record available at https://lccn.loc.gov/2020045351

ISBN: 978-0-367-47999-2 (hbk)
ISBN: 978-0-367-47998-5 (pbk)
ISBN: 978-1-003-03757-6 (ebk)

Typeset in Stone Serif
by codeMantra

eResources accessible at: www.routledge.com/9780367479985

Contents

Introduction		*1*
The Cultural Moment for Music Videos		1
Music Videos: Then and Now		1
Scope and Uses of the Book		7
Using This Book in the Classroom		10
UNIT 1	*Interpreting Music*	*13*
CHAPTER 1	*Form*	*15*
	Two Standard Song Forms	16
	Other Sections	19
	Other Song Forms	22
	Song Form vs. Video Form	24
	Deep Dive: Doja Cat "Juicy" (2019)	26
CHAPTER 2	*Sound Analysis*	*31*
	Instrumentation	31
	Common Instruments	32
	Uncommon Instruments and Effects	38
	Deep Dive: Rihanna (ft. Jay-Z) "Umbrella" (2007)	45
CHAPTER 3	*Lyrics*	*51*
	Pronouns and Persona	52
	Common Themes	55
	Deep Dive: Sia "Chandelier" (2014)	59

UNIT 2 — *Interpreting Visuals* — 63

CHAPTER 4 — *Narrative* — 65

Narrative Strategies — 65

Intertextual Videos — 70

Mise-En-Scène — 74

Deep Dive: Yola "Ride Out in the Country" (2019) — 79

CHAPTER 5 — *Cinematography* — 83

Color and Light — 84

Camera Angles and Movement — 90

Deep Dive: Janelle Monae (ft. Grimes) "PYNK" (2018) — 94

CHAPTER 6 — *Editing and Special Effects* — 101

Editing Basics — 101

Editing to Rhythm and Form — 107

Special Effects — 111

Deep Dive: Travis Scott "Sicko Mode" (2018) — 117

UNIT 3 — *Interpreting Sociology* — 123

CHAPTER 7 — *Sexuality and Gender Diversity* — 125

Sexuality and Gender in Music Video — 126

Women in Music Video — 128

Deep Dive: Avicii (ft. Salem al Fakir) "Silhouettes" (2012) — 136

CHAPTER 8 — *Representing Race and Ethnicity* — 143

Race and Ethnicity in Music Videos — 144

A History of BIPOC Musicians on MTV — 146

BIPOC Musicians after MTV — 151

Deep Dive: Kendrick Lamar "Alright" (2015) — 155

CHAPTER 9 — *Music Video and Politics* — 161

Censorship — 161

Political Music Videos — 167

Deep Dive: The 1975 "Love It If We Made It" (2018) — 172

Index — 179

INTRODUCTION CLIP LIST

YEAR	ARTIST	VIDEO
1986	Peter Gabriel	Sledgehammer
1990	C&C Music Factory	Everybody Dance Now
1999	Limp Bizkit	Nookie
2004	Jay-Z	99 Problems
2006	Tego Calderón	Chillin'
2012	Psy	Gangnam Style
2018	Cardi B and Bruno Mars	Finesse
2018	Drake	In My Feelings
2020	MK XYZ	Pass It
2020	Becky G	My Man

INTRODUCTION

- The Cultural Moment for Music Videos
- Music Videos: Then and Now
- Scope and Uses of the Book
  - *Audience*
  - *Selection of Videos*
  - *Chapter Outlines*
- Using This Book in the Classroom

Introduction

THE CULTURAL MOMENT FOR MUSIC VIDEOS

Over the past 50 years music consumers have grown accustomed to changes in audio media. The LP record gave way to the cassette tape, which eventually led to CDs. However artistic they may have been, music videos aired on cable television networks were conceived as an advertisement for these physical audio media on which an artist's income depended. Of course, YouTube has now replaced cable television as the primary place people watch music videos in the new millennium. But what's remarkable is that YouTube views now account for more than half of all streaming *music*, surpassing CDs, tapes, records, and even audio services such as Apple Music and Spotify. Let's take a minute to examine the gravity of that last fact.

In the new millennium most consumers traded their individual physical recordings for iPods and other portable .mp3 players, and eventually relinquished ownership of audio files altogether in order to access vast libraries of music with subscription-based services such as Apple Music and Spotify. However, all of these media were vessels for audio-only recordings.[1] With YouTube now accounting for a majority of all music accessed, we have seen a seismic shift in which the dominant musical medium is no longer audio, but video. mp4 is the new mp3.[2] Musicians' financial incentives for making videos have also done a 180. With artists earning per-click royalties on YouTube—not to mention revenue through product placements—music videos are no longer advertisements for physical media to be sold. Music videos and live performances have become the vehicles through which artists make money, with royalties from audio-only plays paling in comparison. Many no longer even produce physical media.

These combined shifts in musical media, finances, and access have resulted in what is clearly a cultural moment for music videos. *Interpreting Music Video* introduces students to the musical, visual, and sociological aspects of these changes. The book acquaints students with tools from musical analysis, film and media studies, women, gender and sexuality studies, and critical race theory without requiring previous knowledge of these fields. Because today's students are immersed in music videos (48 of the top 50 current YouTube clips are music videos), these tools are presented as something highly relevant to interpreting their viral pop culture.

MUSIC VIDEOS: THEN AND NOW

For a certain generation, music videos are nearly synonymous with Music Television, better known as the cable network MTV. MTV began in 1981, infamously, as a network for "rock"

2 INTRODUCTION

music videos—meaning that it excluded hip-hop music by African Americans (the long struggle for representation of BIPOC musicians in music videos is addressed in Chapter 8). To honor the best music videos created each year, MTV created their own Video Music Awards (VMA) show. Peter Gabriel's 1986 video "Sledgehammer" (Figure 0.1), with ten awards given in a single night, still holds the all-time record for most awards won by a single video. Despite MTV no longer playing music videos, VMAs are still given each year (largely to videos that are only watched on YouTube), somehow retaining the same gold standard enjoyed by The Emmy Awards for television and The Oscars for film.

In order to add structure to a 24-hour cycle of music videos, and to target advertisements to a select demographic, the network created specially curated shows that focused on a single genre. *120 Minutes* (1986–2000) and *Alternative Nation* (1992–1997) focused on alternative rock and grunge music created by mostly white musicians directed at a mostly white audience. *Yo! MTV Raps* (1988–1995) promoted videos by Black and Latinx artists, though it's important to note that MTV exercised a heavy hand in censoring expression by BIPOC artists (see Chapter 8). C&C Music Factory's listener-friendly dance hit "Everybody Dance Now" (Figure 0.2) was nominated for seven VMAs in 1991 (including Video of the Year), with political/controversial rappers Queen Latifah, N.W.A., and Public Enemy receiving no nominations at all.

Throughout the 1990s MTV also attempted to drum up a buzz around what they considered the most important videos on the network by promoting them as "Buzzworthy," "Buzz Clips," or "From the Buzz Bin."[3] This curatorial role put the network in the position of tastemaker for millions of viewers, which had a direct effect on the artists' success. While in 1991 almost 40% of "buzzworthy" videos were by BIPOC musicians, from 1992 to 1999 that number dropped to just 10%. By the end of the decade MTV was promoting Buzz Clips by white male bands with misspelled names and misogynistic lyrics. Videos such as Limp Bizkit's "Nookie" (Figure 0.3) took musical and visual elements from Latinx and Black culture and packaged them in a more attractive format for suburban audiences.

MTV was not the only cable network on which Americans watched music videos. In the United States alone, Country Music Television (CMT, 1983–), the Canadian network MuchMusic (1984–), and VH1 (1985–) were all dedicated music video networks with wide circulation. While not a dedicated music video network per se, BET (Black Entertainment

Figure 0.1 Peter Gabriel Sledgehammer (1:02)

Figure 0.2 C&C Music Factory "Everybody Dance Now" (2:48)

Figure 0.3 Limp Bizkit "Nookie" (1:03)

Television) played a great deal of live music performances and music videos, including a specialty program called *Rap City* (1989–2008) that was hugely influential in the spread of hip-hop during its golden age. *Rap City* played Jay-Z's controversial video "99 Problems" despite pressure from a number of censorship angles, including graphic gun violence as well as animal rights agencies' concerns over dogfighting in the video (Figure 0.4).

MTV continued to play music videos almost exclusively until around 1994, when their own reality show *The Real World* proved more lucrative. By the turn of the millennium MTV had moved nearly all of their music video programing to separate cable *networks* (MTV2, MTV Tr3s (aka MTV Español), etc.) to free up primetime for reality programming. Customers willing to shell out the money for these premium cable packages could access music videos that were much more popular internationally than in the States. For example, Puerto Rican reggaeton musician Tego Calderón's "Chillin" (2006), a hugely popular Spanish-language video shot on location in Jamaica, was in heavy rotation on MTV Tr3s, yet never reached mainstream US airplay (Figure 0.5).

4 INTRODUCTION

Figure 0.4 Graphic content in Jay-Z "99 Problems" (3:52)

Figure 0.5 Tego Calderón "Chillin'" (1:50)

With few networks playing music videos on harder-to-access cable stations, music videos sagged in cultural relevance in the mid-2000s. It was actually a few years after YouTube was released that music videos became popular on the network—largely due to bandwidth constraints (I remember having the same frustration trying to stream a music video in the late 2000s as I experienced trying to download an .mp3 in my dorm room just a decade earlier). It's hard to overstate the sea change in music videos brought about by the migration from cable networks to YouTube. Perhaps the most important change is the removal of the parallel functions of gatekeeper and tastemaker that cable networks had been playing in the distribution of videos. With artists and record companies able to release whatever they want, whenever they want, the world of music videos was no longer curated by cable networks or censored according to what their advertisers demanded. Music videos are now posted to a number of sites—particularly the artist-only hub VEVO, which links directly to YouTube—but they are circulated in a fully democratic manner through social media. Videos such as "Gangnam Style," by the Korean pop artist Psy, that contained dance sequences likely to be recirculated as memes (Figure 0.6), were particularly prone to going viral. In 2012 "Gangnam Style" became the first video of any type to reach one billion views on YouTube, and remained the most-watched video on the network until 2017.

INTRODUCTION **5**

Figure 0.6 Meme-ready dance sequence in Psy "Gangnam Style" (1:13)

Figure 0.7 Social media influencer Lil' Nas X

This change in distribution has also triggered a change in the kind of content being produced and the kinds of people who get to participate. Several of today's hottest music video stars got their start not with an A&R executive at a major record label, but through music-based social media hubs. American pop star Billie Eilish got her start on Soundcloud.com in 2015, was shortly afterward signed to Interscope, and swept the 2020 Grammy awards, winning five awards including Album of the Year, Record of the Year, Song of the Year, and, of course, Best New Artist.

While Soundcloud and Bandcamp are largely audio-based social media hubs, the multimedia hub TikTok has also produced notable music video stars. Users are able to post short videos of themselves singing, lip-synching, dancing, or responding in any way they want to music—whether they created that music or not. After an amateur Atlanta-based hip-hop artist called Lil' Nas X (Figure 0.7) self-released "Old Town Road" on various internet channels, a viral campaign took over TikTok, in which users performed a choreographed dance to the track. A later remix of the track went on to break a number of records, including the most number of streams in a single week (143 million), and longest run at #1 (17 weeks) on the Billboard *Hot 100*.

6 INTRODUCTION

And although it's true that the broader social acceptance of BIPOC and LGBTQ+ musicians has changed since the days of MTV, it's hard to imagine MTV ever playing a video like "Pass It," by the half-Filipino half-Black queer rapper MK XYZ. While her look, sound, and swagger owe a good deal of debt to Missy Elliott (Figure 0.8), the lyrics and visuals would have never passed muster a generation earlier. MK XYZ holds up photographs of nude women and simulates cunnilingus while rapping explicitly about her emotionless sexual conquests of women.

Being circulated through social media, that marketplace of memes, has allowed music video to respond to viral culture with remarkable speed and fluency. On June 29, 2018, a popular comedian named Shiggy posted a video on Instagram of himself dancing to the track "In My Feelings" by the Canadian rapper Drake. Thirty-four days later, on August 2, Drake released his official video for the track, containing footage of people dancing (mostly amateurs, but also celebrities such as Will Smith, see Figure 0.9). Music video had gone from influencer to influenced.

Of course, not all artists want to be of the moment. The recent popularity of 1990s fashion, as well as drum machine and keyboard sounds associated with 1990s pop and dance music, has led to a few notable "throwback" videos of late. Cardi B and Bruno Mars released

Figure 0.8 MK XYZ "Pass It" (0:12)

Figure 0.9 Will Smith cameo in Drake's "In My Feelings" (7:54)

Figure 0.10 Throwback costumes and set design in Cardi B and Bruno Mars "Finesse" (2:43)

"Finesse" in 2018, in which they dance in bright baggy clothing (as was the fashion of the 1990s) entirely on a soundstage replicating the set design of the iconic 1990s variety show *In Living Colour*. Ironically, while the video bucks the modern 16:9 aspect ratio in favor of the boxier 4:3 common in 1990s television (Figure 0.10), it's shot at a much higher frame rate—60 frames-per-second (FPS)—relative to the 24 FPS television standard, giving the video a flair of the uncanny. Pop stars Charli XCX and Troye Sivan recently collaborated on "1999," a parody video that imagines the millennial duo in iconic 1990s movies (e.g. *Titanic*), advertisements (e.g. Sketchers), and even music videos (e.g. TLC's "Waterfalls"). The lyrics are full of reminiscences about collecting CDs and other things the duo was likely too young for in 1999 (they were born in 1992 and 1995, respectively).

And yet music video continues to respond to the blinding pace of culture with remarkable fluency. Mexican-American singer Becky G's video "My Man," released on July 9, 2020, is one of the first videos to be shot entirely in quarantine due to the outbreak of COVID-19 in the United States, which began to shut down businesses just a few months earlier. Becky sings over a mariachi/reggaeton track while she and her partner (the Argentine-American soccer star Sebastian Lletget) capture their daily life in and around their apartment using amateur handheld and stationary camera angles. The video was then sent off for post-production where it was adorned with annotations evoking video games (Figure 0.11), a commentary on how many of us during the time of quarantine turned normal household activities into a "game" of sorts to keep us occupied, as well as a reflection of the huge influence video games have cast not only on music video graphics but on our culture as a whole.

SCOPE AND USES OF THE BOOK

Audience

The primary market for *Interpreting Music Video* is the large-enrollment undergraduate survey on popular music found at virtually every college and university. My primary argument for replacing (or at least supplementing) the most commonly adopted texts for such a course is twofold. First, in this, the cultural moment for music videos, a course that only or primarily examines recorded audio is missing at least half of the picture for music made after

8 INTRODUCTION

Figure 0.11 COVID-19 quarantine in Becky G "My Man" (1:37)

1981—especially for a contemporary art form that is now conceived *prima facie* as a multimedia product. Second, by analyzing music video, this book opens up myriad possibilities for assessing cinematography, gender, race, and fashion elements that are simply absent in the records, tapes, and CDs discussed in current texts.

For high school or college courses devoted to subjects related to popular music studies— be it media studies, cultural studies, or a dedicated course on music videos themselves (such as I teach at my university)—I have paced the content of this book such that it is possible to cover the topic in either a 16-week semester or 10-week quarter. Since the text is not particularly dense or wordy, reading-intensive courses at both the graduate and undergraduate level can easily incorporate selections from the book as part of a much larger reading list. To support instructors using the book for these purposes, I have included a number of pedagogical resources on the book's website (www.routledge.com/9780367479985), including:

- Slide decks for each chapter (Powerpoint, Keynote, or PDF) for in-class lecture
- Question sets for each chapter to be used for discussion, quizzes, or tests
- Writing prompts for end-of-unit projects, plus a video-creation final project

For those wishing to use this book as an educational resource, my goal is to make it as plug-and-play as possible. If you've wanted to teach students about music videos, but didn't know where to start, this is the book for you.

As a music video scholar, when I started writing this book the early drafts were plagued with parenthetical citations, discussions of published articles dealing with the various topics, and other standard fodder one expects to find in academic journals. But at some point, I realized this was not the niche that this book was meant to fill. With so many scholarly contributions to the field of music video analysis appearing in the past ten years, this book aims instead to guide readers in their own act of *interpreting* music video. My focus throughout the book is to show you how to hear and see what's happening in music videos, and how to use these observations to build your own interpretation. Because I realize that some readers will wish to consult more scholarly sources on some topics, I have provided a few citations and suggestions for further reading as endnotes in each chapter.

This accessibility should also make the book useful to the average music video fan who appreciates, likes, and would like to understand more about music videos. You may know a lot about a certain kind of music video (e.g. 1990s hip-hop videos), but would like to learn more about other styles and genres. This book can also help you understand other facets of music video that you might not have paid much attention to. Perhaps you watch music videos primarily for the music, but had never given much thought as to how the visual component is put together, or the kinds of social groups represented in that visual content? Chapters 1–3 (musical analysis) might be of special interest to you, with the remaining chapters offering new perspectives. It's important to understand that the three units and nine chapters can be read in any order, and entire chapters or units can be skipped without losing too much relevance. Those not really wishing to learn about any sorts of *theory*—musical, visual, or sociological—but who are just interested in deeper readings of music videos themselves, could actually skip directly to the end of each chapter, where I provide a "deep dive" into a single video that illustrates the topics discussed in that particular chapter. Learning more about these nine videos alone could lead to deeper appreciation of the videos themselves.

Selection of Videos

My primary goal in selecting music videos for this book aims to overthrow the exclusionary Canon of popular music from the past century by focusing on recent, extremely popular music videos by women, BIPOC musicians, and the LGBTQ+ community that have *billions* of views on YouTube. When illustrating a particular concept, and given the choice between videos by white, cisgendered, heterosexual men and those by more marginalized groups, I have actively privileged the latter. Of the resulting examples chosen for this book, 83.6% are by a woman and/or BIPOC musician. Even within this frame the book could, of course, not possibly be about *all* music videos. A number of criteria helped narrow which videos I address in this book, and which I did not.

First, as you might have surmised from my brief history of music video earlier in this introduction, the book does not consider music videos that aired prior to 1981, when MTV premiered. Depending on how one chooses to define the art form, it could be argued that music videos are as old as film itself. This makes sense if we define it as simply the union of film and music, since many early films were accompanied by either live or recorded audio. Music variety shows started on the radio, but were then adapted for television shows like *Your Hit Parade* on the American network CBS from 1950 to 1959.[4] Promotional clips released in the 1960s and 1970s such as The Beatles' "Strawberry Fields Forever" and Queen's "Bohemian Rhapsody," both of which were aired on BBC's show *Top of the Pops,* come closer to our modern understanding of music videos.[5] While it's easy enough to identify these major milestones, Andrew Goodwin calls the search for a single moment of music video's origins "a fruitless exercise," so one might as well just start somewhere.[6] I choose to focus on the MTV era onward because it's the moment in this long evolution when music videos by a wide variety of artists exert their strongest cultural influence.

Second, while never attempting to define "music video," this book only takes into account "official" music videos produced in some manner by the musical artist.[7] However popular they may be, fan-generated videos (such as "lyric videos") represent something different entirely. Other kinds of user-generated videos, such as lip-synched and/or choreographed tributes to popular music tracks circulated on Tik-Tok, Snapchat, and other social media, are also not considered. Multimedia products in which the director pays for the right to *use* an artist's song (including commercials, uses of music in television and film, etc.) are also not considered in this book.

Finally, this book aims to be about *popular* music videos. Toward this aim, the majority of my selections are taken from nominees from one or more VMA categories, which continue to be awarded every year despite MTV playing almost no music videos on its main network. When I have gone "off menu" for a video that was not nominated for an VMA, it's either

10   INTRODUCTION

because of a video's capacity to demonstrate something valuable (e.g. satire in The Roots' "What They Do"), because the video is too NSFW to be recognized by MTV (e.g. Peaches' "Rub"), or, rarely, because I am a product of a certain time and culture and cannot help myself (e.g. Fall Out Boy's "Sugar, We're Goin' Down").

Chapter Outlines

Interpreting Music Video treats music videos as truly multimedia works to be interpreted in three primary domains: music, visuals, and culture. Therefore, the book is organized into three larger units, each of which addresses a different aspect that contributes to the whole experience of music video. Rather than proceed chronologically (as would a history of music video), each unit shows how each of these aspects can be applied to a wide range of videos from different eras.

Unit 1 (Chapters 1–3) is devoted to analyzing the sounding music we hear in a music video. Chapter 1 examines the video's formal design, how both the music and visuals structure our experience of time. Chapter 2 is devoted to understanding the instruments, sounds, and special effects we hear in various genres of popular music. Finally, Chapter 3 addresses perhaps the most important component of popular music, the lyrics.

Unit 2 (Chapters 4–6) reveals the somewhat opaque process of visual design that goes into making music videos. We begin broadly in Chapter 4 with an examination of how a narrative is deployed in the visual storyline, and how this visual narrative relates to the song's lyrical narrative. Chapter 5 exposes some techniques and technologies associated with camera angles and lighting used to capture music videos on film. Chapter 6 highlights a number of aspects of the editing process, including how the final product is cut together and how and when special effects are added.

The final unit (Chapters 7–9) delves into what I call the sociology of music videos. Chapter 7 examines how gender and sexuality are expressed in music videos, with particular attention to contributions by women and LGBTQ+ artists. Chapter 8 examines race and ethnicity in music videos, including some non-mainstream music videos from remote corners of the globe that seem less remote due to these spectacular music videos. Chapter 9 attempts to convey some of the more overtly political aspects of music video, focusing on censorship and music videos that relate specifically to recent movements such as #MeToo, Black Lives Matter, climate change, and corporate greed.

USING THIS BOOK IN THE CLASSROOM

There are a few different ways that I have used this text in relation to the courses on music videos I teach at the University of Kansas. I have personally used these materials in a wide variety of class formats, including:

- A first-year seminar on music videos
- A combined undergraduate/graduate degree requirement for music majors and minors
- A large enrollment undergraduate elective course on music videos
- A fully online course

In smaller settings, such as a first-year seminar or degree requirement within the major, using the text as fuel for in-class discussion can be accomplished a number of ways. I had the students read sections of chapters prior to class, make a post on an online discussion board, then reply to two other students' posts. I then began class by highlighting the major topics that came up in their contributions. Most of our class time was spent applying what the students had learned in the chapter to one or two new videos that were discussed in small groups. For example, after reading the section about the male gaze in Chapter 7, groups of students watched Beyoncé's "Run The World" and discussed ways in which the video does or does not subvert the male gaze, reporting their findings back to the whole group before the end of the period.

When teaching this material to a large undergraduate elective audience, I strive for less out-of-class prep, delivering most of the content in lecture format. The provided slide decks are useful here. I spend a lot of time watching videos with the students, pointing out details in real time, "cold calling" on students to do the same, and asking small groups to discuss what they find interesting in videos. I then offer the text as lecture notes so that the students have a thorough accounting of all the terminology. Students are ultimately made responsible for all the material in the text through quizzes given at the end of each chapter, including identifying any video discussed by audio or visual clips alone. This latter "drop-the-needle" approach ensures that the students spend a good amount of their time outside of class immersed in the music videos themselves.

For a fully online version of this course (in which most of us became immediate experts in 2020), there are a number of different levels of engagement possible based on how much prep time the instructor wants to spend. The most streamlined approach is to break up the semester into nine equal parts, assigning one chapter in each of these parts for students to read, and creating a quiz in your learning management system (LMS) that checks for understanding. Again, I recommend including audio clips and screenshots to deepen their immersion. Instructors looking for a more personal connection with their students might also create videos of themselves working through the included slide decks, or even talking in real time through the videos. The nine videos discussed as "deep dives" at the end of each chapter would be excellent candidates for this sort of thing. You can foster community amongst the students themselves by breaking them into smaller teams (I might suggest four to five students) and having the same discussion board practice as I described for the first-year seminar, where students make an original post and respond to the posts made by their team members.

Regardless of which format you teach in, I find that it's always a good idea to include a few larger stakes assignments alongside whatever chapter quizzes or discussion you take on. I have provided four such assignments as downloadable, editable files for you to customize to your own taste. Three of them are end-of-unit short papers that ask students to apply what they've learned in that unit to a video of their choosing. If you have more than ~20 students you may wish to offer a pre-curated list of videos to save yourself the time of having to view a different video for each student. The final project gives students a deeper immersion into the video format itself. Using the "deep dives" as a guide, students create an analytical *video* that highlights aspects of a music video they find interesting. My students have then uploaded their projects to a Vimeo channel that highlights years' worth of students' creative work and serves as a guide for future students.

NOTES

1 Only recently have subscription services such as Apple Music started hosting music videos.
2 Beyoncé's visual album *Black Is King* (2020) represents an extreme example of this shift to a primarily visual medium since it was released—along with the first commercially available stage recording of *Hamilton*—on the cable network Disney+, a service for accessing movies and television shows. Disney

paid huge sums for both, and it's unclear whether the network would have done so at all had it not been for the COVID-19 crisis in which consumers were more willing than ever to spend money to access media on their home entertainment systems.

3 For more on the Buzz Clips series see Brad Osborn, E. Rossin, K. Weingarten, "Content and Correlational Analysis of a Corpus of MTV-Promoted Music Videos Aired between 1990 and 1999," *Music & Science* 3 (2020). DOI <10.1177/2059204320902369>

4 See Heather McIntosh, "Music Video Forerunners in Early Television Programming: A Look at Wcpo-Tv's Innovations and Contributions in the 1950s," *Popular Music and Society* 27, no. 3 (2004): 259–272.

5 Andrew Goodwin, *Dancing in the Distraction Factory: Music Television and Popular Culture* (Minneapolis: University of Minnesota Press, 1992): 29–30.

6 Goodwin, 1992, 30.

7 Carol Vernallis takes the opposite approach, seeing music videos in the YouTube era as an inextricable part of a greater "media swirl" (2013, 3) that includes streaming multimedia of all types; See Carol Vernallis, *Unruly Media: Youtube, Music Video, and the New Digital Cinema* (New York and Oxford: Oxford University Press, 2013).

Interpreting Music

UNIT 1

CHAPTER 1 CLIP LIST

YEAR	ARTIST	VIDEO
1982	Michael Jackson	Thriller
1983	Cyndi Lauper	Girls Just Wanna Have Fun
1986	Prince	Kiss
1987	Whitney Houston	I Wanna Dance With Somebody
1991	Red Hot Chili Peppers	Under the Bridge
1992	En Vogue	Free Your Mind
1992	Rage Against the Machine	Freedom
1997	Radiohead	Karma Police
2003	Outkast	Hey Ya!
2007	Rihanna (ft. Jay-Z)	Umbrella
2014	Taylor Swift	Blank Space
2016	Marshmello (ft. Wrabel)	Ritual
2016	The Chainsmokers (ft. Halsey)	Closer
2018	Nicki Minaj	Barbie Dreams
2018	Childish Gambino	This is America
2018	Carly Rae Jepsen	Party for One

FORM

- Two Standard Song Forms
  - *Verse/Chorus Form*
  - *Strophic Form*

- Other Sections
  - *Postchorus*
  - *Video Intro, Fade-Out, Coda*
  - *Drum Break, Rap Verse*

- Other Song Forms
  - *Terminally Climactic Form*
  - *Super-Simple Verse/Chorus Form (SSVC)*
  - *Electronic Dance Music (EDM) Form*

- Song Form vs. Video Form
  - *Parametric Form Chart*

- Deep Dive: Doja Cat "Juicy" (2019)

C H A P T E R   1

Form

Doja Cat's 2019 hit video "Juicy" gets right to the point. A hip-hop song about her respect for well-endowed derrieres, it starts directly on the chorus, with the song title as its fourth (and fifth) words. Her video doesn't miss a beat either. The first ten seconds summarize the visuals seen over the next three minutes: plain colored backgrounds, various "juicy" fruits, and, of course, derrieres of prodigious size (Figure 1.1).

But the way that Doja Cat keeps the viewer's interest has much to do with the way that the video shapes time, both musically and visually. It's a delicate balancing act of providing *enough* premium shots and sounds in the opening seconds while reserving plenty for later. This shaping of musical and visual time is what this chapter analyzes as a video's **form**. Changes in musical form and visual form are highly coordinated in music videos. Paying attention to one usually leads to a deeper understanding of the other.

This chapter begins by looking at two standard song forms that shape the majority of music videos: verse/chorus form and strophic form. After this overview we'll zoom in a bit more to understand some individual sections that make these forms work. I will then demonstrate three alternative strategies for organizing musical time that depart from these standard forms. Finally, we'll compare the formal structure of a video's music with the time flow of the visuals themselves. Only then can then we take a deeper dive into "Juicy" to fully understand how a song and video that is so seemingly straightforward keeps our interest over time.

Figure 1.1 Introduction of Doja Cat (ft. Tyga) "Juicy" (0:08)

TWO STANDARD SONG FORMS

Verse/Chorus Form

Because uncovering a video's formal design piece by piece can obscure the smoother flow of time we experience in a music video, it will be helpful for readers to watch the entirety of Whitney Houston's "I Wanna Dance With Somebody" to get a sense of the song's form—the way it organizes time—as part of my analysis. As I go through the smaller sections that make this video work, try not to lose the sense of perpetual flow that makes Houston's video so enjoyable.

The video begins with an introductory section, often shortened as **intro**. Like the layers of a cake, the various instruments are added one at a time: percussion, then the bass (0:30), and finally the main riff played by keyboards and horns. This technique is called a **buildup**, and it's common in intros.[1] Adding these layers one at a time keeps the listener's interest before Houston's vocals even enter.

Houston begins the **verse** (0:57) wondering how she'll chase her blues away. The mood is rather somber. She seems a bit more optimistic in the **prechorus** (1:14). Her higher vocal range complements the lyrics that state how fine the daytime hours are. But what she's really looking forward to is dancing this evening. The **chorus** (1:28) is the highlight of standard verse/chorus songs. Houston belts out the memorable melody in her highest register yet, beginning immediately on the title lyric. She only sings higher than this once in the song. Listening to chorus two (2:04) and chorus three (3:37) back to back reveals that everything— not just her vocals but also the instrumental tracks—has been shifted up in pitch. Pitching the final chorus up is a special technique called the **pump-up chorus**,[2] and it's especially common in 1980s songs.

This overall formal shape is called **verse/chorus form**. It's one of two standard song forms that make up the majority of music videos. Lyrically, verses typically set up and advance a narrative, while the chorus either reflects on that narrative or drives home its main message. Notice how the chorus contains the song's title, and its lyrics are the same every time. By contrast, the verse's lyrics are different each time, even though they appear over the same backing music.

Music videos respond visually to musical sections in nuanced ways. Just like the lyrics change from verse one to verse two, so does the cinematography between these two verses (Figure 1.2). Comparing the camera's point of view, verse one centers on Houston's face in verse one, while verse two uses a side-angle shot. The lighting also changes from back-lighting to side-lighting. Houston's costume and hairstyle both change in verse two as well. Chapters 5 and 6 go deeper into the specific techniques of cinematography in music video, but these things are integral to experiencing a video's form.

It can be helpful to keep track of the song's overall flow with a **form chart** (Table 1.1). Form charts can vary in their level of detail. Table 1.1 simplifies the form by noting only the timing of the video, the section name, and a brief description. Formal descriptions can include myriad details, including which instruments are present, what camera angles are used, or, as I have done here, the meaning of Houston's lyrics in each section.

As long as a song has verses and choruses, it's considered a verse/chorus form. But those aren't the only sections that appear in verse/chorus forms. Houston's song, for example, contains a prechorus between the verse and chorus. To count as such, prechoruses must be noticeably different from the verse that precedes them.[3] Houston's prechorus melody at 1:14 becomes higher and different, and the keyboards become more active. Some listeners may also hear that the beginning chord of the prechorus is a different chord than the beginning chord of the verse.

FORM **17**

(a)

(b)

Figure 1.2 Cinematography changes in Whitney Houston "I Wanna Dance With Somebody" (0:56, 2:05)

Table 1.1 "Form chart for "I Wanna Dance With Somebody"

TIME	SECTION	DESCRIPTION
0:01	Intro	Buildup: percussion, bass, horns and keyboard
0:56	Verse 1	Lyrics about getting through the day
1:14	Prechorus	Lyrics about loneliness at night
1:27	Chorus	Begins with title lyric
2:04	Verse 2	Different lyrics than verse 1
2:20	Prechorus	Begins differently than prechorus 1, ends the same
2:34	Chorus	Same as first chorus
3:06	Bridge	Independent music, dependent lyrics
3:23	Prechorus	Same lyrics as prechorus 2
3:37	Chorus	Pump-up chorus (higher)
4:09	Outro	Dependent, based on chorus

18 INTERPRETING MUSIC

Houston's song includes another transitional section, called a **bridge**, between the first two verse/chorus pairs and the final chorus. Bridges are commonly heard in pop and rock songs from the 1960s all the way through the early 2000s. Modern pop songs have started omitting them to get right to the chorus (the same is true of intros). Bridges can be based on previously heard material, known as *dependent* bridges, or, can consist of entirely new material, resulting in *independent* bridges. Houston's bridge actually kind of splits the difference: its backing music is independent, but the lyrics ("somebody who") are obviously dependent on the chorus. Such ambiguity is not uncommon in bridges.[4]

Taylor Swift's "Blank Space" (2:53–3:13) features a fully independent bridge. Director Joseph Kahn responds to Swift's brand-new melody and lyrics by introducing several new elements at the onset of this section (Figure 1.3): a new prop (the apple); a new plot twist (the apple acts like a voodoo doll); and the tightest close-up shot of Swift's face thus far.

The only remaining section in "I Wanna Dance With Somebody" is the **outro**. Unlike bridges, outros are always dependent on previously heard material. Houston's outro is so dependent on the chorus that it barely constitutes a new section. It seems to flow out of the chorus, continuing the backing track long after the catchy lead vocal melody has subsided.

Strophic Form

Verse/chorus forms don't appear in popular music until the 1960s. But a much older and simpler form, called **strophic form**, has been the basis for songs for hundreds of years (including the oldest folk songs) and is still alive in popular music today. Strophic songs consist of several verses, but they lack a contrasting chorus.

Again, I'll suggest that the reader watch an entire strophic video—Prince's "Kiss" this time—before consulting my form chart. Table 1.2 reveals that the video is composed of three long verses. Labeling each of these verses as the "A" section and the bridge as "B" helps to discover a larger **AABA form** to the video. Though strophic songs can vary in their number of verses, and don't need to contain a bridge, most conform to this AABA configuration: two verses, a bridge, and a final verse. Relative to Houston's video, Prince's compensates for these longer verses by containing shorter intros and outros, and also omits the long buildup. Its bridge section also contains no lyrics, consisting entirely of a guitar solo.

Instead of a contrasting chorus, each verse in strophic songs usually contains a **refrain**, a short statement containing the title lyric (rather than an entire section that celebrates that lyric over and over again, like a chorus). Since Prince's refrain happens at the end of each verse, it's known as an *end*-refrain. Cyndi Lauper's "Girls Just Wanna Have Fun" is another strophic song with end-refrain. But refrains can happen at the beginnings of verses too, as in each verse of The Beatles' "Hey Jude" and Radiohead's "Karma Police." Since both of these songs start their verses on the title lyric, they contain *beginning*-refrains.

Figure 1.3 Independent bridge in Taylor Swift "Blank Space" (2:53)

FORM   **19**

Table 1.2 Form chart for Prince "Kiss"

TIME	SECTION	DESCRIPTION
0:05	Intro	All layers presented at once (no buildup)
0:16	Verse 1 (A)	Vocals enter, end-refrain
1:08	Transition	Same as intro
1:16	Verse 2 (A)	Different lyrics than verse 1, same end-refrain
2:08	Transition	Same as intro
2:17	Bridge (B)	Guitar solo
2:51	Verse 3 (A)	Different lyrics than verse 1, same end-refrain
3:43–3:54	Outro	Intro, but with fade out

Prince's verses in this strophic song exemplify the **12-bar blues** (Table 1.3), an important unifying structure in African-American music since the early twentieth century. Variations on this structure abound, but it essentially involves playing the one-chord for four bars ("Kiss" is in the key of A, so we call A "one"), then the four-chord for bars 5–6 (D), returning to the one-chord for bars 7–8. Bars 9–12 start on the five-chord (E), and then musicians tend to add their own twist on things. The most common pattern for bars 9–12 would be E–D–A–A.[5] But Prince repeats the E–D so that he can play the original A chord only after he's delivered the song title at the very last moment in bar 12, almost like a punctuation mark.

OTHER SECTIONS

Every verse/chorus song has a chorus. Every strophic song has a verse. Having discussed some of the most likely other sections encountered in these forms, I'll now define some that happen less frequently. All of the following sections can and do appear in verse/chorus forms from time to time, and most can appear in strophic forms as well.

Postchorus

As its name suggests, the postchorus is a separate section that follows the chorus (this means it can't occur in strophic forms). A postchorus continues the basic accompaniment heard in the previous chorus, but features a different vocal melody.[6] Carly Rae Jepson's video "Party for One" contains a clear postchorus (Table 1.4). Without a prechorus, the video moves directly from verse two into its chorus at 2:28, with Jepsen singing the song title right at the beginning. The postchorus begins at 2:59, when Jepsen stops singing the words of the chorus, and

Table 1.3 Twelve-bar blues in "Kiss"

Bar 1	Bar 2	Bar 3	Bar 4
Chord: A7			
Lyrics: You don't have to be beautiful...		I just need your body...	
Bar 5	Bar 6	Bar 7	Bar 8
Chord: D7		A7	
Lyrics: You don't need experience...		You just leave it all up to me...	
Bar 9	Bar 10	Bar 11	Bar 12
chord: E7	D7	E7	D7
Lyrics: You don't have to be rich...	You don't have to be cool...	Ain't no particular sign...	...and your kiss

20 INTERPRETING MUSIC

Table 1.4 Postchorus in Carly Rae Jepsen "Party for One"

TIME	SECTION	DESCRIPTION
2:12	Verse 2	Unique lyrics, medium volume
2:28	Chorus	Title lyric, memorable vocal hook
2:59	Postchorus	Preserves chorus beat, untexted vocals

sings instead untexted syllables ("ah-ah-ah..."). Postchoruses featuring short syllabic vocals are common, including Lady Gaga's "Alejandro" (3:21), Dua Lipa's "One Kiss" (1:18), and Little Mix's "Woman Like Me" (1:56). Other postchoruses, like Sia's "Chandelier" (1:28), have just as many lyrics as the chorus, though they are less memorable than the chorus.

Video Intro, Fade-Out, Coda

Some musical intros only last a few seconds ("Kiss"), and some take significant time building up all the layers ("I Wanna Dance With Somebody"). Music video offers the possibility of a completely non-musical intro in the visual domain only. The first 24 seconds of Nicki Minaj's "Barbie Dreams" do not appear on the **album version** of the track, the version you might hear if you accessed the audio on a streaming service. What you see and hear is a **video intro**, which helps to build the setting of the video (known in film theory as mise-en-scène, which I'll discuss further in Chapter 4) before the song starts (Figure 1.4).

Once the album version does begin, its musical intro features the drum beat and guitar riff from The Notorious B.I.G.'s 1994 song "Just Playing (Dreams)." This practice of **sampling** another artist's work as part of a new creation has been part of hip-hop music since its inception in the 1970s, when DJs would play drum breaks (to be defined shortly) from one or more funk records while another musician rapped. Minaj's use of the sample works on a number of levels. First, both tracks contain the word "Dreams," with Minaj singing the rest of B.I.G.'s song title ("I'm *just playin'*/but I'm sayin'") in each of the two choruses. More importantly, Minaj flips the script on B.I.G.'s original track, in which he brags about several imagined sexual conquests. Each verse of Minaj's version imagines the poor sexual performance of several rappers, which are portrayed as puppets in the video. Surprisingly, many of these same rappers appear on her record!

A short outro begins at 3:24, and the track begins a **fade-out**. Whereas this gradual reduction in volume almost always happens at the end of a video, the timer reveals that there is still nearly a minute and a half to go. At 3:38, just as things go silent, Minaj begins rapping again, and a totally new beat starts. The beat picks up at 4:30 and Minaj's rapping reaches an impressive fever pitch just before the track ends. This ending, on completely new material unrelated to anything else heard in the song, is called a **coda**. Whereas outros that depend

Figure 1.4 Video intro in Nicki Minaj "Barbie Dreams" (0:09)

on material heard before (namely the chorus) are common in all genres, unrelated codas like the one in "Barbie Dreams" are relatively rare, though they do seem to be occurring with some frequency in recent hip-hop.

In music videos, codas are almost always accompanied by a change in lighting, scenery, or other visual elements. The aforementioned puppets appear throughout the earlier verse/chorus portion of Minaj's video, but in the coda all of these distractions are removed so the viewer can focus on Minaj's impressive rapping. In Childish Gambino's "This is America" (Figure 1.5), there is a change from high-key bright lighting in the warehouse to a darkened, nearly pitch-black lighting scheme when the coda kicks in at 3:40.

Drum Break, Rap Verse

En Vogue's "Free Your Mind" is a notable video for seamlessly blending rock, funk, and hip-hop genres. Following the second chorus (2:50) the listener might expect a bridge, but En Vogue's track features only drums. This **drum break** is a special kind of bridge that features no vocals. Hip-hop producers in the 1980s and 1990s sampled these drum breaks (especially from funk records) to rap over. Fortunately, since drum breaks like this one usually start with one layer, the drums, then gradually add more layers one at a time—cowbell, guitar, bass—DJs had a lot of flexibility in exactly which part they wanted to sample.

Rapping doesn't only happen in rap songs. Sometimes singers insert a single **rap verse** into songs that are otherwise sung. Rap verses are usually performed by "featured" guests, such that "Umbrella," by Rihanna, will usually include the words "featuring Jay-Z." Rap verses often occur later in the song, but Jay-Z actually gets the *first* verse (0:12) in Rihanna's track.

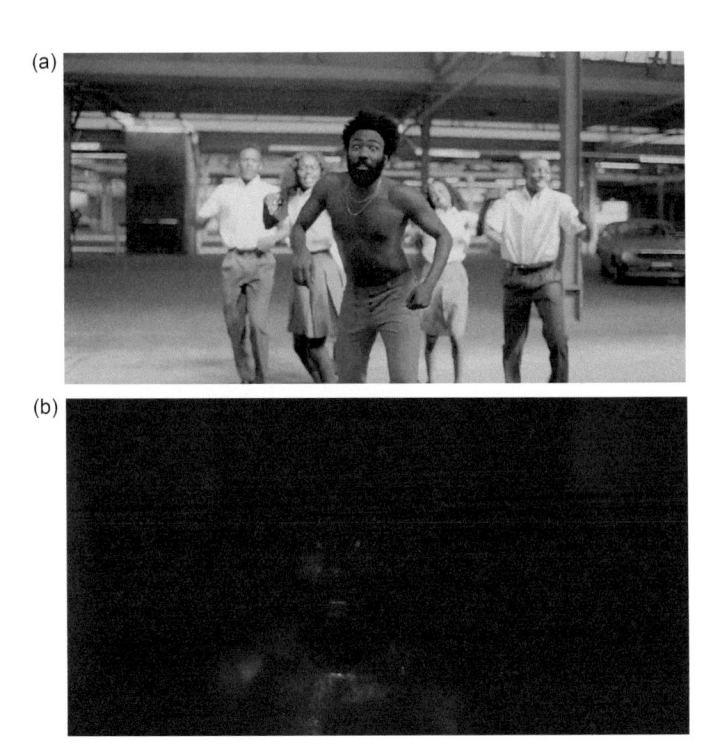

Figure 1.5 Change in coda lighting in Childish Gambino "This is America" (1:12, 3:49)

OTHER SONG FORMS

Terminally Climactic Form

Choruses, and, to a lesser extent, refrains, usually serve as the memorable high point of the song. These are the parts that a listener is most likely to remember and sing throughout the day. Unsurprisingly, these lyrics often contain the song's title as well. But some special verse/chorus songs actually reserve their most memorable singalong on the song title for the ending. A memorable ending section that appears only once at the end of the song is called a **terminal climax**.[7]

Table 1.5 shows the form for a video in **terminally climactic form**, Red Hot Chili Peppers' "Under the Bridge." The song begins like any other verse/chorus form. But the chorus, while more memorable than the verse, still feels like it's missing something. It's not that much louder than the verse, and it doesn't contain the song title. Both of these usual chorus functions, left unfulfilled in their usual section, are heard instead only in the terminal climax starting at 3:13. Whereas the chorus only hints at a bad experience had by the narrator ("I don't ever wanna feel like I did that day..."), the terminal climax makes clear exactly what the bad experience was: a heroin overdose. That the terminal climax is sung by a literal chorus of voices (where the song section gets its name) and the chorus is sung by only the lead singer is further proof that the terminal climax is fulfilling expectations usually reserved for the chorus. The high-voiced choir of angels at the end of this video is especially suggestive of a near-death experience.

Terminally climactic forms are usually heard in rock music, rather than hip-hop (Frank Ocean's "Self-Control" is a notable exception), and they occur much more frequently after 1990. "Karma Police" is another example of a terminally climactic form we've already seen in this chapter, as is Dashboard Confessional's video "Hands Down." It's important to separate codas (new, but not memorable) from terminal climaxes (new AND memorable). "This is America" closes with brand new coda material, but the beginning-refrain on the song title far outshines the auto-tuned melody of the coda. Thus, the Childish Gambino video is *not* in terminally climactic form.

Super-Simple Verse/Chorus Form (SSVC)

Terminally climactic forms add even more contrast to an already contrasting verse/chorus song; but SSVC **forms** do the opposite by actually reducing the amount of contrast heard throughout the song. There is still a difference between a verse and a chorus in an SSVC form (unique lyrics vs. repeated lyrics), but songs in SSVC form use the same *accompaniment* material for both the verse and the chorus.

Table 1.5 Terminally climactic form in Red Hot Chili Peppers "Under the Bridge"

TIME	SECTION	DESCRIPTION
0:01	Intro	Solo electric guitar
0:28	Verse 1	Lyrics about Los Angeles
0:58	Verse 2	Narrator continues to praise Los Angeles
1:27	Chorus	Lyrics hints at a bad experience
1:50	Verse 3	Narrator feels lonely, but comforted by the city
2:29	Chorus	Lyrics hint at a bad experience
3:13	Terminal climax	Song title appears, describes heroin overdose

FORM 23

Table 1.6 Super-Simple Verse/Chorus in Outkast "Hey Ya"

A. VERSE

1	2	3	4	5	6	7	8	9	10	11	12	13	14
	thank	god	-for	mom	and dad	-for	stick in'	two	to- ge-	-ther	cause we	don't	know

15	16	17	18	19	20	21	22
how					(Clap)	(Clap)	(Clap)

B. CHORUS

1	2	3	4	5	6	7	8	9	10	11	12	13	14
hey				ya								he-	y

15	16	17	18	19	20	21	22
ya					(Clap)	(Clap)	(Clap)

After a long video intro, Outkast's video "Hey Ya!" features a verse (1:09) with many lyrics, then a sung chorus (1:42) on the song title. But listening to the rest of the musical instruments reveals that these sections are made of the same backing music. "Hey Ya!" makes this especially easy to hear since its sections contain an unusual number of beats. Most popular music is based on groups of four, but this one seems to subtract two beats in its fourth bar (Table 1.6). A listener paying attention to the number of beats could count to 22 over and over again in both of these identical sections.

Electronic Dance Music (EDM) Form

Since 2011 a lot of popular music has started absorbing some of the sonic characteristics of EDM in a way that has fundamentally altered the formal structure of these songs. Instead of the familiar four pop sections (verse, prechorus, chorus, postchorus) these songs feature two new ones, resulting in the four-part design verse, **riserchorus**, **drop**, postchorus.

As its name implies, a riserchorus blends the catchiness of a pop chorus (usually featuring the song title) with the anticipation heard in an EDM riser. EDM risers are named for a constantly rising pitch heard in some or all of the section. They also contain a rhythmic buildup that involves a drum rhythm accelerating exponentially (twice as fast, then four times as fast, etc.). Both the rising pitch and the rhythmic build continue until the drop, the moment where the song's beat finally returns.

Marshmello's "Ritual" (featuring Wrabel) is a video in **EDM form** (Table 1.7). The verse at 1:56 is like any other verse, featuring lyrics that are unique each time. Prechoruses in EDM feature the same lyrics each time they return, and usually thicken the texture by adding synth and percussion layers not heard in the verse. But at 2:30 all these layers drop out. There is a nice vocal hook, eventually featuring the song title, but it's accompanied by a riser and

Table 1.7 EDM form in Marshmello "Ritual" (ft. Wrabel)

TIME	SECTION	DESCRIPTION
1:56	Verse 2	Medium volume, unique lyrics
2:13	Prechorus	Added layers, recurring lyrics
2:30	Riserchorus	Vocal hook w/song title; rising pitch, rhythmic build
3:05	Drop	Beat returns
3:23	Riserchorus–Drop	Riserchorus vocals over drop beat

a build instead of a big thick chorus. At the beginning of the riser, the drum hits once every two beats, then once every beat (2:48), twice every beat (2:57), four times every beat (3:01), finally ending up in a blur just before the drop. This rhythmic blur blends seamlessly with the highest point of a riser that reaches a screeching pitch at this very moment.

The entire point of a riserchorus is to lead to the drop, which happens at 3:05. Notice how Marshmello actually pulls back all the cacophony at the last second to highlight Wrabel singing the title. The video actually shows Marshmello doing this on the DJ console (Figure 1.6). Drops usually do not contain lyrics. If they do contain vocals, they are usually short, syllabic samples, often with heavy vocal effects added.[8] In this way, they function similarly to a postchorus. Since EDM forms are made using extensive libraries of samples (for vocals, drums, bass, etc.), it's really easy for producers to reorder and recombine these samples however they want. At 3:23, for example, Marshmello actually puts the catchy riserchorus vocal sample together with the drop beat for the first time. This is a really common way to end EDM forms, resulting in a climactic mega section called the *riserchorus-drop*.

SONG FORM VS. VIDEO FORM

Parametric Form Chart

Thus far each of my form charts has been based on a video's musical characteristics. But music videos project their own visual and narrative pacing alongside the music.[9] Changes in lighting, scenery, or plot can all shape our sense of how time passes in a music video. A new tool, the **parametric form chart**, can measure the passing of time in both music and visuals simultaneously.

A parametric form chart for the video "Closer," by The Chainsmokers (featuring pop superstar Halsey), appears as Table 1.8. The left two columns display a basic musical form chart with timings and sections. Note that the song is in EDM form, though its drop repeats a lyric heard in the riserchorus ("we ain't never getting older"). Any additional columns can be used to measure parameters that relate to the passing of time in the video. In "Closer," these include: who is singing; the video's changing setting; and the plot regarding two central characters (who are also the track's singers).

Who is singing and at what time will eventually relate to the video's plot. Arranged as a duet, Drew Taggart sings verse one and Halsey sings verse two. The first riserchorus hook is only sung by Taggart—the higher frequencies are produced by a vocoder (see Chapter 2), not Halsey. When that hook appears after the second verse, those high frequencies are Halsey's actual voice. Singing together signifies their healthy relationship at this point in the video. After the breakup, we hear Taggart singing alone again, reminiscing about their past relationship, with Halsey only joining him for the line "we ain't never getting older."

Figure 1.6 DJ Marshmello preparing for the drop in "Ritual" (3:01)

FORM **25**

Table 1.8 Parametric form chart for The Chainsmokers "Closer" (ft. Halsey)

TIME	SECTION	SINGER	SETTING(S)	PLOT
0:01	Intro	n/a	Hotel bar	Breakup foreshadowed
0:11	Verse 1	Taggart	Bedroom #1, party	Couple first meets
0:30	Prechorus			
0:50	Riserchorus		Bedroom #1, kitchen	Couple kisses (on countertop)
1:12	Drop			
1:32	Verse 2	Halsey	Bedroom #1, pool	Halsey becomes increasingly distant
1:52	Prechorus			
2:12	Riserchorus	Both		
2:33	Drop		Bedroom #2, underwater	
2:52	Riserchorus (extended)	Taggart (both)	Bedroom #3, hotel bar	Couple breaks up, lives separately
3:33	Drop		Hotel rooftop	Taggart attempts to win Halsey back

Using foreshadowing as a narrative technique, the video's first and last setting are the same (a hotel bar), with both scenes set in the present. Drew Taggart's first verse is set as a throwback shot to the time and place where he first met Halsey at a party. They kiss on the counter, and then in the first of the three bedrooms. These changing bedrooms—three over the course of the video—are central to the plot. The second bedroom is the one they live in together as a couple. After the couple falls apart Halsey appears in her own, third bedroom (Figure 1.7), wearing a new outfit and sporting a new haircut.

A parametric form chart is a useful tool for understanding how a video's plot can be affected by musical and visual parameters simultaneously. In "Closer," all of these parameters seem to work in concert with one another to strengthen the plot. But a parametric form chart can also help make sense of more complex music videos in which the visual form departs drastically from the musical form. Such a disparity occurs in Michael Jackson's celebrated epic "Thriller" (Table 1.9). Jackson's video is ten minutes long, even though the album version of this song is only around six. Column two of the parametric form chart shows that the video gains most of these extra minutes through an extended video intro, lasting about four minutes. But it also modifies the song form significantly, skipping the chorus for all three of the first verses. It does so to withhold the climactic chorus for the video's visual climax, when Jackson turns into a zombie to perform one of the most famous choreographed dance sequences in music video history (Figure 1.8). Unlike the repeated verse/chorus form of the album version, the video actually transforms this song into a terminally climactic form, withholding the one-and-only chorus until the very end!

Figure 1.7 Halsey's own bedroom in "Closer" (2:56)

26   INTERPRETING MUSIC

Table 1.9 Parametric form chart for Michael Jackson "Thriller"

TIME	SONG FORM	VIDEO SETTING
0:01	n/a (video intro)	Couple on date, movie theatre
4:14	Intro (extended)	
4:42	Verse 1	City streets, Jackson acting like a zombie
5:16	Verse 2 (chorus skipped)	
5:47	Verse 3 (chorus skipped)	
6:20	Drum break (with voice-over)	Graveyard, zombies emerging
8:02	n/a (music stops)	Couple encounters zombies on the street
8:29	Drum break continues	Jackson turns into a zombie, dances with other zombies
9:41	Chorus	

Figure 1.8 Terminally climactic dance scene in "Thriller" (9:03)

DEEP DIVE: DOJA CAT "JUICY" (2019)

Let's finally return to the video we watched at the beginning of this chapter, "Juicy." Table 1.10 is a parametric form chart showing the song's musical design alongside the video's defining visual formal characteristic: the gradual introduction of various "juicy" fruits. In addition to acting as a clear metaphor for plump derrieres, Doja Cat explains in an interview that the fruits are all about enhancing the video's color palette.[10] For instance, the cherry in the video's opening informs an overall red/white color palette until the watermelon arrives, which changes the video's color palette to red/green/white.

Though "Juicy" is best described as a verse/chorus form, it does have a couple of peculiarities. Like many pop songs after about 2014, "Juicy" begins on its chorus, more properly a chorus-verse form than a verse-chorus one.[11] There are perhaps a number of reasons for this evolution, but the most obvious theory would be that, in the streaming age, it's all too easy for a user to skip to the next song/video if it doesn't catch their attention immediately. This chorus not only features the song title straight away, but is followed by an incredibly catchy postchorus that repeats the syllable "back" (remembering that many postchoruses feature repeated syllables).

Upon hearing the verse it's difficult to tell if the three different subsections (0:33, 0:46, 0:57) constitute some kind of greater verse-prechorus design. Two sections at 0:33 and 0:57,

Table 1.10 Parametric form chart for Doja Cat ft. Tyga "Juicy" (2019)

TIME	SECTION	MUSICAL DESCRIPTION	FIRST APPEARANCE OF FRUITS/COLORS
0:01	Intro	Solo synth filter sweep preparing chorus "drop"	Cherry
0:11	Chorus	Song title	
0:22	Postchorus	Back back back	
0:33	Verse 1a (Doja)	Rap-like delivery, sans bass	Watermelon
0:46	Verse 1b	Higher singing, bass returns	Watermelon and cherry
0:57	Verse 1a	Bass drops out, rap delivery returns	
1:08	Chorus	Recap chorus	Banana and Peach (lime)
1:19	Postchorus	Recap postchorus	
1:31	Verse 2a (Tyga)	Sans bass	Yellow backdrop (strawberry, kiwi, lemon)
1:42	Verse 2b	Bass returns	
1:53	Verse 2a	Bass drops out	Blueberry
2:04	Chorus	Recap chorus	
2:15	Postchorus	Recap postchorus	
2:27	Bridge	Repeated lyric hook (quiet)	*Luchador* mask, purple
2:50	Chorus	Recap chorus	
3:00	Postchorus	Recap postchorus	

both sung in a rap-like delivery without any bass, act as symmetrical bookends to the higher sung melody that coincides with the entrance of the synth-bass at 0:46. Table 1.10 simply labels these three parts as verse 1a, 1b, and 1a, since it's clear that the second section is not a prechorus, and the third section is the same as the first.

Normally in a verse/chorus form this three-part structure would return for verse two (1:31). In verse two Tyga's delivery consists entirely of rapping, so the low-high-low singing profile of verse one is absent. It's also important to note that this video is for a *remix* of the track that features Tyga. In the album version, sung entirely by Doja Cat, her flow in the middle section is radically different, stringing together 64 consecutive rapped syllables, one on every sixteenth note. Despite these differences in versions, the same synth-bass pattern heard in verse one (absent-present-absent) is present in all versions of verse two, helping to clarify the section's role in the song form as a whole.

For the sake of concision, Table 1.10 shows only the *first* appearance for each new fruit, though each fruit generally reappears several times later in the video. This creates a visual rhythm that runs parallel to the timing shaped by the song form. It matters when exactly these changes of scenery occur. Notice that the introduction of each new fruit coincides with the beginning of a new musical section. Watermelons appear at the onset of verse one, and the striking yellow backdrop with its ocean of lemons appears right with verse two. While a change of musical section would seem to be a *necessary* condition for a change of scenery, it is not a *sufficient* condition; the cherry lasts three sections, for instance.

This gradual introduction of new color palettes keeps a viewer's interest throughout the song, as does the reappearance of previously seen palettes. The bridge at 2:27 introduces the final novel color palette: the purple background paired with a *luchador* mask. Tracking each of these color-recaps along with the song's beat reveals a remarkably clear musical-visual rhythm: Red (2:39, bar 1/beat 1); Green (2:40, bar 1/beat 3); Purple (2:44, bar 3/beat 1); Green (2:45, bar 3/beat 3). When the chorus comes back at 2:49 right on beat one as we expect, it marks the ending of this clear pattern: 1, 3…1, 3…1.

28   INTERPRETING MUSIC

Table 1.11 Lingo you should know

Intro	Strophic form	Drum break
Buildup	AABA form	Rap verse
Verse	Refrain	Terminal climax
Prechorus	12-bar blues	Terminally climactic form
Chorus	Postchorus	Super-simple verse/chorus form
Pump-up chorus	Album version	Electronic dance music form
Verse/chorus form	Video intro	Riserchorus
Form chart	Sampling	Drop
Bridge	Fade out	Parametric form chart
Outro	Coda	

This practice of cutting images to the beat is largely the provenance of the video's editor, a practice we'll discuss more in Chapter 6. Editors thus play a crucial role in how we understand form in music video. As a viewer and listener, we can have a deeper understanding of form in music videos by paying attention to the simultaneous visual and musical rhythms that constitute the final product.

NOTES

1 For more on the buildup technique see Robin Attas, "Form as Process: The Buildup Introduction in Popular Music," *Music Theory Spectrum* 37, no. 2 (2015): 275–296.

2 On pump-up modulations see Adam Ricci, "The Pump-Up in Pop Music of the 1970s and 1980s," *Music Analysis* 36, no. 1 (2017): 94–115.

3 Summach provides a thorough history of the prechorus from the 1960s onward; see Jay Summach, "The Structure, Function, and Genesis of the Prechorus," *Music Theory Online* 17, no. 3 (2011), <https://mtosmt.org/issues/mto.11.17.3/mto.11.17.3.summach.html>

4 See Trevor de Clercq, "Embracing Ambiguity in the Analysis of Form in Pop/Rock Music, 1982–1991," *Music Theory Online* 23, no. 3 (2017), <https://mtosmt.org/issues/mto.17.23.3/mto.17.23.3.de_clercq.html>

5 Like most Blues-based music, each of these chords contains a minor-seventh (E7, D7, A7). Blues and jazz regularly includes sevenths and other chordal extensions (ninths, elevenths, thirteenths).

6 This definition comes largely from Mark Spicer, "(Per)Form in(g) Rock: A Response," *Music Theory Online* 17, no. 3 (2011), <https://www.mtosmt.org/issues/mto.11.17.3/mto.11.17.3.spicer.html>

7 I have written extensively of terminally climactic forms, a term which I coined in a series of articles and talks given in the 2000s; see Brad Osborn, "Subverting the Verse—Chorus Paradigm: Terminally Climactic Forms in Recent Rock Music," *Music Theory Spectrum* 35, no. 1 (2013): 23–47 <DOI: 10.1525/mts.2013.35.1.23>

8 Barna calls this section the "dance chorus"; see Alyssa Barna, "The Dance Chorus in Recent Top-40 Music," *SMT-V* 6, no. 4 (2020), <http://www.smt-v.org/bibliographies/6_4_Barna.pdf>

9 This method of separating the analysis of visuals and music before ultimately combining them owes a huge debt to the work of Lori Burns. See, for example, Lori Burns, "Multimodal Analysis of Popular Music Videos," in *Coming of Age: Teaching and Learning Popular Music in Academia*, edited by Carlos Xavier Rodriguez (Ann Arbor, MI: Maize, 2017), <http://dx.doi.org/10.3998/mpub.9470277>

10 Access the entertaining interview "Doja Cat Explains 'Juicy' to a Classical Music Expert," <https://www.youtube.com/watch?v=cHqf2M0SqFI>

11 I take this reversal from the title of a talk given by Jeffrey Ensign, "From Verse-Chorus to Chorus-Verse," Paper given at the joint meeting of Music Theory Southeast and South-Central Society for Music Theory, Kennesaw State University, Kennesaw, GA, April 1–2, 2016.

CHAPTER 2 CLIP LIST

YEAR	ARTIST	VIDEO
1981	Joan Jett and the Blackhearts	I Love Rock N Roll
1981	Laurie Anderson	O Superman
1983	Herbie Hancock	Rockit
1988	The Pixies	Gigantic
1991	Nirvana	Smells Like Teen Spirit
1992	My Bloody Valentine	Only Shallow
1996	The Smashing Pumpkins	Tonight, Tonight
1997	Save Ferris	Come On Eileen
1999	Marc Anthony	I Need to Know
2003	Outkast	Hey Ya!
2005	Fall Out Boy	Sugar We're Goin' Down
2008	Lil' Wayne (ft. T-Pain)	Got Money
2011	Sia and David Guetta	Titanium
2017	Slowdive	Sugar For the Pill
2018	Galantis (ft. Sofia Carson)	San Francisco
2018	Carrie Underwood	Cry Pretty
2019	Alicia Keys	Raise a Man
2019	Judah & The Lion (ft. Kacey Musgraves)	Pictures
2019	Ingrid Andress	More Hearts Than Mine
2019	Brittany Howard	Stay High (Acoustic version)

SOUND ANALYSIS

- Instrumentation
  - *Four Layers*

- Common Instruments
  - *Acoustic Instruments*
  - *Electronic Instruments*

- Uncommon Instruments and Effects
  - *Uncommon Instruments*
  - *Uncommon Timbres and Effects*

- Deep Dive: Rihanna (ft. Jay-Z) "Umbrella" (2007)

CHAPTER 2

Sound Analysis

It's hard to imagine that the inimitable Barbadian pop singer and entrepreneur Rihanna was ever anything other than an international megastar. But in 2007, her video for "Umbrella" (ft. Jay-Z) catapulted her into success. The single broke a record in the UK, holding fast at #1 for ten consecutive weeks, and the corresponding album *Good Girl Gone Bad* is still her best-selling record in the U.S.

There are several reasons for the success of this video, but one obvious (if overlooked) reason is that it *sounds* good. In order to understand the details of that hit sound, it's necessary to identify the sound's component parts. This chapter will explore how to recognize, by ear, what sounds, instruments, and effects are regularly heard in music videos. While a number of these sounds appear in a diverse array of genres, there are certain sounds that are linked to a particular genre and, therefore, help the listener to place a video within that genre. Finally, because modern pop music rarely uses unprocessed "natural" sounds, this chapter will examine the most common effects used to enhance and modify the instruments heard in a recording.

INSTRUMENTATION

Four Layers

Nearly all genres of music organize the instruments used into four different layers[1]:

- **The beat layer:** keeps the beat using non-pitched percussion instruments like drum set
- **The melody layer:** the instrument, usually a voice, that plays memorable tunes
- **The bass layer:** the lowest sounding instrument, usually playing one note at a time
- **The chord layer:** fills in the middle, playing multiple notes at the same time (chords)

Listening to how these layers are articulated in a famous grunge song from the 1990s, Nirvana's "Smells Like Teen Spirit," will help to further elucidate this concept of the four layers. Like most tracks, this one begins with a buildup where instruments are added gradually, usually one at a time. Table 2.1 shows exactly when each instrument enters in this video.

32 INTERPRETING MUSIC

Table 2.1 Four instrumental layers in Nirvana "Smells Like Teen Spirit"

LAYER	0:01	0:07	0:09	0:18	0:26	0:42
Melody				Lead guitar	Voice	
Chord	Rhythm guitar					Rhythm guitar
Bass			Electric bass guitar			
Beat		Drum set				

The video begins with guitarist Kurt Cobain strumming chords on an electric guitar. Calling this the **rhythm guitar** part helps to distinguish it from when a guitar plays only single notes in a melody. This **lead guitar** part plays the two-note melody at 0:18, just before the voice enters. At 0:26 Cobain begins to sing, taking over the role of melody layer previously held by the lead guitar.

The bass layer enters at 0:09 and remains constant throughout the track, provided by Krist Novoselic on the electric bass guitar. Drummer Dave Grohl (now better known as the lead man of the Foo Fighters) enters just before that with the beat layer at 0:07 played on the drum set. Visually, the camera responds to this buildup by steadily panning from right to left, focusing gradually on each of these instruments in the order in which they enter.

The specific instruments and effects used to articulate these four layers help to place a particular video within the genre(s) a song participates in. These four instruments are used in other genres as well, but rock music nearly always features vocals, guitar, bass, and drums. Since those four instruments are also heard in funk music, they might be deemed a necessary but not sufficient condition for the rock genre.

But the high level of distortion on the electric guitar (in the chorus), the manner of playing the bass with a pick (rather than with the fingers), Dave Grohl's hard-hitting style, and especially Cobain's rough and aggressive manner of singing all work together to make "Smells Like Teen Spirit" sound like a song in the rock genre, rather than funk. There are further subtleties that separate this rock song from, say, The Foo Fighters' "Big Me," even though both songs use exactly the same instruments (and even the same drummer!). Aggressively distorted sounds place the former in a subgenre known as grunge, while the softer, cleaner edge of the latter is an example of alternative rock.

Determining exactly the subtleties at the level of instrumentation and effects that make grunge and alternative rock different requires close attention to each instrument in the ensemble, the way that instrument is played, and the effects used to modify that sound. This chapter will provide an overview of the most common instruments and effects, and which genre(s) those are most likely to be heard in.

COMMON INSTRUMENTS

Acoustic Instruments

Besides the voice, the **electric bass** guitar is probably the most common instrument across all genres of popular music. The player strikes the strings, and the vibrations of the string are transferred through the electric pickups to a high-powered amplifier that makes them audible. Andre 3000 plays electric bass with his fingers in "Hey Ya" (Figure 2.1). It's especially easy to hear the instrument's low frequencies exposed at the beginning of each verse (e.g. 1:09 in the video).

SOUND ANALYSIS **33**

Figure 2.1 Electric bass (fingers) in Outkast "Hey Ya!" (3:48)

Figure 2.2 Electric bass (pick) in The Pixies "Gigantic" (0:21)

Because the fictional setting in this video is referencing The Beatles' performance on the Ed Sullivan show, Andre is using a vintage Rickenbacker four-string model quite similar to the one Paul McCartney played. Though four-string electric is the most common setup, acoustic basses (like acoustic guitars) are sometimes heard in softer styles, and some virtuosic bass players play five- and even six-string models. Andre 3000 plays the bass by plucking with his fingers, as is common in softer genres. By contrast, The Pixies' bassist Kim Deal rakes the strings with a pick in their hit "Gigantic" (Figure 2.2), which lends a brighter, more articulate sound to the bass.

Based on these two examples, one might conclude that rock musicians play with a pick and hip-hop musicians play with their fingers. But genre is more complex than that, and Outkast is a perfect example of genre flexibility. A hip-hop group from Atlanta, they released

34 INTERPRETING MUSIC

a groundbreaking, genre-defying double-album called *Speakerboxxx/The Love Below* in 2003. "Hey Ya!" is only representative of half the tracks, which have a softer pop sensibility drawn from Andre 3000's varied influences. The other half of the album, created by rapper Big Boi, helped establish the Atlanta hip-hop sound, especially its signature trap beat deriving from the Roland 808 drum machine.

Besides the bass guitar, two other guitars are used regularly, especially in rock, country, and folk genres. Unlike the bass, six-string rhythm guitars almost always play more than one note at a time and, therefore, constitute the chord layer. Brittany Howard plays an **acoustic guitar** in "Stay High" (Figure 2.3). It's the only sound besides her voice and the tapping of her right foot in this stripped-down version of the song recorded particularly for this video. The acoustic guitar's large, resonant, hollow cavity allows it to project in this wide-open space.

Unlike the acoustic guitar, the **electric guitar** needs amplification to be heard on recordings. When the strings are strummed, it regularly fulfills the same chord layer role as the acoustic guitar. Joan Jett plays the chord layer on an electric guitar in "I Love Rock and Roll" at 2:30 in the video (Figure 2.4). But the electric guitar can also play melodies, especially in guitar solos like the one heard at 1:49 in the same video. Both of these uses of the electric guitar—as chord and melody layer—rely on an effect known as distortion that makes the sound angular, sharp, and fuzzy. Distortion is by far the most common effect added to the electric guitar. Genres have a lot to do with the amount of distortion added to an electric

Figure 2.3 Acoustic Guitar in Brittany Howard "Stay High" (0:20)

Figure 2.4 Electric Guitar in Joan Jett "I Love Rock N Roll" (2:26)

SOUND ANALYSIS   **35**

guitar: light distortion appears in pop, country, and alternative genres, while heavy distortion is reserved for hard rock, grunge, and metal.

The **drum set** is actually a collection of acoustic instruments, including: the kick drum (biggest, played with a pedal); the snare drum (a sharp cracking sound); resonant toms (ranging from high to low); and a series of brass or bronze cymbals. Listen for the drums alone at the beginning of Fall Out Boy's "Sugar We're Goin' Down" (Figure 2.5). The drums play solo at the beginning, with the cymbals joining as the rest of the band enters.

The particular cymbal on which the drummer plays often correlates with a song's form: quiet closed hi-hat cymbals at the beginning of the verse; washy hi-hat sounds as the track gets louder; and ringing crash cymbals in the chorus. An acoustic drum set is one of only two common beat layer instruments, the other being electronic drum machine. Traditionally, rock, pop, and country genres used acoustic drum sets while EDM, hip-hop, and R&B used drum machines but these once-stable genre boundaries are becoming more fluid.

Ingrid Andress's country ballad "More Hearts than Mine" showcases the versatility of yet another acoustic instrument, the **piano** (Figure 2.6). Her voice provides the melody layer, but the piano fulfills the remaining three layers simultaneously. Andress's left hand plays the lower bass layer, while her right hand plays the chord layer. Before the drum set enters at 0:32 the piano actually provides the beat layer as well, with the right-hand chords sounding evenly, right on the beat, keeping time.

Figure 2.5 Drum set in Fall Out Boy "Sugar We're Goin' Down" (0:44)

Figure 2.6 Piano in Ingrid Andress "More Hearts Than Mine" (0:04)

36   INTERPRETING MUSIC

Electronic Instruments

Each instrument in the preceding section is able to make a sound (however soft, in the case of the electric guitar) by vibrating a column of air (voice), a string (guitars, piano), or a resonant surface (drums). Some of these acoustic instruments rely on voltage to make them louder. For example, an electric guitar or bass transmits its vibration into an amplifier through electromagnetic pickups. But in the early 1980s it became commonplace to use voltage and digital technology to create synthetic sounds from scratch, doing away with the acoustic instrument altogether. This family of instruments, known as **synthesizers**, became the basis for various emerging electronic music genres, especially hip-hop, 1980s synth pop, and EDM.

Synthesizers (or synths) can either mimic traditional acoustic instrument sounds, or create new ones for which there is no analog in the real world. One of the first hit videos to use synths extensively is "Rockit" by jazz legend Herbie Hancock. Again, paying attention to the track's buildup reveals which sounds are providing the four layers. It begins with only the beat layer, provided by a **drum machine**, accompanied by percussive record scratching. A single distorted guitar chord sounds at 0:17, which is actually a sample from a Led Zeppelin song. Along with the swelling synth sound at 0:20 that mimics bowed strings, this constitutes a very sparse chord layer (these middle chord layers are often called **synth-pads**). A very low bass layer appears at the same time performed either on an electric bass guitar, or a synthesized mimicry of a bass—a **synth-bass**. Finally, at 0:28 the track's melody layer is performed on a bright, sharp sounding synthesizer. Since this sound playing the lead melody doesn't seem to be mimicking any acoustic instrument, it's known simply as a **synth-lead**.

It is hard to overstate the importance of one particular synthesizer heard here, the drum machine, on the future of popular music. The first widely used drum machine, the Roland 808 (Figure 2.7), was released in 1980. Housed in a durable metal box, the 808 contained a number of drum sounds that could be placed in any one of the 16 positions in the beat (snare almost always goes on positions 5 and 13). After creating exactly which sounds go where in the beat, the user could then adjust the volume and tone of each individual instrument to create the final product. The Roland 808 is so important for the development of hip-hop that it gets name-dropped in numerous tracks (e.g. "I know y'all wantin' that 808…" in Outkast's "The Way You Move").

Later drum machines replaced the clunky knobs and switches of the 808 with rubber pads that allowed the user to play beats using their fingers. Some drum machines look like full-size drum kits, which allows a user to play large rubber pads with drum sticks in real time (even live). The most recent evolution of drum machines has actually moved beyond synthesis altogether. Sampling programs, such as Apple's Logic software (Figure 2.8), allow a user

Figure 2.7 The Roland 808 drum machine

to manipulate actual recorded samples of drums to create a sound nearly indistinguishable from the real thing.

Today's pop hits are laden with electronic sounds of some kind (Brittany Howard's acoustic version of "Stay High" is a rare exception). Hip-hop tracks and EDM-influenced pop hits typically use synthesizers to create or modify nearly every sound. Most rock and country songs that use some acoustic instruments still use soft synth chord layers to thicken the sound. Many tracks that sound like they are using acoustic instruments are actually using samples to achieve a polished studio sound. Table 2.2 provides a quick point of reference for

Figure 2.8 Drum sampling in Logic

Table 2.2 Common acoustic and electronic instruments in various genres

LAYER	INSTRUMENT	HIP-HOP/ R&B	COUNTRY	SOFT ROCK/ POP	HARD ROCK/ METAL	EDM/ EDM-POP
Melody	Voice	x	x	x	x	x
	Synth-lead	x				x
	Piano right hand		x	x		
	Lead guitar		x	x	x	
Chord	Acoustic guitar		x	x		
	Electric guitar (clean)	x	x	x		
	Electric guitar (distorted)				x	
	Piano		x	x		
	Synth pads	x	x	x		x
Bass	Bass guitar	x	x	x	x	
	Piano left hand	x	x	x		
	Synth-bass	x				x
Beat	Drum set		x	x	x	
	Drum machine	x				x

38   INTERPRETING MUSIC

which instruments, both electronic and acoustic, provide each of the four layers in various genres of music.

UNCOMMON INSTRUMENTS AND EFFECTS

Uncommon Instruments

It would be impossible to list every instrument heard in every song in this chapter. Most important are those instruments that tend to occur as stylistic markers in particular genres. Figure 2.9 shows two instruments common to bluegrass, folk, and Americana genres, the **mandolin** (left) and the **banjo** (right), in Judah & The Lion's "Pictures" (ft. Kacey Musgraves). Along with all the guitars, the mandolin and banjo round out a family of stringed instruments known as "plucked" strings because a player makes the sound by plucking the string with either their fingers or a pick.

Country music uses plucked strings extensively, including one that is ubiquitous in that genre, the **pedal steel guitar**. Figure 2.10 shows the typical manner of playing this instrument, which involves sitting down so that one can operate the pedals. The pedal steel is most notable for its ability to slide gracefully between notes, and for its wide vibrato and sustain—qualities that it shares with the human voice. In the quiet verse of Carrie Underwood's "Cry Pretty," for example, it sounds as if it's "singing" a duet with her from 0:44 to 1:02.

Figure 2.9 Mandolin and banjo in Judah & The Lion "Pictures" (2:39)

Figure 2.10 Pedal steel guitar in Carrie Underwood "Cry Pretty" (2:52)

SOUND ANALYSIS **39**

Whereas all of the above stringed instruments are plucked, an entirely different family of **bowed strings** (along with their synthesized equivalents) regularly adds melody, chord, and bass layers in nearly all genres of popular music. The Smashing Pumpkins' video "Tonight Tonight" (Figure 2.11) shows three-quarters of the bowed string family, the low **cello** (two in front), the mid-range **viola** (back right), and the high **violin** (back left). Each of these instruments is played by rubbing a bow (traditionally made of taut horsehair) across the strings.

Figure 2.12 shows the largest member of the bowed string family, the **upright bass** (aka "double bass") in Alicia Keys's "Raise a Man." It differs from the other three in a number of ways. First, it is so large that it requires the player to be standing. Second, its increased body cavity size relative to the other three allows it to be plucked in addition to bowed. Jazz and R&B styles regularly feature the former, while the latter is heard in classical symphonies.

Drum set and drum machine still provide the primary beat layer in Latin musical genres, but they are almost always accompanied by **auxiliary percussion** instruments ("Latin" is a catch-all genre term used by *Billboard* for number of distinct musical traditions from a number of countries and regions, most of which are sung in Spanish). Several of the most common appear in Marc Anthony's 1999 video "I Need To Know," one of the first Latin videos on MTV. The easiest to hear include a metallic cowbell on every beat (0:08), punctuated by scrapping noises on the wooden *guiro* (0:14), and quasi-pitched *congas* throughout (pictured in Figure 2.13).

Figure 2.11 Cello, viola, and violin in Smashing Pumpkins "Tonight, Tonight" (0:18)

Figure 2.12 Upright bass in Alicia Keys "Raise a Man" (2:38)

40   INTERPRETING MUSIC

Figure 2.13 Auxiliary percussion in Marc Anthony "I Need To Know" (0:17)

Figure 2.14 Wind instruments in Save Ferris "Come On Eileen" (0:31)

"I Need to Know" also uses trumpet, a **wind instrument**. All wind instruments are created by blowing air through or across a cylindrical bore. The woodwind family (wind instruments that use a wooden reed), while essential to classical music, regularly lends only one instrument to popular music, the saxophone. Trumpets and trombones, members of the brass family (wind instruments activated by buzzing a mouthpiece) are also common. Ska (and ska-punk), a niche genre of music that became extremely popular in the late 1990s mainstream, uses wind instruments extensively. Figure 2.14 shows the most common arrangement of trumpet, trombone, and saxophone in Save Ferris's 1997 commercially successful cover of "Come on Eileen." Note that, even though the saxophone is *made of* brass, it is not considered a brass instrument because the sound is produced by a reed.

Uncommon Timbres and Effects

Thus far I have only discussed the sounds heard in music videos in terms of what instrument produces them. But the guitars in "Sugar We're Goin' Down" and "I Love Rock N Roll," both of which are electric and distorted, sound different. The term **timbre** refers to the exact sound produced by an instrument. Specific timbres in popular music are often the result of the exact studio recording environment used—including the size of room and exact placement of microphone—and also the **effects** used to process those sounds.

To demonstrate the concept of timbre, imagine two women whom you know well (perhaps your mother and your sister) both singing "ah" on the same pitch at the same volume. Since sound waves are only composed of frequency (pitch) and amplitude (volume), one might assume that you couldn't tell them apart. But humans are exceptionally good at identifying the vocal timbres of other humans. We evolved this trait as a survival strategy (it's good to know who's sneaking up on you!).[2] Timbre is exactly this nuanced difference between two sounds that differ in neither pitch nor amplitude,[3] what you might call the "tone" of the instrument or voice. Timbre describes the nuanced difference between your mom's and sister's voices, and also the difference between the guitars in Fall Out Boy and Joan Jett.

Effects applied to instruments and voices regularly result in the creation of their specific timbres. A class of effects known as **vocal manipulation** are most common in EDM-influenced pop music. The most common vocal manipulation effect, **auto-tune**, began not as an effect at all, but rather as an imperceptible cosmetic coverup to erase the imperfections of human singing. Changing a singer's pitch is simply done with the software's graphical interface. The record producer or engineer sees red squiggly lines wherever a singer's actual pitches are out of tune, and simply drags the errant pitch up or down to align with straight blue bands that represent a perfectly tuned pitch.

At some point in the late 1990s producers began making the traces of this heretofore imperceptible machine intentionally audible by increasing the speed at which the software "snaps" the pitch to the blue band (Cher's 1998 hit "Believe" is often heralded as a watershed moment). Because the human voice naturally slides slowly between pitches, the faster it is tuned to a specific pitch the more robotic and unnatural it sounds. Southern hip-hop musician T-Pain used it to such an extreme degree that to many the timbre is known simply as the "T-Pain Effect." Listen at 1:42 in "Got Money" (Figure 2.15) where the effect is applied liberally not only to T-Pain's singing voice but to Lil' Wayne's rap as well.

Heil Sound originally manufactured their **Talk Box** (Figure 2.16) as a guitar effect. Peter Frampton made this sound famous in the 1970s, and it would later be used by The Foo Fighters and Tool. The performer plugs their instrument (e.g. a guitar) into the box, which amplifies the sound and plays it through the surgical tube rather than a speaker. With the surgical tube inserted into their mouth, guitarists would then simply open their mouths in front of a microphone to form vowel sounds and it would sound like the guitar is "talking."

Figure 2.15 The "T-Pain" effect (auto-tune) in "Got Money" (0:48)

42 INTERPRETING MUSIC

Figure 2.16 Heil talk box

Figure 2.17 Harmonizer effect in Imogen Heap "Hide and Seek" (0:44)

French EDM duo Daft Punk has used this effect (along with other vocal manipulation effects) extensively. Instead of powering the talk box with a guitar, they use a synthesizer, which produces a cleaner, more intelligible sound such that we actually perceive what is coming out of their mouth cavity as words and sentences, rather than just abstract vowel sounds. Talk boxes are especially clear in their songs "Around the World" and "Digital Love" (while both have videos, neither Daft Punk nor their talk boxes appear in them).

Perhaps the most famous video to use another vocal manipulation effect, the Digitech **Harmonizer**, is Imogen Heap's 2005 hit "Hide and Seek." Unlike auto-tune or the talk box, the harmonizer doesn't actually use the singer's voice at all. Rather, it adds synthesized "robot" voices to harmonize with the singer. Whereas the original idea was to "smart" harmonize with the singer using built-in presets, Heap hacks the interface by connecting a keyboard controller and specifying exactly which harmonies she wants. While the official video doesn't show this happening, a number of live performances (such as that in Figure 2.17) demonstrate her mastery of the technology.[4]

SOUND ANALYSIS   **43**

Recently a vocal manipulation tool called the **vocoder** has taken on a level of popularity rivaled only by the auto-tune in the mid-2000s. Vocoders first appeared in music videos in the early 1980s. Laurie Anderson's "O Superman" features its most extensive use, though many listeners are more familiar with its novelty use as the "Mr. Roboto" voice at the beginning of Styx's song by the same name.

In "O Superman," the camera focuses on the vocoder as a complex combination of a microphone and keyboard (Figure 2.18). The user sings into the microphone but plays the pitch(es) they want on the keyboard. What we hear is then the vocal articulation of Anderson's consonants (e.g. the "s" in "Superman") combined with the pitch of the vowel sounds (e.g. the "u" in "Superman") being replaced by a keyboard. Recent EDM-pop hits use this effect extensively, usually through digital interfaces rather than Anderson's mess of keyboards and cables. "San Francisco," by EDM producers Galantis and vocalist Sofia Carson, features the vocoder prominently in its first verse. With Galantis layering Sofia Carson's vocoded voice in harmony, the overall effect is somewhat like Imogen Heap's, though the vocal timbre itself stems from Carson's, rather than a robot.

In addition to the human voice, the electric guitar is the other instrument regularly subjected to various effects in popular music. Most of these effects are controlled by the guitarist in real time using **stompboxes** such as those shown in Figure 2.19. The individual effects

Figure 2.18 Vocoder in Laurie Anderson "O Superman" (1:29)

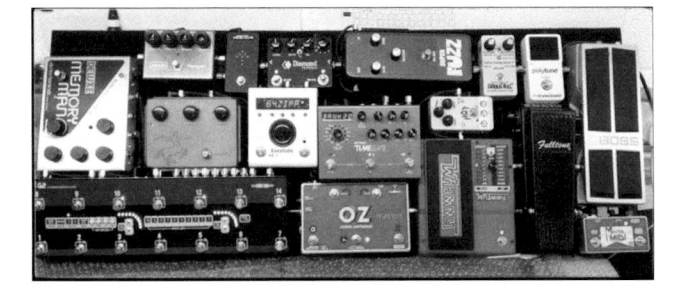

Figure 2.19 Stompbox effects arranged on a guitarist's pedalboard

44   INTERPRETING MUSIC

Figure 2.20 Reverb in My Bloody Valentine "Only Shallow" (2:34)

on a guitarist's pedalboard are myriad, though three are most common. Distortion, which is demonstrated clearly in the introduction to "Smells Like Teen Spirit" when Kurt Cobain's guitar turns from relatively clean and precise to fuzzy and diffuse, is the most ubiquitous.

The other most common guitar effects are **reverb** and **delay**. Reverb increases the length of time it takes a sound to decay. With every sound lasting longer, the entire soundscape tends to fill up like a fog bank socking in a city. Gargantuan guitar reverb fills the beginning of My Bloody Valentine's "Only Shallow" (Figure 2.20). In an interesting visual parallel, the multiple, cloudy images seem to respond to the swirl of guitar noise. Just like reverb causes sounds to stick around longer than they would normally, this image is constructed of multiple superimposed shots that each fade away gradually.

Instead of prolonging a single sound, delay multiplies it, like an echo. At the beginning of Slowdive's "Sugar For the Pill," for instance, four different chords are played four times each. But because the guitarist is using a delay pedal, the strings are only struck once at the beginning of each chord, then the delay pedal causes it to echo three times before the next chord. Figure 2.21 shows a convincing parallel in the video's visual design. A large square on the outside gets softer as it multiplies into smaller repetitions, just as the delay effect on the guitar weakens the volume of the echo each time.

My Bloody Valentine and Slowdive are both rock bands that operate in a niche subgenre known as shoegaze.[5] These effects were just as integral to the shoegaze sound as the instruments themselves. Likewise, in today's EDM and pop hits, certain effects—especially sidechaining and filter sweeps—have become synonymous with the genre.

The drop section in Sia and David Guetta's "Titanium" (e.g. 1:16) features one such effect, in which the high frequencies cut in and out on every beat. This effect is known as **sidechaining**. Figure 2.22 shows what sidechaining looks like on a **spectrogram**, a visual representation of sound. The high frequencies are sidechained to the kick drum, which means that every time the kick drum sounds, the high frequencies are cut out. They resurface momentarily between each kick drum attack, almost as if they are "breathing" with the beat.

This gradual attenuation of frequency also forms the basis of a **filter sweep**,[6] another effect heard regularly in EDM. By letting in more and more high frequencies gradually (called a high-pass filter), the pitch of a single synthesized tone gradually rises, which builds up

SOUND ANALYSIS **45**

Figure 2.21 Delay in Slowdive "Sugar For the Pill" (0:15)

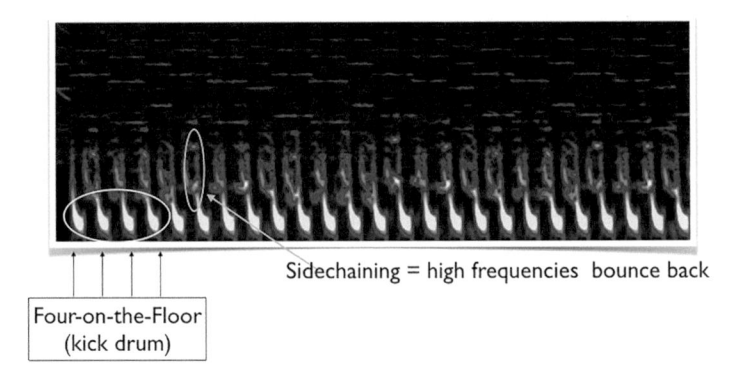

Figure 2.22 Sidechaining in Sia and David Guetta "Titanium"

tension to be released at the onset of the drop section. Listen for this gradual "whooshing" pitch from 1:12 to 1:18 in "Titanium."

DEEP DIVE: RIHANNA (FT. JAY-Z) "UMBRELLA" (2007)

Like most pop songs in the new millennium, "Umbrella," credited to Rihanna featuring Jay-Z, is a collaboration involving several producers and songwriters working more or less behind the scenes. The track began in an Atlanta studio when three musicians (Terius "The Dream" Nash, Christopher "Tricky" Stewart, and Kuk Harrell) got together to create new material from scratch, with no idea who would eventually be singing on the track. Songwriting often works this way. A backing track is created, sent to labels and A&R representatives, and then a deal is worked out. Singers listen to prospective backing tracks like actors read a script. Before Rihanna sang the hit, the team attempted to get no fewer than three singers, including A-list stars Britney Spears and Mary J. Blige. To better understand this backing track, Table 2.3 breaks it down into its four component layers.

46 INTERPRETING MUSIC

Table 2.3 Four instrumental layers in Rihanna "Umbrella" (ft. Jay-Z)

LAYER	0:01	0:11	0:33	0:56
Melody	Jay-Z's rap		Rihanna's singing	
Chord		Lead synth	Lead synth	Synth pads
Bass			(Synth bass)	Synth bass
Beat	Drum machine			

Table 2.4 Garageband "Vintage Funk Kit 03" in box notation

	5	E	+	A	6	E	+	A	7	E	+	A	8	E	+	A
H	x		x		x	x	x	x	x	x	x	x	x		x	
S				x									x	x		
K	X						x				x					

Table 2.5 Rihanna "Umbrella" beat in box notation

	5	E	+	A	6	E	+	A	7	E	+	A	8	E	+	A
H	x		x		x	x	x	x	x	x	x	x	x		x	
S				x									x	x		
K	x	x					x				x					

The buildup begins with a drum machine featuring voluminous reverb on the kick drum. Despite serving as an immediately identifiable sonic signature for the track (I'd imagine most listeners familiar with the track could identify "Umbrella" in just one to two seconds based on this beat), the beat is taken almost verbatim from a beat contained in Apple's Garageband software called "Vintage Funk Kit 03" ("VFK"). Both VFK and "Umbrella" are eight counts long, and the first four counts of both beats are exactly the same. But close scrutiny reveals that the second four counts are actually different. Counts 5–8 of VFK are presented in **box notation** in Table 2.4. The X-axis of a box notation subdivides counts 5–8 into their four component parts (called "sixteenth notes" in traditional music theory), resulting in 16 total boxes. Reading left-to-right, these are counted as "5-ee-and-uh," "6-ee-and-uh" etc. The box's y-axis lists the beat's principal instruments, in this case hi-hat, snare drum, and kick drum.

There was actually a bit of controversy on the internet surrounding what many listeners perceived as using a stock loop from Garageband's library. It is interesting that such a controversy arose in the first place, given that the song's primary genre, hip-hop, was invented by people who not only took inspiration for their beats' ideas from other artists, but in fact sampled them, verbatim. Nevertheless, a box notation of "Umbrella" (Table 2.5) reveals that there is a difference between the two patterns on the "e" of count 5. Whereas the Garageband beat uses a single kick drum on beat 5, "Umbrella" has a quick double-kick on "5-e." While the musical effect of this difference may seem subtle, it proves that the producers did not use the stock Garageband sample, but in fact programed it on their own.

This beat, along with two overlaid tracks of Jay-Z's rapped vocals, forms the backdrop of the track's buildup. Jay-Z's rap, like most rap, is distinctive in that its melody is often composed of notes that are not necessarily tuned to the same pitches on the piano (unless, of course, it's auto-tuned). This means that when the lead synth enters at 0:11 it complements, rather than competes with, Jay-Z's voice for the melody layer. Using a technique called *arpeggio* (Italian: to play in the manner of a harp), the synth part is playing up and down the individual notes of the chords rather than all at once.

Having so much reverberant low-end coming out of the kick drum sound disguises the fact that there is actually no bass layer in the first 33 seconds of the track. The bass doesn't actually enter until Rihanna's voice does, at 0:33. Even then it only plays short notes right on the beat. This serves two functions. First, just like Jay-Z's rap and the synth arpeggio make plenty of room for one another by existing in two different registers, the bass plays short notes in order to complement Rihanna's sustained, drawn out melody. Second, reserving the bass's long sustained tones for the entrance of the chorus at 0:56 helps elongate the buildup even further. Whereas the chord layer has been filled with only sparse arpeggios thus far, the chorus also supplies thick rich chord pads to help round out the sound.

Despite the backing track being made exclusively with highly processed and effected electronic sounds, Rihanna's voice is presented decidedly *au naturel,* with little to no vocal manipulation. Listening closely at 0:33 reveals some tasteful reverb and delay effects added to fill out the otherwise sparse texture, but these are present in nearly every modern recording. For example, delay effects provide for each of Rihanna's phrases to be echoed exactly one beat later. Her opening statement, ending on "had-my-heart" (1-and-a), echoes back exactly one beat later (2-and-a). This pattern of precise tempo delay continues throughout the verse.

One can never account for the gargantuan success of a hit like "Umbrella" through sound analysis alone. A number of factors go into making a hit, including lyrics, marketing, celebrity, and reception. Even if there were truly a musical formula, ostensibly, every song would use it. Nevertheless, paying attention to details of sound design, however subtle, can help identify successful songwriting strategies. The undeniably pleasing sonic design of "Umbrella" can be broken down into a three-component process: patiently building up the texture over 56 seconds; using synth layers in slightly unconventional ways (for example, using the kick drum as bass layer and the lead synth as chord layer); and showcasing the textural contrast between a fully synthetic backing track and a minimally processed lead vocal. Of course, if the producers had gone with a different lead vocalist than Rihanna or a different rapper than Jay-Z, who knows if it would have been a hit?

Table 2.6 Lingo you should know

Beat layer	Synthesizer	Vocal manipulation
Melody layer	Sample	Auto-tune
Bass layer	Synth-pad	Talk box
Chord layer	Synth-lead	Harmonizer
Buildup	Drum machine	Vocoder
Rhythm guitar	Mandolin	Stompbox
Lead guitar	Banjo	Distortion
Electric bass	Pedal steel guitar	Reverb
Acoustic guitar	Auxiliary percussion	Delay
Electric guitar	Wind instruments	Sidechaining
Drum set	Timbre	Spectrogram
Piano	Effects	Filter sweep

NOTES

1 Though I have simplified the names and definitions of these layers, I take the idea of the four layers from Allan Moore, *Song Means*: *Analysing and Interpreting Recorded Popular Song* (Farnham: Ashgate, 2012): 21.

2 For more on the evolutionary basis of our perception of timbre, see Eric Clarke, *Ways of Listening: An Ecological Approach to Musical Perception* (Oxford: Oxford University Press, 2005).

3 Megan Lavengood identifies this among multiple possible definitions of the word timbre in the first chapter of her dissertation; see Megan Lavengood, "A New Approach to the Analysis of Timbre," PhD dissertation, City University of New York, 2017. <https://meganlavengood.com/research/dissertation/>

4 See, for example, her 2009 performance on Indie 103: https://www.youtube.com/watch?v=AcHjk1fVav4

5 David Blake analyzes the ways in which particular timbres reflect an overall "indie" vibe in indie rock genres; See David K. Blake, "Timbre as Differentiation in Indie Music," *Music Theory Online* 18, no. 2 (2012), <https://mtosmt.org/issues/mto.12.18.2/mto.12.18.2.blake.php>

6 For more on sidechaining, filter sweeps, and the sonic design of modern EDM-influenced tracks see Asaf Peres, "The Sonic Dimension as Dramatic Driver in 21st-Century Pop Music," Ph.D. dissertation, University of Michigan, 2016.

CHAPTER 3 CLIP LIST

YEAR	ARTIST	VIDEO
1994	Soundgarden	Black Hole Sun
1995	TLC	Waterfalls
2006	Shakira (ft. Wyclef Jean)	Hips Don't Lie
2008	Adele	Make You Feel My Love
2015	Kendrick Lamar	Alright
2015	Drake	Hotline Bling
2016	Alessia Cara	Scars to Your Beautiful
2019	Mustard (ft. Roddy Rich)	Ballin'
2019	Anderson.Paak	Make it Better
2019	Yona	One

LYRICS

- Pronouns and Persona
  - *Pronouns*
  - *Persona*

- Common Themes
  - *Breakup (Jealousy)*
  - *Self-positivity (Empowerment, Success)*
  - *Desire (Love, Sex)*
  - *Politics/Social Justice*
  - *Surreal/Nonsense Lyrics*

- Deep Dive: Sia "Chandelier" (2014)

CHAPTER 3

Lyrics

For a lot of people who listen to popular music (dare I say, most), the lyrics are the most important thing. Our desire to hear, understand, and empathize with lyrics carries on into the music video, even though the lyrics are now not only competing with the musical instruments for attention but also the video's complex visuals.

Take, for example, Sia's 2014 hit video "Chandelier." Are its catchy melodic hooks, soaring melody, and relatable yet deeply meaningful lyrics *weakened* by the video's singular visual focus on celebrity dancer Maddie Ziegler (Figure 3.1)? Surely not. If this were the case, the video would not have received the over 2 billion views on YouTube it has garnered at the time of this writing. By contrast, Sia's record has sold 2 million units, and Maddie Ziegler's most-watched YouTube video (excluding the numerous Sia music videos she's in) has only been viewed 30 million times.

What makes the lyrics of "Chandelier" so moving, and why do they work even better when paired with a video of Maddie Ziegler dancing in an abandoned house? To answer that question, this chapter untangles the web of personalities involved in music video, including Sia (the artist), Ziegler (the actor), and the presumed narrator of the lyrics. Then, by examining the seven most common lyrical themes in popular music videos, we'll see how much of the song's raw emotional power comes from cleverly combining two themes not often heard together in a single song: partying and self-negativity.

Figure 3.1 Maddie Ziegler in Sia "Chandelier" (1:37)

PRONOUNS AND PERSONA

Pronouns

Just like in fiction, poetry, and prose writing, lyrics can be told from the first-person, second-person, or third-person perspectives.[1] **First-person** singular narration uses "I" as a pronoun to connote that the narrator was or is part of the action; first-person plural uses "we" or "us" to connote that the narrator was or is part of a group. **Second-person** narration, which relies on the pronoun "you," usually does one of two things in popular music. It could literally be speaking to another person (e.g. "you broke my heart"), or can more abstractly reference a general feeling one gets (e.g. "you know it when you see it"). Finally, **third-person** narration uses either singular or plural pronouns to address somebody else (e.g. "Maria, come back" or "Boys play games") or reference some inanimate object (e.g. "get this party started").

Unlike first and second person, third-person narration can use **feminine pronouns** (e.g. she/her/hers), **masculine pronouns** (e.g. he/him/his), or can be **gender-neutral** (e.g. ze/zir/zirs, or simply "they," which is now used as either singular or plural). "I," "we," and "you" are already gender-neutral pronouns, though listeners often collapse this neutrality when they know the artist's gender while interpreting a song.

To see just how this works, consider the situation in which you have been asked to write a review of Adele's video "Make You Feel My Love" for a music blog. Since the song is narrated in entirely the second person ("you"), you might find yourself writing something like "her lover is undergoing many trials and tribulations from which she wants to rescue him." There are at least two assumptions in this sentence that need unpacking. First, the analysis is **heteronormative**, in that it assumes that a woman must be singing about a man. Second, and more surprising, it assumes that the narrator is a woman. Assessing how this may or may not be true rests on the broader concept of persona in lyrics.

Persona

The analysis of music video deals with visuals, music, and lyrics. Analyzing persona involves disentangling the several different personalities, or **personas**, present in the combination of all three. Returning to the Adele example, while it is obviously heteronormative to guess the gender of the narrator's love interest (as expressed in the lyrics), it is also problematic to guess the narrator's gender. After all, this song was originally written not by Adele, but by Bob Dylan! And yet one shouldn't even assume that the gender of the author (Adele or Dylan) is the same as the gender of the lyrical narrator.

Astute readers of fiction, especially in genres like fantasy, adventure, etc., are already used to disentangling narrators from authors. After all, nobody really believes that Edgar Allan Poe (an author) went through the harrowing tales of the first-person narrator ("I") in *The Fall of the House of Usher*. Furthermore, there are plenty of examples of first-person narrators whose gender differs from that of their author (e.g. the first-person male narrator throughout Anna Kavan's novel *Ice*).

Therefore, in "Make You Feel my Love," the analyst must disentangle the **human persona**—Adele Laurie Blue Adkins, MBE, who identifies as a woman—from the **narrator persona**, identified only through the pronouns "I" and "my," and bearing no gender pronouns. A more accurate sentence for your review of this video might then read: "ze undergoes many trials and tribulations from which the narrator hopes to rescue zir." You could also use "they" and "them" in place of ze and zir. You could also preserve the gender-neutrality of the statement by omitting pronouns altogether.

LYRICS 53

After demonstrating the utility and validity in separating the human and narrator personas, I am now going to go one step further and suggest that one should, to varying degrees, separate the human persona from both the **actor persona** and the **artist persona**. Actor personas are only present in music videos, where the actor is shown playing a character. Figure 3.2 shows the fictional character in "Make You Feel My Love" played by the actor Adele—in this case, the fictional character goes unnamed. Believing that Jennifer Lawrence is a separate human from all of the characters she has played (Katniss Everdeen in *The Hunger Games*, for example) is the same as believing that Adele is playing an unnamed character here. Some artists, such as the rock band Tool, never appear in the music videos associated with their music, and thus never perform the actor persona.

Just like actors differ from the characters they play, humans can differ from the artist(s) they perform as.[2] Therefore, technically "Adele" is an artist persona performed by the human Laurie Blue Adkins, MBE. The human, David Eric Grohl, is the musician solely responsible for all of the sounds heard on the first Foo Fighters record, the drums on all but one Nirvana record, and has contributed to countless other projects, including a solo project as the artist "Dave Grohl."

If it feels unnecessary to distance a human from their artist persona(s), consider the extreme example of the French EDM duo known as Daft Punk (Figure 3.3). This is the artist

Figure 3.2 Actor persona in Adele "Make You Feel My Love" (0:58)

Figure 3.3 Daft Punk (artist persona)

persona adopted by two humans who, until relatively recently, were never pictured without their masks (behind-the-scenes photos have recently surfaced on the internet revealing that they are, indeed, "human after all"). It's even conceivable that different humans could have, at one time or another, performed as the artist Daft Punk without the audience even realizing it.

Whereas DJs such as Daft Punk, Marshmello, and other masked entities seem to revel in their anonymity, certain genres of music thrive on collapsing two or more personas into one believable, authentic self. Most gangsta rap, for example, operates on the assumption that the listener believes, to some degree, that the narrator of the track is telling a story that the human lived through. There is therefore little perceived difference between the artist and any of these expressions of persona. Take the case of the artist known as 50 Cent. Several of 50 Cent's songs prominently feature stories of the narrator being shot; 50 Cent is the artist persona portrayed by the human Curtis James Jackson III, who, on May 24, 2000, was himself shot. 50 Cent's image of authenticity relies on the fans believing that all of these personas are more or less the same, which he encourages by displaying his gunshot wounds prominently in music videos and public appearances.

Modern collaborative music-making practices can also complicate various levels of persona. The artist known as Flo Rida had a massive hit in 2012 called "Whistle." Writing credits for that song are awarded to no fewer than six humans, only one of which is Tramar Lacel Dillard—the human perceived as Flo Rida. If more than one person wrote the song, how can one assume that the narrator of a story is even the same as the artist, let alone the human? Since massive collaborations have become one of the most surefire ways to make money in the past decade, it can sometimes make just as much sense to conceive of an artist (e.g. Flo Rida) as a brand, or corporation, rather than as a single human. Technology has now in fact made it possible for artificially intelligent (AI) artists such as Yona (Figure 3.4) to be run entirely by corporations without a human artist at all.

These various personas have a profound impact on lyrical themes. Bearing in mind the difference between these various personas, it's a worthwhile exercise to consider which videos' lyrics seem fully fictional, sung by a human who had no similar experience, and which are drawn from that human's lived reality. Similar considerations can be given to the character played by the actor in a video. While some seem like "authentic" versions of the artist and/or human, in other videos the human seems to portray a fully fictional character.

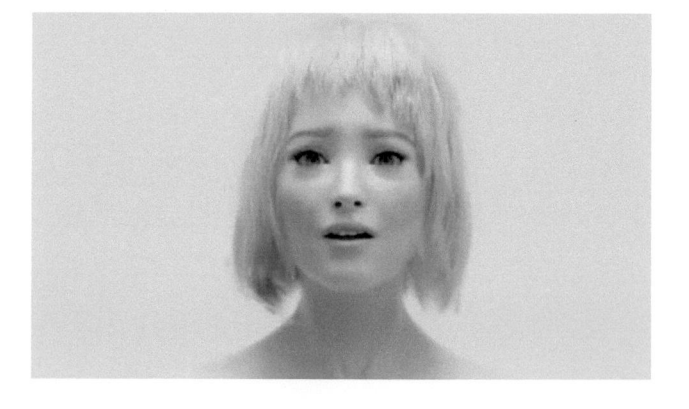

Figure 3.4 Yona (AI Musician) in their (?) video for "One" (0:27)

LYRICS **55**

COMMON THEMES

Breakup (Jealousy)

Anderson.Paak's 2019 hit "Make it Better" (ft. Smokey Robinson) is a song about breaking up. More properly, it's about living through the aftermath of a breakup and trying to figure out how to get back together with a lover. The video features plenty of imagery of a couple breaking up (Figure 3.5). From the perspective of the lyrics' continued use of the past tense ("we fell right out of touch"), as well as their description of the present ("now we're strangers in the night"), this is likely a flashback. But about half of the video shows the happy couple, which is therefore either an older flashback from before the breakup, or, perhaps an optimistic foreshadowing of the couple getting back together in the future. Chapter 4 details how music videos don't always tell exactly the same story as a song's lyrics do. In the case of "Make it Better" it seems like the video is more ambiguous in its meaning than the lyrics alone, and the combination of the two makes for a rich possibility of interpretations.

Nowhere in the lyrics or the video do we get the sense that the narrator, or Paak's character in the video, is jealous of their lover's new life. On the contrary, the narrator pines for a new start. But other breakup songs, such as Drake's "Hotline Bling," are essentially jealous demonizations of women's sexual activities after a breakup. The narrator of "Hotline Bling" comments on the "reputation" of their former lover, and criticizes them for being sexually active and wearing revealing clothing. Drake's song is both misogynistic and patriarchal since such jealousy both disproportionately affects women and reinforces male power structures.

Self-positivity (Empowerment, Success)

Generally speaking, breakup songs are not the most positive, though, in the case of "Stay Together," they may be melancholic or even aspirational. Lyrics that are explicitly positive tend to cluster around two categories: empowerment and success. Empowerment lyrics are those that describe a feeling of satisfaction in a situation that may not seem resoundingly positive. "Scars to Your Beautiful" [sic], by the Italian-Canadian singer Alessia Cara, describes the process of seeing beauty in all sorts of people. The video is remarkable in that it contains a number of diegetic voice-overs from actors other than Cara describing (and showing off) their unique bodies, as well as describing hardships society has placed on them. The woman shown in Figure 3.6, for example, describes her albinism as "weird things that make you seem strange," but reassures viewers that such unique features may end up being your "greatest strengths."

Figure 3.5 Breakup theme in Anderson.Paak "Make it Better" (2:06)

56 INTERPRETING MUSIC

Figure 3.6 Empowerment in Alessia Cara "Scars to Your Beautiful" (3:15)

Figure 3.7 Success lyrics in DJ Mustard and Roddy Rich "Ballin'" (2:46)

Success lyrics represent a different category of self-positive lyrics in that they typically focus on power or status gained by the narrator. In rap, such lyrics are frequently described as "braggadocio." Most of Roddy Rich's lyrics in DJ Mustard's track "Ballin,'" for example, detail the wealth he has accumulated, and how this wealth has led to increased social status and sexual partners. The video shows Mustard and Rich displaying this wealth, power, and fame in a strip club (Figure 3.7) and also driving a Lamborghini convertible down a closed freeway.

Desire (Love, Sex)

Songs about love and sex might represent the greatest overall proportion of lyrics in music. Such a universal topic transcends genres, appearing in country, hip-hop, rock, jazz, and classical songs. Most of the time, these songs do not actually describe sex in the current or past tense, but rather, the *desire* to have these encounters with a specific person in the future. The lyrics of "Hips Don't Lie" form a duet between the Colombian pop singer Shakira and Haitian musician Wyclef Jean. The narrator voiced by Wyclef is attracted to Shakira's dance moves, while the narrator voiced by Shakira is charmed by the suitor's attempt to woo her in Spanish. We hear Shakira singing of "the attraction" and "the tension," but never an actual physical encounter.

Since the music video for "Hips Don't Lie" features both Shakira and Wyclef as actors, it collapses the distinction between narrator-, artist-, and actor-personas. We perceive Wyclef as

Figure 3.8 Desire in Shakira "Hips Don't Lie" (2:55)

being attracted to Shakira and vice versa. But even in the video, the desire in the lyrics never materializes into a physical encounter. The shot in Figure 3.8 is actually the closest, physically, we ever see the two artists to one another. Furthermore, this shot comes at one of the only times in the song where the two are not singing about their desire, but rather a political non-sequitur about the CIA's mistreatment of both Colombians and Haitians.

Politics/Social Justice

The lyrics of En Vogue's 1996 hit "Free Your Mind" stress the importance of expanding one's perception of people beyond popular stereotypes. It teaches lessons about race and ethnicity, including not judging someone's ethnicity or their sexual preferences by their physical appearance, not assuming that revealing clothing insinuates prostitution, and not equating hip-hop music and fashion with criminal behavior.

"Free Your Mind" is one example from a broad category of lyrics that concern politics and social justice. Entire chapters will be devoted to lyrics that address gender and sexuality (Chapter 7), as well as race and ethnicity (Chapter 8). Others lyrics are more specific than that, usually concerning matters that may be particularly important to movements of a certain time. Atlanta R&B/hip-hop group TLC released the hit single "Waterfalls" during the AIDS crisis in the mid-1990s.[3] Though the lyrics are somewhat coded, its "three letters" refer to HIV, which we see a character in the video contracting after sexual contact with a woman. But, like the lyrics, the video's portrayal of HIV is also subtle. The only HIV symptom it shows—other than death—is a brief glimpse of an associated condition known as Kaposi's Sarcoma (Figure 3.9) as the character who has recently contracted the disease looks in the mirror.

A more contemporary example, "Alright," by the Pulitzer Prize-winning rapper Kendrick Lamar, addresses police brutality toward Black men. Though this has a centuries-old history, Lamar's hometown of Compton, California and the surrounding Los Angeles area has seen a profound increase in this violence since the 1990s. There's nothing subtle or coded about his lyrics "We hate popo/wanna kill us in the street fo' sho,'" or the stylized depiction of this in the song's video, shown in Figure 3.10.

58   INTERPRETING MUSIC

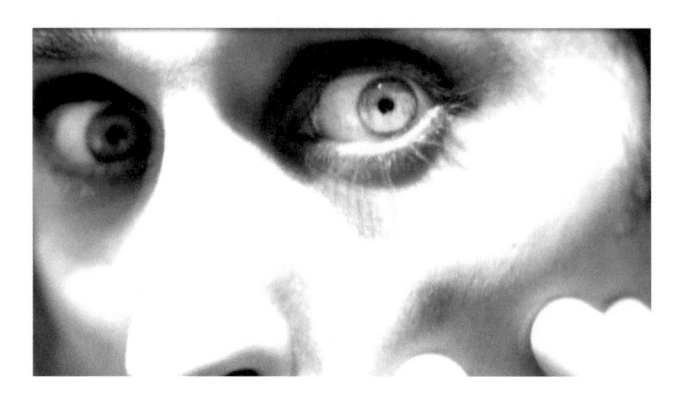

Figure 3.9 HIV symptoms in TLC "Waterfalls" (3:23)

Figure 3.10 Police brutality in Kendrick Lamar "Alright" (5:54)

Surreal/Nonsense Lyrics

Occasionally it can be difficult to decipher what relationship a song's lyrics have to any broader concept or theme, if any. Many songwriters, such as the Canadian multi-instrumentalist Moonface, source lyrics from accounts of their own dreams as recorded in dream journals. Still more popular musicians draw inspiration from thoughts or visions that they might have had under the influence of drugs. Regardless of the inspiration, whenever a song's lyrics seem to have little bearing on reality they usually evoke the surreal, or perhaps, even the nonsensical.

Soundgarden's 1994 video "Black Hole Sun" pairs its surrealist lyrics with equally surreal visuals (Figure 3.11) made possible through newly available techniques of computer-generated imagery and digital intermediate (see Chapter 6). Singer Chris Cornell's lyrics in the chorus are not only surreal but also oxymoronic. The sun cannot be a black hole, since black holes come about after a star has collapsed. And how would sunlight wash away rain?

Surreal lyrics are a little less common than they were in a period between the late 1960s and early 1970s, when musicians were openly experimenting with psychotropic drugs, as well as actively creating music that was designed for those undergoing similar body/mind experiments. One still hears echoes of this psychedelic trope in surrealist lyrics from the 1990s and 2000s, including The Smashing Pumpkins' "Bullet With Butterfly Wings," and The Mars Volta's "The Widow."

Figure 3.11 Surreal imagery in Soundgarden "Black Hole Sun" (3:36)

DEEP DIVE: SIA "CHANDELIER" (2014)

After reviewing the most common lyrical themes in popular music we are now in a better position to understand the clever way in which Sia pairs two of those—partying and self-negativity—in a clever way. Table 3.1 adapts the same kind of form chart seen in Chapter 1 to the analysis of lyrics. Charting these themes by section, along with some particular keywords, shows that the two themes interact with the song's verse-prechorus-chorus-postchorus design in an interesting way. Two of those sections mix the two themes, while each is given its own section.

Verse one starts with a first-person narration in which the narrator identifies herself as feminine ("party girls"). On the surface, these lyrics might seem to be about partying, but the narrator quickly reveals a self-negative side to this behavior, in which she admits that perhaps she's using drinking to push down feelings she doesn't feel entitled to express outwardly. In the second half of the verse she sarcastically proclaims that she "feels the love" of her friends and perhaps even lovers who only seem to enjoy her company while partying.

At the prechorus the narrator throws caution to the wind, forgets about her insecurities, and just drinks ("one, two, three"). This leads to the song's emotional climax in the chorus, in which the narrator swings from a chandelier. A listener who just hears the beginning of the chorus would likely miss out on the broader self-negative context. Maybe it's a joyous moment, surrounded by friends, doing something a little unsafe but completely memorable. However, the narrator reminds us in the third line of her sadness, with the whoosh of the chandelier acting to dry her tears.

Table 3.1 Lyrical themes in Sia "Chandelier"

TIME	SECTION	THEME(S)	KEYWORDS
0:10	Verse 1	Party, self-doubt	Party girl, push it down
0:33	Prechorus	Party	Drink
0:44	Chorus	Party, self-doubt	Swing, chandelier, tears
1:28	Postchorus	Self-doubt	Holding on, glass full
1:50	Verse 2	Self-doubt, escape	Run from this

60 INTERPRETING MUSIC

As a corrective, the postchorus swings the narrative fully back to the realm of the self-negative. Holding onto the swinging chandelier is a metaphor for drinking as a way to cope, to "hang on for dear life," with her larger problems. She mentions keeping her glass full as a double entendre; there is little optimism in this sentiment, only a glass full of booze to keep her medicated until the morning.

Verse two begins the next morning with the narrator a mess, looking for a way out. These two lines are actually the last two unique lines heard in the song. Almost immediately the track cuts to the second prechorus, chorus, and postchorus, featuring exactly the same lyrics as before. Whereas verse one was four lines in length, verse two is just half that. In a clever parallel to the spirals of alcoholism and depression, the narrator is back to drinking and self-medicating quicker than ever.

But how, if at all, are these lyrics portrayed in the video? The video features dancer Maddie Ziegler (then aged 11 years) dancing in a neglected house captured in exceptionally long shots, giving the illusion that the video might have been filmed in a single take. Based on this description it may seem like the video then has nothing to do with the lyrical themes described here.

Chapter 4 tackles the four different relationships the narrative in a song's lyrics can have with the narrative advanced by its music video. Two options seem most probable in the case of "Chandelier." First, that this video actually lacks a visual narrative, that a child dancing in a room doesn't have the familiar exposition-rising action-climax-denouement structure of a well-formed story.[4] Second, perhaps Ziegler's dance tells some kind of story, but that it's a different story than that told by Sia in the lyrics.

While both of these interpretations are possible, humans seem to have a propensity for neatly summarizing seemingly disparate elements—such as a set of lyrics and a long dance sequence—into a broader, single narrative that encompasses both. And though I think the two possibilities I have provided (no story, no relationship) are defensible, I would imagine that most viewers actually are creating some sort of larger meaning that relates Ziegler's dance to Sia's lyrics.

One might start this process of multimedia meaning creation by paying attention to the house itself (Figure 3.12), which looks either like a flophouse that the occupant doesn't have the energy to care for (tattered furniture, sparse decoration), or a party house (graffiti and other damage). In either case it's easy to imagine the narrator of Sia's song there. The house is also quite empty. Metaphorically, this could relate to the emptiness Sia's narrator is feeling throughout the song, which she attempts to fill through alcohol and shallow relationships.

But the most fruitful avenue to pursue comes about only by paying close attention to Ziegler's movements and how closely they animate the particular lyrics sung by Sia at that point in the video.[5] Some are so explicit that they border on pantomime, such as that shown

Figure 3.12 Flop house/Party house in Sia "Chandelier" (0:08)

LYRICS   **61**

in Figure 3.13, in which Ziegler does a familiar cup-stacking routine timed perfectly with the "one, two, three" lyrics. And though Ziegler doesn't swing from a chandelier along with the title lyrics at 0:46, her kaleidoscopic pirouettes effectively animate the same sentiment.

But other movements are less explicitly tied to single words or phrases, and can only be interpreted with respect to the broader themes of the lyrics. In the second postchorus, for example, Ziegler wraps herself in various ways among the window dressings. Her face becomes panicked as she imagines herself being choked by the curtains. It is also possible that she's treating the curtains as a frame in which to simulate drowning, since she gradually moves higher and higher in the frame (Figure 3.14) until her eyes are no longer visible, all the while drawing the closed curtains up closer to her gasping face.

In either interpretation of this movement, it would be easy to see how this could relate to the postchorus's lyrics. In barely keeping her face above the rapidly closing curtains Ziegler is perhaps "holding on for dear life." Or maybe Ziegler is interpreting Sia's "glass full" metaphor rather literally, with the curtains acting like rising water. Even more broadly, the constriction Ziegler feels in the curtains surely has a parallel in the ongoing self-destructive cycles the narrator finds herself in that are difficult to escape.

"Chandelier" was the first of several music video collaborations between Sia and Ziegler. The two have, to some extent, become part of the same brand. While Sia rarely appears in her own videos, Ziegler almost always wears Sia's signature blond square-cut wig, suggesting that the actor Ziegler might be portraying some version or persona of Sia herself. Clearly this unorthodox strategy has been successful; their total collaborative output has been viewed over 4 billion times on YouTube. Perhaps this statistic alone might serve as evidence that viewers are finding deeper connections between the song's lyrics and the video's interpretation of those lyrics.

Figure 3.13 Explicit pantomiming of lyrics in Sia "Chandelier" (0:33)

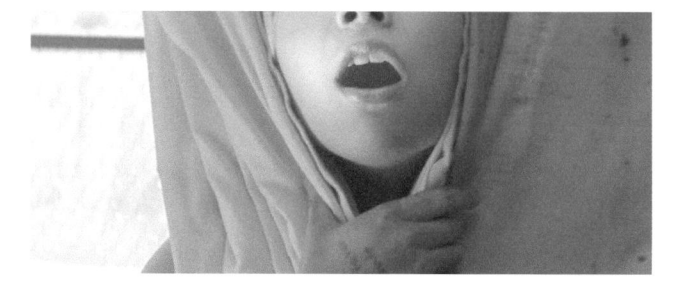

Figure 3.14 Thematic interpretation of lyrics and visuals in Sia "Chandelier" (3:03)

Table 3.2 Lingo you should know

First-person	Feminine pronouns	Narrator persona
Second-person	Gender-neutral	Actor persona
Third-person	Heteronormative	Artist persona
Masculine pronouns	Human persona	

NOTES

1 For more on this perspective, see Lori Burns, "Multimodal Analysis of Popular Music Videos," in *Coming of Age: Teaching and Learning Popular Music in Academia*, edited by Carlos Xavier Rodriguez, n.p. (Ann Arbor: University of Michigan Press, 2017).

2 For more on persona in music video, see Philip Auslander, "Framing Personae in Music Videos," in *The Bloomsbury Handbook of Popular Music Video Analysis*, edited by Lori Burns and Stan Hawkins, 91–109 (London: Bloomsbury, 2019).

3 Of course, we cannot neatly separate the AIDS crisis from the broader social justice movements it was linked to, especially gender and race. A number of social and political factors, including wealth inequality, access to treatment, social stigmas concerning transparency among sexual partners, etc. lead to white, cisgendered men having higher rates of survival from HIV.

4 Carol Vernallis takes the position that music videos rarely have well-formed narrative structures and that they compensate for this lack by creating interest through rhythmic editing techniques; see Carol Vernallis, "Strange People, Weird Objects: The Nature of Narrativity, Character and Editing in Music Videos," in *Medium Cool: Music Videos from Soundies to Cellphones*, edited by Jason Middleton and Roger Beebe, 111–151 (Durham, NC and London: Duke University Press, 2007).

5 Maeve Sterbenz uses this method to derive broader meanings about sexuality and masculinity from a video by Tyler the Creator; see Maeve Sterbenz, "Movement, Music, Feminism: An Analysis of Movement-Music Interactions and the Articulation of Masculinity in Tyler, the Creator's 'Yonkers' Music Video," *Music Theory Online* 23, no. 2 (2017).

UNIT 2

Interpreting Visuals

CHAPTER 4 CLIP LIST

YEAR	ARTIST	VIDEO
1987	Guns N Roses	Paradise City
1992	Pearl Jam	Even Flow
1994	Rage Against the Machine	Freedom
1994	Crash Test Dummies	Mmm Mmm Mmm Mmm
1994	Beastie Boys	Sabotage
1995	Dr. Dre	Keep Their Heads Ringin'
1995	Coolio	Gangsta's Paradise
1996	Foo Fighters	Big Me
1996	The Roots	What They Do
2002	Linkin Park	In the End
2005	Sleater-Kinney	Jumpers
2007	Rihanna (ft. Jay-Z)	Umbrella
2008	Beyoncé	If I Were a Boy
2009	Lady Gaga	Alejandro
2009	The Chicks	Goodbye Earl
2011	Sia and David Guetta	Titanium
2012	Bruno Mars	Locked Out of Heaven
2016	HAIM and Calvin Harris	Pray to God
2016	Beyoncé	Formation
2017	Lorde	Green Light
2018	Halsey and Benny Blanco	Eastside
2018	Lady Gaga and Bradley Cooper	Shallow
2018	SZA and Kendrick Lamar	All the Stars
2019	Rag N Bone Man and Calvin Harris	Giant
2019	Anuel AA and Karol G	Secreto
2019	Lizzo	Juice

NARRATIVE

- Narrative Strategies
  - *Performance Video*
  - *Narrative Music Video*
- Intertextual Videos
  - *Parody and Satire*
  - *Movie Music Videos (MMV)*

- Mise-en-Scène
  - *Settings*
  - *Imagery*
- Deep Dive: Yola "Ride Out in the Country" (2019)

CHAPTER 4

Narrative

Yola's "Ride Out in the Country" has one of the most unexpected surprise endings in the history of music video. This surprise is so effective because the video's lyrics and its visual universe tell stories that are deeply rooted in certain expectations associated with certain genres.

"Ride Out in the Country," like all sung music, presents a story through its lyrics. But how does that story change when we consider the music video, which also presents a story through its visuals? Considering the ways in which these different types of stories interact yields four different narrative strategies. Some videos tell the same story as their lyrics, some tell different stories, and others, like Yola's, do both.

To really appreciate Yola's complex narrative web, this chapter begins by addressing types of music videos that don't tell a visual story at all. After dealing with music videos that do tell a visual story, I'll present a number of videos called "intertextual videos" that derive their meaning through relationships to other media. This chapter also examines an important cinematic term—mise-en-scène—which helps explain how music videos use settings and imagery to enhance these stories.

NARRATIVE STRATEGIES

Performance Video

Every video has the capacity to tell stories. But sometimes a director, an artist, or both, may forego a narrative story in order to showcase the musical performance itself. Videos such as these, which highlight singing, dancing, or instrumental performance for the majority of their duration, are known as **performance videos**.[1]

The performance video is only one of many approaches to structuring narrative in music video. Furthermore, videos that are *entirely* performance-based are quite rare. Many videos presented in this chapter feature performance footage intermixing with other narrative types as the video unfolds.

Some videos are actually just recorded footage of the band playing live. These **live-performance videos** can be subdivided further into whether the audio track is taken from that same performance or whether the live footage is synced to the album version of the track. Pearl Jam's "Even Flow" (Figure 4.1) showcases the raw, live audio recorded on-site along with the visuals. By contrast, the audio in Guns N Roses' "Paradise City," despite the stitched-together footage of live performances (note the "behind-the-scenes" authenticity in Figure 4.2) sounds much more polished because it's taken directly from the album version of this track.

66 INTERPRETING VISUALS

Figure 4.1 Live performance (live audio) in Pearl Jam "Even Flow" (0:56)

Figure 4.2 Live performance (studio recording) in Guns N Roses "Paradise City" (0:48)

More commonly, artists don't use actual live performance footage, but rather construct live performances on controlled studio soundstages. These **simulated-performance videos** benefit from a feeling of "live-ness" while retaining the control of a modern production studio. Shot at the height of his international fame, Bruno Mars's video for "Locked Out of Heaven" (Figure 4.3) seems like he's performing in a small club. But there is no way Bruno Mars would actually be playing in a club that size. Usually the audience members have been cast as extras in the video. Simulated live-performance videos use the same studio recordings heard on the album version.

There is also a more general category of performance videos that do not make any attempt at "live-ness" whatsoever. This category of **soundstage-performance videos** includes all footage of singers singing and musicians performing instruments in a cinematic environment. To keep a viewer's interest, such scenes are often interspersed with non-performance footage. Rock band HAIM is shown singing in highly unusual settings throughout "Pray to God," especially a constructed forest (Figure 4.4) with lions, bears, and wolves. Sleater-Kinney performs in front of a white studio screen in "Jumpers." The bland white backdrop (Figure 4.5) resonates with the mundane office work, which acts as a foil to the band rocking out with their instruments.

Figure 4.3 Simulated live performance in Bruno Mars "Locked Out of Heaven" (0:21)

Figure 4.4 Soundstage-performance in HAIM and Calvin Harris "Pray to God" (2:22)

Figure 4.5 Soundstage-performance in Sleater-Kinney "Jumpers" (1:02)

68 INTERPRETING VISUALS

Figure 4.6 Choreographed performance in Lizzo "Juice" (0:52)

Videos in dance-friendly genres, like hip-hop and dance-pop, often feature elaborately choreographed performances. Dancing in these **choreographed-performance videos** serves largely the same role as footage of a rock band playing in soundstage-performance videos. The costumes and movements often relate to the video's broader themes. In Lizzo's "Juice," for example, the 1980s costumes and exercise movements (Figure 4.6) match the video's overall "throwback" theme.

Narrative Music Video

Watching these six performance videos with the sound muted reveals that none of them tells a story through their visuals alone. In describing the "plot" of these videos, one would just say that a bunch of people were singing and dancing in costumes somewhere. When a video does tell a story with a developed plot, without the aid of the music or lyrics, it is said to be a **narrative music video**.[2] Since most song lyrics tell stories as well, narrative music videos enable four different relationships between a video's musical story and its simultaneous visual story.[3]

Explicit-narrative music videos tell the same visual story as that told in the lyrics. Each of the three verses in The Crash Test Dummies' video for "Mmm Mmm Mmm Mmm" tells a lyrical story that is reenacted, visually, as a school play (Figure 4.7). In these verses, the listener hears about a boy getting into a car accident (verse 1), a girl with birthmarks (verse 2), and dancing in a church (verse 3). A viewer would experience exactly the same plot if they watched the video on mute.

But it's also possible that a video can describe a completely different story than the lyrics, resulting in an **extra-narrative** video. Watching Sia and David Guetta's "Titanium" with the sound switched off results in the following visual plot:

- A boy comes to amidst a scene of destruction at a school.
- He flees home and realizes he's the one who caused the destruction.
- The police try and apprehend him but he uses his supernatural powers to evade capture (Figure 4.8).

But listening to Sia's lyrics alone reveals a very different plot. Broadly, the lyrical theme is one of self-positivity (see Chapter 3). More particularly, these lyrics are about resilience in the face

NARRATIVE **69**

of a verbally abusive person. Therefore, the video presents an extra narrative through visuals not heard in the music.

Most music videos are not so extremely explicit or extra, but rather somewhere between. They often provide a **complementary-narrative** that reinforces some of the lyrics, but which also provides a slightly different spin on those lyrics. Beyoncé's "If I Were a Boy" is an excellent example. In the first verse Beyoncé pays little attention to her attire ("roll out of bed in the morning/and throw on what I wanted and go") and acts friendly with her co-workers ("kick it with who I wanted…"). However, the lyrical story has nothing to do with the police-officer character she plays in the video (Figure 4.9). The lyrics "drink beer with the guys" are also not shown explicitly in this verse. The visuals complement the lyrics yet do not explicitly trace them.

Finally, though rare, it is possible that a video can provide a **conflicting-narrative** that is antithetical to the lyrical plot. "Eastside," by Halsey, Khalid, and Benny Blanco, features lyrics about a childhood crush who the narrator wishes would "come away" with them and "start a new life." Watching this video with the sound off is especially instructive since it uses subtitles to describe not the lyrics, but the visual narrative itself. Unlike the plot of the lyrics, there is no indication that the two lovers will end up together. Instead, the narrator's crush—Ash, now a grown woman (Figure 4.10)—doesn't even seem to remember Benny, or the vivid story that he's telling in the lyrics.

Figure 4.7 Explicit narrative in Crash Test Dummies "Mmm Mmm Mmm Mmm" (0:38)

Figure 4.8 Extra narrative in Sia and David Guetta "Titanium" (3:43)

70   INTERPRETING VISUALS

Figure 4.9 Complementary narrative in Beyoncé "If I Were a Boy" (0:37)

Figure 4.10 Conflicting narrative in Halsey and Benny Blanco "Eastside" (2:20)

INTERTEXTUAL VIDEOS

Parody and Satire

Narratives are rarely self-contained within the unique universe of a single music video. Music videos borrow narrative devices and structures just like books do (like every story that begins with "once upon a time"). Some videos go even further, in that understanding their narrative relies on the viewer recognizing the music video's relationship to another specific media product. Such videos are known as **intertextual videos**, since their full comprehension relies on the knowledge of one or more additional "texts" (be they visual, audio, or lyrical).

Two of the most common types of intertextual music videos involve parody and/or satire. **Parody** music videos mimic another text largely for entertainment value, while **satire** music videos draw the viewer's attention to that text in order to highlight its shortcomings.

Aired in 1995, Foo Fighters' video for "Big Me" parodies a popular series of commercials for the breath-mint brand Mentos. Just like the commercials, the band members find themselves in a confounding situation but then, fueled by the energy of their breath mints (re-labeled "Footos" in Figure 4.11), come up with an ingeniously zany solution. Three such

NARRATIVE **71**

Figure 4.11 Specific parody (Mentos) in Foo Fighters "Big Me" (1:19)

Figure 4.12 Genre parody in Beastie Boys "Sabotage" (1:21)

vignettes, each aligned with a verse of the song, comprise the music video. Since the video parodies something so specific, it's best described as a **specific-parody video**.

While the Foo Fighters video relies on the viewer's knowledge of a specific text, some music videos draw on a broader concept or genre. Lizzo's "Juice" (Ex 4.6), for example, parodies talk shows, home shopping, and 1980s workout tapes. Likewise, The Beastie Boys' "Sabotage" parodies the conventions of 1970s cop dramas (Figure 4.12). Because these videos refer to a genre of texts, rather than one specific text, both are examples of **genre parody**.

The Roots' video for "What They Do" also draws on the conventions of a genre: the hip-hop music video. But, since it does so in order to point out the flaws—conceivably so that the viewer perceives The Roots as transcending those flaws—it's an example of satire. Throughout the video the band acts out several worn-out tropes in hip-hop videos, drawing the viewer's attention to each with explanatory Chyron text (Figure 4.13).

72 INTERPRETING VISUALS

Movie Music Videos (MMV)

Music videos often intertextually reference a feature film, especially when that song appears on the movie's soundtrack. These MMVs either contain actual footage from the movie, or, in some cases, contain newly produced footage featuring actors from that film.[4] Dr. Dre's "Keep Their Heads Ringin'" (from the film *Friday*) is an example of the former. Seemingly an unrelated video involving some kind of high-tech heist, it nevertheless incorporates scenes from *Friday* throughout. Usually these appear as unrelated "jump cuts" (see Chapter 6). But sometimes the film is interwoven into the video plot, such as when the robbers attempt to confuse the security guards by playing *Friday* on the closed-circuit security monitor (Figure 4.14).

Coolio's song "Gangsta's Paradise" was featured on the soundtrack of the film *Dangerous Minds* (starring Michelle Pfeiffer). The music video does feature some footage from the film itself but is more notable for starring Pfeiffer alongside Coolio. Coolio interrogates Pfeiffer (and vice versa) in this newly filmed footage (Figure 4.15) amidst scenery designed to look like the dilapidated high school in the film.

Figure 4.13 Satire in The Roots "What They Do" (3:56)

Figure 4.14 Incorporation of film footage in Dr. Dre "Keep Their Heads Ringin'" (3:10)

Since not everyone who watches these music videos has seen the film referenced within, the question is: what happens to the meaning of an MMV, or any other intertextual music video, when the viewer does not "get" the allusion to another text? Does this mean they don't "get it?" On the contrary, I'd like to suggest that, while a viewer who does not understand the intertextual reference might not get the meaning *intended* by the video's producer, they are then given wider freedom to interpret the meaning of the video in myriad ways not yet imagined by that producer.

Take for example SZA and Kendrick Lamar's video for "All the Stars." The song appears on the soundtrack of the 2018 blockbuster *Black Panther*, but contains neither footage from the movie nor newly filmed scenes with the actors. Perhaps the most direct intertextual reference to the film can be seen in a shot that features Lamar walking with actual black panthers (*Panthera pardus,* see Figure 4.16)—creatures that never actually appear in the film. A viewer who doesn't know that this song is on the soundtrack, and doesn't get it from this allusion,

Figure 4.15 Newly filmed MMV scene in Coolio "Gangsta's Paradise" (2:01)

Figure 4.16 Subtle intertext in SZA and Kendrick Lamar "All the Stars" (1:51)

74   INTERPRETING VISUALS

Figures 4.17 (a) and (b) Trailer-MMV in Lady Gaga and Bradley Cooper "Shallow" (2:25) (2:48)

might then hear the song's lyrics about violence ("confrontation ain't nothin' new to me/ you can bring a bullet, bring a sword") in relation to real-world violence, rather than the fictional violence depicted in the film—especially since the video introduces a mild conflicting narrative by showing these tribal warriors to be from the African continent, whereas the film focuses on tribal warriors in the (fictional) nation of Wakanda.

On the opposite end of the spectrum, there also exist MMVs that are fully dependent on their corresponding movie for any and all narrative. Such MMVs are usually wholly composed of footage from the film, and thus blur the line between MMV and movie trailer. This typically occurs in music biopics where the musical artist of the MMV and actor of the film are the same. Lady Gaga and Bradley Cooper's MMV for "Shallow," from the film *A Star is Born*, starring Lady Gaga and Bradley Cooper, for example, contains two kinds of shots: footage from the film (Figure 4.17a); and footage of the musicians performing the song in front of an audience (Figure 4.17b). But since the on-stage performance is also taken directly from the film, the entire MMV is composed of footage from *A Star is Born* and thus behaves like a musical movie trailer.

MISE-EN-SCÈNE

Telling a story in music videos relies on narrative devices and relationships with other texts. But music video directors enhance these stories by building a visual world to support them. The term **mise-en-scène** originally comes from the world of theater, where it literally means "building a scene."[5] In music video, mise-en-scène can be broken down into two categories: settings and imagery. Just as the universe of unique lyrics can be categorized by their broader themes (see Chapter 3), so can settings and imagery, which are either produced physically (like theater sets), or created virtually with computer-generated imagery (CGI).

NARRATIVE **75**

Settings

"Green Light," by the New Zealand pop star Lorde, features each of the three most common types of setting in music video: club, driving, and urban. Lorde is shown singing and dancing in the club setting (Figure 4.18). She escapes the club for the privacy of a hired car but proceeds to hang out the window and dance on top of it (much to the chauffeur's chagrin). Lorde also walks the streets of her native Auckland singing along with her earbuds (to her own song?). Through a technique known as **cross-cutting** (see Chapter 6), the video editor continually cuts between shots filmed in each of these settings to produce the illusion that these scenes all have something in common.

There are of course many possible music video settings other than these three. While some may be one-offs (e.g. the four-treadmill setting in OK GO's "Here it Goes Again"), a few other common settings are worth mentioning. The **CGI setting** is a world produced virtually, entirely in post-production, with actors filming in front of a green screen. These were common in the early 2000s when the technology was new and exciting. Linkin Park's "In the End" features flying whales, vines growing several stories tall in a desert, and many other fantastical elements only possible through CGI (Figure 4.19). Since then, music video directors have followed the trend in feature film production to incorporate CGI and live action elements as seamlessly as possible; improvements in CGI technology have made it increasingly difficult to tell the difference anymore.

On the opposite end of the spectrum, some music video directors prefer to show the viewer exactly how the video was filmed. To draw yet another parallel to theater, this is the

Figure 4.18 Club setting in Lorde "Green Light" (3:01)

Figure 4.19 CGI setting in Linkin Park "In the End" (1:36)

music video equivalent of breaking the fourth wall, admitting the artifice of the media itself to the viewer. These **reflexive settings** usually happen when one camera zooms out to reveal other cameras and microphones on set. They can also make the viewer privy to the camera technology itself. Beyoncé's "Formation" contains several scenes that simulate the camera operator's viewfinder (Figure 4.20). Almost like leaving a forensic trace of the production process, the viewer sees the raw footage through the eyes of its creators. One might also interpret this scene as a "throwback" to VHS technology. Both the "play" icon in the lower right-hand corner and the grainy quality of the video support this reflexive interpretation.

Videos occurring in **nature settings** often center around bodies of water. In R&B singer Rag N Bone Man's video "Giant," nature represents an escape from the protagonist's depressing urban life. He runs all the way from his housing complex, through a forest, and ultimately into a clearing where he meets like-minded individuals. To celebrate, they have a dance party in the rain. Along the way, we see cameos of EDM producer Calvin Harris (Figure 4.21), who is depicted as the pastoral ideal man, foraging mushrooms in the forest and fishing for his dinner from a canoe.

Travel settings often highlight the success and ambition of a musician. The premise of travel settings is that the viewer is privy to a "behind the scenes" look at what it's like to be a pop star. Anuel AA and KAROL G's "Secreto," for example, highlights not only the luxurious places to which the duo travel, but also how they travel there: by limousine, helicopter, four-wheeler, or jet (Figure 4.22). Aside from a passing shot of the two artists performing this song on a stage somewhere, there is no performance element. Largely, the narrative action of the video details the two musicians' real-life love and the excitement of world travel when a wealth of riches is at your disposal.

Figure 4.20 Reflexive setting in Beyoncé "Formation" (2:28)

Figure 4.21 Nature setting in Rag N Bone Man and Calvin Harris "Giant" (1:13)

NARRATIVE **77**

Figure 4.22 Travel setting in Anuel AA and KAROL G "Secreto" (1:19)

Figure 4.23 Classic film imagery in Rihanna and Jay-Z "Umbrella" (2:04)

Imagery

Setting refers to the location (either real or simulated) where a video takes place. That location also contains imagery—props, signs, symbols, icons, or other visual messages—that helps advance the video's mise-en-scène. The most common imagery seen in music videos includes that which is borrowed from classic films, or imagery that is either religious or political in nature.

Rihanna and Jay-Z's "Umbrella" uses umbrellas in a manner similar to several classic films. For viewers familiar with *Singing in the Rain* (1952) and *My Fair Lady* (1964), Rihanna's dance scenes with these props will evoke a timeless classic. This resonates with the Elizabethan architectural setting seen in some of these dance scenes (Figure 4.23). The added orange filter and Rihanna's costume—far too sexy for a mainstream film in the mid-century—provides an interesting conflict with this classic association.

Religious imagery in music videos can be sacred, but it's more often profane. Such imagery in Lady Gaga's video "Alejandro" drew sharp criticism from The Catholic League, and, perhaps more surprisingly, Katy Perry. Her underwear features an upside-down cross, long associated with acts of rebellion against the church (Figure 4.24). But it was probably her act of *theophagy* (literally, eating of a god) that riled up the most viewers. At once profane and sexual, it calls to mind several related images in Madonna's "Like a Prayer."

Music videos have long served as sites for both sexual and political rebellion. Mexican-American rock band Rage Against the Machine produced several videos in the early 1990s that advertised the injustices volleyed against Indigenous peoples in North America

78 INTERPRETING VISUALS

(Figure 4.25). One such example is "Freedom," which details the case for Leonard Peltier, a Chippewa Indian and leader of the American Indian Movement who was captured by the FBI at the Pine Ridge Reservation in 1975. Later chapters will be devoted to videos that address issues of race and ethnicity (Chapter 8) and those that promote political viewpoints (Chapter 9).

Figures 4.24 (a) and (b) Religious imagery in Lady Gaga "Alejandro" (5:12, 5:14)

Figure 4.25 Political imagery in Rage Against the Machine "Freedom" (4:44)

NARRATIVE   **79**

DEEP DIVE: YOLA, "RIDE OUT IN THE COUNTRY" (2019)

Yola's 2019 video "Ride Out in the Country" makes a fascinating study piece for each of this chapter's foci: narrative, intertext, and mise-en-scène. Of course, all of these are, to a certain extent, dependent on one another. The lyrics alone tell a familiar story of trying to get over heartbreak. They are at once sad and optimistic, with the narrator opining that falling out of love with their former lover isn't easy but also reveling in the fresh country air and freedom of a drive as a means of forgetting about those troubles. While this is a universal tale that could be heard in songs spanning various genres, a number of timbral and rhythmic factors place this song squarely in the country-ballad genre: strummed chords on an acoustic guitar; tasteful leads on a pedal steel guitar; a relaxed drum pattern with quiet ride cymbal; and a relaxed ballad tempo.

The video's opening seconds also situate this track, visually, within the country genre. The setting is literally out in the country, with the actor-persona Yola (also the video's character-protagonist) driving an old pickup truck (Figure 4.26). By introducing this setting and imagery in the opening seconds the video immediately creates a rural country mise-en-scène that shapes how we perceive everything within it.

It's worth stating the obvious that one important part of this video does not fit squarely into the country genre—Yola herself, a strong, full-figured Black woman in a genre that has been historically dominated by cisgendered, straight, white men. But genre conventions seem to be unraveling in the past decade, particularly regarding the race, sexuality, and ethnicity of musicians associated with certain genres. Some of the most successful folk/Americana hits of the mid-2010s were recorded by Mumford & Sons (British) and First Aid Kit (Swedish), and 2019 was also the year that a gay Black man (Lil' Nas X) topped the country charts.

Once the musical and visual mise-en-scène puts us in the country genre, a host of expectations derived from other country songs and videos comes with it. And this is what makes the video's ending so surprising. Everything from the tempo, the timbre, the setting, the imagery, and the bright yet undersaturated lighting sets up an expectation of *wholesomeness*. One assumes that Yola is just out for a drive in the country to escape a past lover. After all, this is what the lyrics describe. It is then a massive plot twist when, at 1:47, she parks the truck, walks around to the back, and pulls back the tarp to uncover her cargo: two dead bodies wrapped in blankets (Figure 4.27).

"Ride Out in the Country" is not a parody video or a satire video. Yola is actually a country artist; she's not playing on the conventions of the country genre to prove a point. Because the universe of country videos sung by women about killing former lovers and stuffing them into a vehicle is small enough, there is a potent intertext here with a 2009 video by The Chicks called "Goodbye Earl" (Figure 4.28).[6]

Figure 4.26 Mise-en-scène in "Ride Out in the Country" (0:22)

80   INTERPRETING VISUALS

Figure 4.27 Plot twist in "Ride Out in the Country" (1:47)

Figure 4.28 Intertext with The Chicks "Goodbye Earl" (3:37)

Figure 4.29 Yola breaking the fourth wall in "Ride Out in the Country" (1:53)

Yola's video departs from The Chicks' in a number of ways. First, unlike the dark humor of the latter (which features a zombie-like, deceased Earl conducting and singing along with the band), Yola's only hint at humor is a knowing grin, not quite a wink, she gives the viewer in the seconds following the plot twist (Figure 4.29). Unlike television and feature films, most music video performers look directly into the camera as a matter of course (including Yola throughout this video). But this particular gaze does seem to break the fourth wall, acknowledging the irony, with Yola telling the viewer "see what I did there?"

Table 4.1 Lingo you should know

Live-performance video	Complementary-narrative video	Cross-cutting
Simulated-performance video	Conflicting-narrative video	CGI setting
Soundstage-performance video	Specific-parody video	Reflexive setting
Choreographed-performance video	Genre-parody video	Nature setting
Explicit-narrative video	Satire video	Travel setting
Extra-narrative video	Movie music video	

Yola's video is drastically different from "Earl" in that nothing in the song's lyrics prepares the viewer for this plot twist. "Goodbye Earl" is about as explicit as explicit-narrative videos get. Because its visuals tell exactly the same story as the lyrics, a viewer who heard the song on the radio prior to watching the video wouldn't be surprised in the least. Even small details in the lyrics, such as Earl not liking the taste of his wife's black-eyed peas, are rendered explicit in the video. But the question remains: while "Ride Out in the Country" is clearly not an explicit-narrative video, what is the relationship between its visual plot and its lyrical plot?

I might start by ruling out a conflicting relationship. While the viewer has no reason to *expect* the video's plot twist, nothing in the lyrics rules out its possibility. The narrator mentions "forgetting about you," and "letting it all go like I ain't got a care." A listener might *assume* a wholesomeness in those lyrics (or at least the absence of double homicide), but the video causes the viewer to interpret both of those lyrical ideas (retrospectively) as being perfectly plausible explanations for the narrator's relief after killing her former lover.

For that reason, I am tempted to say that Yola's video is an interesting case of complementary narrative that borders on extra narrative. It's easy enough to understand how the video and lyrics may be about the same experience. But a viewer's expectations—cued instantly by the country-ballad genre—suggest so strongly a wholesomeness that all but rules out double homicide that it seems like the video presents a different story than the music and lyrics. Since there are *two* bodies in the back of the truck, the video does suggest a potential reason for the dissolution of the narrator's relationship with the now-dead partner (infidelity), which is also an example of blurring the line between complementary and extra narratives.

NOTES

1 Martina Elicker identifies the performance video genre in "Popular Music in the Age of the Video Clip," *AAA: Arbeiten aus Anglistik und Amerikanistik* 23, no. 1 (1998): 69–89.

2 Vernallis suggests that narratives in music videos of the new millennium are more developed and less fragmented than those of the 1980s; see Carol Vernallis, "Music Video's Second Aesthetic?" in *The Oxford Handbook of New Audiovisual Aesthetics*, edited by John Richardson, Claudia Gorbman, and Carol Vernallis, 437–465 (Oxford: Oxford University Press, 2013).

3 These four categories of narrative in music videos were originally put forth by my PhD advisee Matthew Ferrandino; see Matthew Ferrandino and Brad Osborn, "Seeing Stores, Hearing Stories in Narrative Music Video," *SMT-V* 5, no. 5 (2019), <https://vimeo.com/357096231>

4 Brent Ferguson provides an extensive study on the ways to analyze intertextuality in movie music videos; see Brent Ferguson, "Intertextuality in the Movie Music Video," Ph.D. dissertation, University of Kansas, 2020, <https://dissexpress.proquest.com/dxweb/doc/2433285236.html?FMT=AI&desc=Intertextuality+in+the+Movie+Music+Video>

5 For more on mise-en-scène in music video see Michel Chion, *Audio-Vision: Sound on Screen* (New York: Columbia University Press, 1990).

6 The artist formerly known as The Dixie Chicks changed their name to The Chicks in 2020 to distance themselves from images of the antebellum South.

CHAPTER 5 CLIP LIST

YEAR	ARTIST	VIDEO
1987	Whitney Houston	I Wanna Dance With Somebody
1990	Sinead O'Connor	Nothing Compares 2 U
1994	Green Day	Basket Case
1999	Jennifer Lopez	If You Had My Love
1999	Macy Gray	I Try
1999	Destiny's Child	Jumpin, Jumpin
2000	NSYNC	Bye Bye Bye
2002	Johnny Cash	Hurt
2007	Feist	1, 2, 3, 4
2016	The Weeknd	False Alarm
2018	Dua Lipa and Silk City	Electricity
2018	Drake	God's Plan
2019	Khalid	Talk
2019	FKA Twigs	Cellophane
2019	Yola	Faraway Look
2019	Ariana Grande and Victoria Monét	Monopoly

CINEMATOGRAPHY

- Color and Light
  - *Hue, Saturation, Brightness (HSB)*
  - *Digital Intermediate (D.I.)*
  - *Interpreting HSB Values*

- Camera Angles and Movement
  - *Point-of-View (POV)*
  - *Eye-Level*
  - *Low-Angle/High-Angle*
  - *Panning and Tracking Shots*
  - *Handheld Shots, Shaky Camera*

- Deep Dive: Janelle Monae (ft. Grimes) "PYNK" (2018)

CHAPTER 5

Cinematography

When Janelle Monae approached music video director Emma Westerberg about the concept for her upcoming music video "PYNK," Monae's only directive, supposedly, was that the video should contain a lot of the color pink (Figure 5.1). This chapter's deep dive will reveal that Monae's video is about so much more than the color pink, including gender, sexuality, and the rich intellectual tradition of Afrofuturism. Many of those concepts are nevertheless animated or made beautiful by Westerberg's various uses of the color pink, which she executes through skilled control of the various parameters of color and light that music video directors manipulate to create their final product.

The technology music video directors use today to manipulate color and light is drastically different than the technology used in the 1980s and 1990s. This chapter shows how it was done in both eras. More importantly, this chapter leverages observations about color and light into interpretations that take into account the bigger picture of music videos. Cinematography in music videos all ultimately hinges on a camera operator's ability to master various camera angles and movements that bring music videos to life, a process discussed in the chapter's second half.

Figure 5.1 The color pink in Janelle Monae "PYNK" (4:07)

84 INTERPRETING VISUALS

COLOR AND LIGHT

Hue, Saturation, Brightness (HSB)

Like the Guns N Roses performance video from the same year (1987), Whitney Houston's "I Wanna Dance With Somebody" begins with black and white footage of a backstage performance to set up a sort of "behind the scenes" authenticity. But after this introduction the camera leaves behind the world of the backstage performance, with most shots occurring on a blank soundstage. This blank soundstage gives the director maximum control of color and light.

In the late 1980s the primary way directors and the rest of a music video crew controlled color and light was analog, through lamps fitted with thin, colored **gels**. Videos were also filmed using analog tape—digital video formats weren't used for music videos until the 1990s. The only color editing that could be done to tape was by using a **telecine** machine. A primitive device mainly used to convert professional studio-grade tape into cassette formats for home playback, its color editing function was limited to changing the color of the entire image, rather than individual elements. This is all to say that in the pre-digital era, there was a premium on getting color right the first time, because it was nearly impossible to fix it later. Figure 5.2 shows four shots from "I Wanna Dance with Somebody" that neatly demonstrate the range of colors directors could achieve using gels alone.

These four shots also demonstrate the way that film professionals talk about color, which is in terms of **HSB values**. **Hue** is what most people mean when they refer to color. To identify the individual colors of the rainbow as "ROYGBIV" is merely to name seven distinct

Figures 5.2 (a)–(d) Gels in Whitney Houston "I Wanna Dance With Somebody" (1:04)

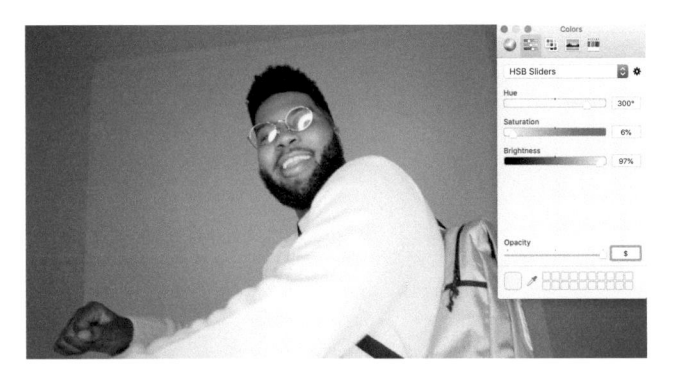

Figure 5.3 HSB values in Khalid "Talk" (0:39)

points on a spectrum of visible light frequencies. Accordingly, Figure 5.2a–d might be said to contain the hues magenta, yellow, green, and blue. A more specific way of identifying hue is to use an integer value between 0 and 359 on a color wheel. Red starts around 0 degrees, giving way shortly to orange and yellow around 30 and 55. Greens and blues appear between 110 and 220, becoming violet and purple around 230 and upward until reaching red again. The magenta in Figure 5.2, for example, is around 298 degrees.

Saturation is how much of that hue is present. The fullest expression of a hue one can imagine is at 100% saturation—the bluest blue—while 0% of any hue is either black or white, depending on brightness (more on that shortly). Comparing Whitney Houston's magenta to a similar color seen throughout Khalid's "Talk" (Figure 5.3) illustrates some differences in saturation. The far left and right edges are the most saturated (67%), while the pink on his shirt is nearly colorless, at only 6% saturation. The reason that his shirt appears nearly white (rather than black) is not only because it lacks saturation but also because it's at a very high level (97%) of **brightness** (aka "lightness"—you'll sometimes hear "HSL" values instead of "HSB"). Any hue at any saturation level will appear black with a brightness level of zero. Bear in mind that all of this variation in color perceived in Figure 5.3 occurs when the actual *hue* remains nearly identical, 298 on the wall versus 300 on the shirt, small enough to be a mere margin of error in measurement.

Digital Intermediate (D.I.)

Getting the color right in real life was key in the age of Whitney Houston's music video. But in the early-to-mid 1990s a new tool called D.I. (also known as "color grading") emerged that gave filmmakers the ability to manipulate color for individual objects in a shot in post-production.[1] Instead of filming to analog tape and editing the entire image with a telecine, now music video creators were filming to digital tape and editing the final product on computers. One of the first feature films to reveal this technology was *Pleasantville* (1998), which imagines a culturally conservative community in the mid-century that is actually black and white. The dramatic shot shown in Figure 5.4 occurs when Joan Allen's character begins to acquire hue as a metaphor for the heretofore forbidden emotions she feels. Everything else in the shot, including Pleasantville itself, remains black and white.

Green Day's video for "Basket Case" was one of the first to utilize D.I. technology. It was actually filmed entirely in black and white; every color was added later, digitally, using a computer. Since the song's lyrics are about paranoid delusions resulting from drug use, the

86   INTERPRETING VISUALS

Figure 5.4 Dramatic use of digital intermediate in *Pleasantville*

Figure 5.5 Digital intermediate in Green Day "Basket Case" (1:41)

video's setting, a mental institution, seems fitting. As shown in Figure 5.5, the colorist chose only deeply saturated, neon hues with medium brightness, which lends a surreal quality to the video because these colors appear "abnormal."

Interpreting HSB Values

Identifying which colors are present in a music video usually acts as the first step toward interpretation. Though it's often said that there are universal interpretations of certain colors (e.g. green = envy, red = rage), there are a few problems with this approach. First, such associations are rarely human universals and are more likely culturally conditioned for only a subset of humans in a certain place at a certain time. A color that connoted sadness for one civilization at one time may very well connote prosperity for a different group of people today.

A better approach is to consider the interpretation of color in music videos as contingent. Specific colors take on a specific context within an individual music video. Certain directors may favor certain color schemes or designs throughout their oeuvre. Colors associated with brands may take on referential meaning. Drake's "Hotline Bling," for example, likely brings to mind a number of T-Mobile ads for millennial viewers just as color schemes in The 1975s "Love it If We Made It" (see Chapter 9) remind an older generation of Apple's iPod ads.

Macy Gray's "I Try" is an example of a video that uses color as a narrative device within the video. Director Mark Romanek uses a stark color contrast—cool blues versus warm oranges and reds—to advance a narrative in which blue represents "playing it cool" while the warmer colors represent bottled up feelings the protagonist is trying to repress. Figure 5.6 shows this most concisely on Macy Gray's wardrobe. When she's alone in the hotel room by herself she wears only the orange shirt ("We should be together babe") but when she enters the public sphere she attempts to cover up these emotions ("I play it off but I'm dreaming of you"). Romanek represents this cover-up literally, with the cool blue jacket somewhat but not fully covering the orange shirt.

Along with the settings and imagery discussed in Chapter 4, colors can also help to establish a music video's mise-en-scène. Dua Lipa and Silk City's "Electricity" is a fictional retelling of the August 2003 blackout in New York City, in which nearly all of the city's residents lost power. British directing duo Bradley and Pablo begin the video with archival footage from 2003, then cut directly to the shot of Dua Lipa in Figure 5.7. Despite the two shots having different aspect ratios (more on this later), the blue hues in various levels of brightness instantly transport us to an evening in an urban area that has lost power.

Figures 5.6 (a) and (b) Representative colors in Macy Gray "I Try" (0:29, 0:41)

88 INTERPRETING VISUALS

Color can also work on an intertextual level by enabling interpretations that may not be present in the song's lyrics alone. The lyrics in FKA Twigs's song "Cellophane" are self-negative and autobiographical in nature, reflecting the artist's struggles after sustaining injuries both physical and emotional. Director Andrew Thomas Huang and set designer Fiona Crombie worked together to create an image of Twigs as a moving bronze statue, showcasing her athleticism as she performs aerial stunts (Figure 5.8a). Greek statues immediately come to mind. So, when a winged Pegasus enters the visual narrative it makes sense within the visual and material world of Greek mythology created in the visuals (Figure 5.8b) despite this having nothing to do with the lyrics. That Twigs eventually ends up in a sort of underworld furthers this Greek mythology intertextual arc.

Figure 5.7 Color as mise-en-scène in Dua Lipa and Silk City "Electricity" (0:19)

Figures 5.8 (a) and (b) Color as intertextual reference in FKA Twigs "Cellophane" (0:49, 2:26)

CINEMATOGRAPHY   **89**

Johnny Cash's video for his cover of the Nine Inch Nails song "Hurt" uses a different kind of gold. His is light and lowly saturated to dramatize Cash's failing health. Especially effective are moments that juxtapose such shots with film footage of Cash as a younger man. These throwback images are full of bright, highly saturated blues. Such images not only connote youthfulness but help the viewer appreciate the differences in color palettes between film stocks created nearly half a century apart (Figure 5.9).

Directors often use "throwback" looks such as these in music videos (and film) by altering colors in a way that references different film stock used in previous eras. Yola's "Faraway Look" (Figure 5.10) goes over the top in evoking a 1970s aesthetic by including not only

Figures 5.9 (a) and (b) Color as temporal contrast in Johnny Cash "Hurt" (0:15, 2:25)

Figure 5.10 Anachronism in Yola "Faraway Look" (1:54)

90   INTERPRETING VISUALS

lower film speed, different color profiles, and simulated film scratches but also psychedelic color swirls around the edge of the frame that evoke the trippyness of the period. Particularly jarring are the anachronistic moments such as the one shown in Figure 5.10 where iPhone screens, playing a video-within-a-video, are depicted in 1970s color and light.

CAMERA ANGLES AND MOVEMENT

Though the history of film and music videos might be said to contain a nearly infinite number of unique camera angles and movements, several are common enough to recognize as well-worn tropes. This section focuses on these most commonly encountered angles and movements.

Point-of-View (POV)

A **POV** camera angle occurs when a camera appears to be positioned on the face (or perhaps even inside the eyes) of the protagonist. While this is incredibly common in video games—especially first-person shooter games—it is rare in film and music video. More often film and music videos rely on **simulated POV**, in which an editor's quick cut from a subject's eyes to the object of their gaze leaves the viewer with the impression that they are seeing what the subject sees. At 2:11 in "Cellophane," for example, the cut from Twigs's upward gaze to the Pegasus above makes the viewer feel like they are looking upward right over her shoulder.

With the influence of gaming culture seeping into both film and video, actual POV music videos have become more common in recent years. Canadian hip-hop star The Weeknd's "False Alarm" is essentially a first-person shooter video, a classic example of an extra narrative wholly unrelated to the lyrics (Figure 5.11). The plot has just as much to do, if not more so, with the video's director, Illa Naishuller, who has directed a number of first-person POV action videos for his own band Biting Elbows, as well as the first-person POV feature film *Hardcore Henry*.

Eye-Level

Eye-level shots are those in which the viewer perceives that the camera is directly in front of the subject. These tight shots are achieved either through close camera placement or close zoom. Eye-level shots do something like the opposite of POV shots. Instead of the viewer feeling like they are seeing the world through the eyes of the subject, eye-level shots make

Figure 5.11 Point-of-view in The Weeknd "False Alarm" (1:30)

the viewer feel as if the subject is addressing them directly. Irish singer-songwriter Sinead O'Connor's cover of Prince's "Nothing Compares 2 U" makes extensive use of eye-level shots (Figure 5.12). The lyrics concerning the subject's painful breakup seem confessional in a way, and thus generate a profound sense of empathy.

Low-Angle/High-Angle

We have already seen a **low-angle shot** (also called a "worm's eye" shot) in The Roots' satirical video "What They Do" (see Chapter 4), which they subtitle the "beatdown shot." Low-angle shots give the viewer the illusion that the camera (and thus the viewer) are in or near the ground looking up at the subject. "What They Do" is playing on a well-worn trope in machismo rap and nü-metal, in which masculine power is emphasized by this higher position, literally looking down on the viewer. Low-angle shots have other, unrelated uses, especially in dance scenes, where they can emphasize the dancers' footwork. Figure 5.13 shows such use of the low-angle shot in Latin pop star Jennifer Lopez's "If You Had My Love."

Figure 5.12 Eye-level shot throughout Sinead O'Connor "Nothing Compares 2 U" (0:16)

Figure 5.13 Low-angle dance sequence in Jennifer Lopez "If You Had My Love" (3:10)

92 INTERPRETING VISUALS

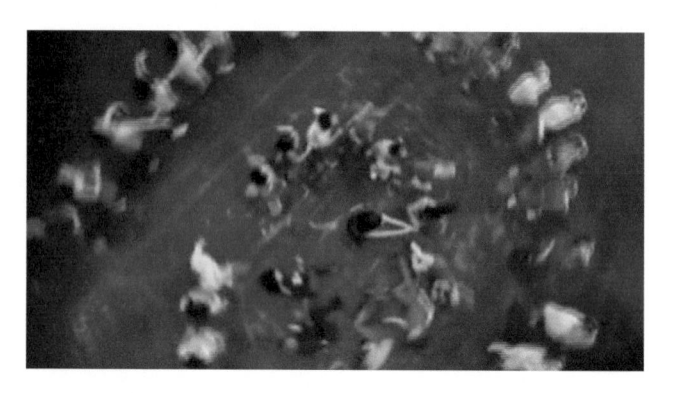

Figure 5.14 High-angle choreography in Feist "1, 2, 3, 4" (1:24)

Figure 5.15 Camera drone in Drake "God's Plan" (3:55)

The opposite of a low-angle shot, the **high-angle shot** (also known as "bird's eye") is typically used to give the viewer a broad overview of a setting. It does so by not only pulling up but also zooming out, and in this way is actually quite different than the low-angle shot. High-angle shots are useful for showing choreography among large numbers of dancers, as in Canadian folk-singer Feist's hit "1, 2, 3, 4" (Figure 5.14).

Remote-controlled, aerial vehicles equipped with cameras, commonly known as **camera drones**, have recently made possible shots from even higher above the subject that would have been impossible with even with the largest camera cranes. Drake's video for "God's Plan," which centers on the artist giving away the entire budget allocated for the music video to various causes and people in need, uses a camera drone to show the artist addressing a large crowd at the University of Miami (Figure 5.15) where he has just given away a $50,000 scholarship to undergraduate student Destiny Paris James.[2] In the past five years the technology for camera drones has become so affordable that amateur filmmakers can pick them up at local department stores.

Panning and Tracking Shots

Music videos are known as being distinct from classic films in that they constantly seem to be in motion. Not only do cuts happen much quicker in music videos relative to film,[3] but the camera itself is stationary less frequently. Two of the most common types of camera movements involve tracking and panning. A **tracking shot** actually moves the camera—usually on a mechanical dolly—in order to give an illusion of movement relative to a relatively motionless subject. Figure 5.14 is actually a dizzying high-angle tracking shot. It tracks Feist (center) in a circular motion as she spins in place, while the stationary subjects around the outside stay planted as they fall one-by-one to her imaginary gun.

By contrast, a **panning shot** involves the camera rotating on a stationary base in order to capture a subject in motion. It is, in essence, the inverse of the Feist shot—the camera spins instead of her. One of the more famous examples occurs in the feature film *Forrest Gump*, in which Gump runs toward the camera, then turns left down a road with the stationary camera panning right 45 degrees to capture the subject-in-motion.

Handheld Shots, Shaky Camera

Whereas controlled smooth movements afforded by a camera dolly lend slick professionalism to videos, the opposite is also common. **Handheld shots** lend a sense of authenticity by promoting the idea that the viewing subject is privy to some minimally edited "real" experience. As such, they are common in not only documentaries but in faux-documentary television series, both humorous (e.g. *The Office*) and dramatic (e.g. *Friday Night Lights*). This behind-the-scenes approach to music video can be thrilling when it gives the viewer the illusion that they have unfiltered access to A-list pop stars. Such personal footage (however staged) in Anuel AA and KAROL G's "Secreto" (see Chapter 4) makes the viewer seem privy to the couple's jet-setting. An extreme example of handheld footage occurs throughout Ariana Grande and Victoria Monét's "Monopoly." The video is composed of handheld shots taken on a low-quality camera phone by Grande herself (Figure 5.16), as well as simulacra of such shots made to look low-quality through video compression (more on that later). The video's narrative conceit is that the viewer is watching an impromptu Tik-Tok style video shoot happening between two friends on a roof. Such playfulness is amplified by goofy emojis and flying text cluttering the screen throughout.

One byproduct of handheld footage, intentional or not, is the inevitable shakiness that comes from attempting to hold a camera still in one's hand. At some point this **shaky**

Figure 5.16 Handheld footage in Ariana Grande and Victoria Monét "Monopoly" (1:05)

94   INTERPRETING VISUALS

Figure 5.17 Shaky camera effect in NSYNC "Bye Bye Bye" (1:09)

camera effect became not only something sought after but also artificially amplified. Through digital effects, directors sometimes add extra shakiness to existing footage. This is usually to promote the effect of a "shockwave" emanating from particularly powerful dance moves. Not coincidentally, directors usually time this effect to land simultaneously with the dancers' feet and the hard hit of a kick drum. Figure 5.17 shows a still of this effect in NSYNC's "Bye Bye Bye" where the simultaneous downbeat of a kick drum and the dancers' five pairs of feet hitting is amplified with a shaky camera effect (note the motion blurring low in the frame). The effect is amplified further through a low-angle shot, putting the viewer right at the epicenter of the percussive action. Destiny's Child's "Jumpin' Jumpin'" is a cautionary tale of how this effect can lose its power if used throughout, especially when not aligned with the beat.

DEEP DIVE: JANELLE MONAE (FT. GRIMES) "PYNK" (2018)

Applying these cinematography concepts to Janelle Monae's celebrated video for "PYNK" can highlight some of the video's central messages: queer love, self-love, and female empowerment. Monae has said the following about the video:

> PYNK is a brash celebration of creation. self love. sexuality and pussy power! PYNK is the color that unites us all, for pink is the color found in the deepest and darkest nooks and crannies of humans everywhere… PYNK is where the future is born.[4]

I read Monae here as talking not only about empowerment but also about how pink is the shared color of flesh that unites all humans, as well as creation and birthing.

Director Emma Westerberg approaches this video similarly, as a mediation on the color pink. She derives this hue using two distinct methods: (1) color grading through a D.I.; (2) by working with the natural pink hues in the video's desert setting. Regarding the former, the director herself has commented "I love color grading—it's like painting."[5] Figure 5.18a and 18b depict the color grading Westerberg uses in the video, showing the naturally captured desert setting on top, and its digitally manipulated final version below. The top screenshot already has a naturally occurring pink (hue = 14 degrees), while the

CINEMATOGRAPHY   **95**

edited version shifts that hue downward by 41 degrees (333 degrees) and increases the saturation from 23% to 42%.

The other way that Westerberg creates stunning pinks in this video is by capitalizing on a neat coincidence: infrared cameras, when used in the daytime, render the abundant sunshine of the desert as pink. Figure 5.19 shows a close-up of Monae shot with an infrared camera. In this way, color is linked directly to the setting. Filming this same video with the same

Figures 5.18 (a) and (b) Color grading in "PYNK" (0:12)

Figure 5.19 Daytime infrared appears pink (1:06)

96   INTERPRETING VISUALS

Figure 5.20 Floating car as Afrofuturism in "PYNK" (0:06)

camera in the cloudy Pacific Northwest, for example, would not afford enough sunshine to produce the intended effect.

But the setting of "PYNK" is not just an actual place (the desert), it's a fictional one as well. Arguably the crux of the video's mise-en-scène hinges in a quick shot in the video intro, in which Monae and their crew roll up in a floating car (Figure 5.20). Of course, the car is not actually floating. The wheels and tires were removed while CGI dust was added in their place, along with a high-frequency/high-tech "whirring" sound.

Recognizing the floating car forces a viewer to realize that Monae's video does not take place in any current setting but rather in an imagined future. This interpretive move places "PYNK" within the long intellectual tradition of Afrofuturism.[6] Janelle Monae's vision of the future is a feminist utopia, where strong Black women of all body types are welcomed to a celebratory hotel in the desert. Westerberg helps us picture the women in this setting with a number of different cinematic techniques. First, the two dominant camera angles are detailed close-up shots and wide establishing shots. The close-ups tend to be used for political messages. Both the middle fingers in the air (Figure 5.21a) and the "I GRAB BACK" on the decidedly unsexy underwear (Figure 5.21b) resonate with contemporaneous social movements promoting awareness of sexual misconduct and discrimination towards women, especially #MeToo and #TimesUp. The latter responds directly to Donald Trump's infamous "grab 'em by the p***y" valorization of sexual assault.

Westerberg reserves the wide establishing shots for pulled-back images of large dancing ensembles. The most famous of these sequences features women in yonic pants (Figure 5.22). Other dancing scenes, particularly those that happen inside and just outside the diner, use only mid-range shots to give us the illusion that the viewer is involved in the dance party. One particularly hard-hitting bass drop in this dance party (3:25) is amplified by the same shaky-camera-effect seen in the NSYNC video nearly 20 years earlier.

In addition to these contrasting camera angles, Westerberg curiously uses two different **aspect ratios** throughout the video. Aspect ratios measure the width of an image's wide axis relative to its narrow one. Most of the video is shot in 16:9 aspect ratio, a relatively standard ratio at the time of this writing that looks good on wide-screen televisions, laptop computer screens, and smartphones in portrait mode. But selected shots, such as that shown in Figure 5.23, revert to 4:3, a boxier standard from decades ago that was designed for pre-widescreen televisions.

Why does Westerberg introduce such discontinuity? One clue has to do with the **compression** of these 4:3 shots relative to the crisp realism of the 16:9. Compression is basically

CINEMATOGRAPHY   **97**

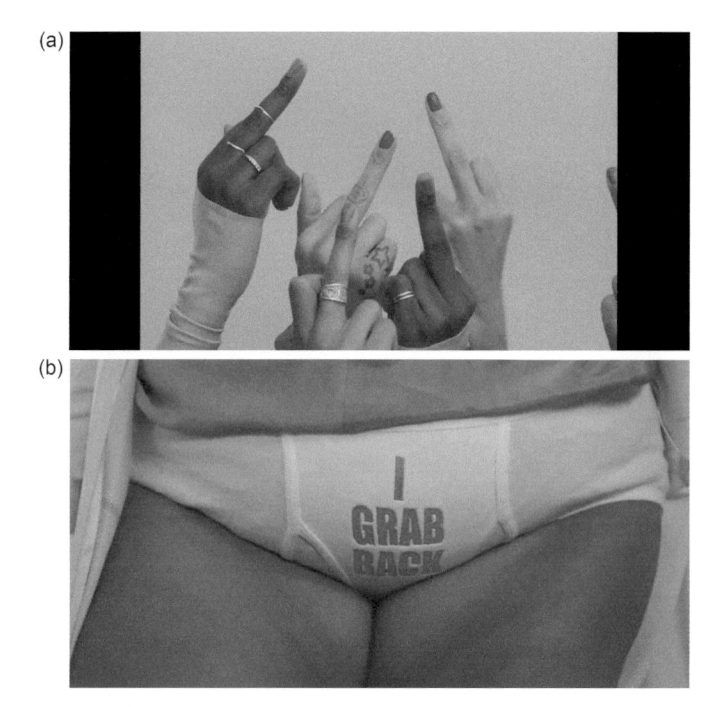

Figures 5.21 (a) and (b) Close up shots with political messages in "PYNK" (3:59, 2:26)

Figure 5.22 Wide establishing shots of yonic pants in "PYNK" (1:12)

how much information is lost in order to keep file size to a minimum. Low compression, seen throughout the video, looks realistic, whereas highly compressed shots, such as those seen in 4:3 aspect ratio, look grainy. Canadian musician Grimes (the track's producer) responds to this change in video quality by using a high-pass filter. The high-pass filter, which temporarily cuts out all of the track's high frequencies, acts as a sonic analog to the video compression's reduction of visual information.

That these grainy shots likely call to mind VHS playback and even home camcorder is part of the point. Westerberg is trying to make these 4:3 shots look like "throwback" home-video footage to introduce a sense of nostalgia and feeling into the video. This has

98   INTERPRETING VISUALS

Figure 5.23 4:3 aspect ratio shot in "PYNK" (2:44)

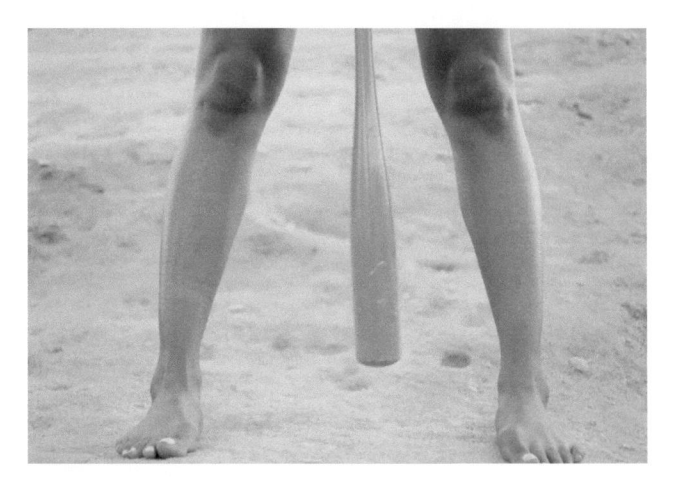

Figure 5.24 Monae's commitment to trans women in "PYNK" (1:16)

an interesting parallel with the all-video album *Dirty Computer* from which "PYNK" is taken, which is full of 1980s "throwback" synth and drum machine sounds, and it creates a rich perceptual dissonance between an album/video about Afrofuturism and sounds/shots meant to evoke the past. Beyoncé's *Black is King* (2020), another album-length music video, uses this same play with compression and aspect ratios in an Afrofuturistic setting.

Like "Make Me Feel" and other videos from *Dirty Computer*, "PYNK" shows Janelle Monae beside their creative and romantic partner, Tessa Thompson (Figure 5.1).[7] In this Afrofuturistic utopia, women can and do have all imaginable body shapes and sizes, and people are free to love whomever they choose. In a shot that goes by rather quickly (Figure 5.24), Monae also affirms their commitment to trans women through a metaphorical shot using a pink baseball bat. We will return to the broader topic of LGBTQ+ themes in music videos in Chapter 7.

Table 5.1 Lingo you should know

Gels	Point-of-view (POV)	Tracking shot
Telecine	Simulated POV	Handheld footage
HSB values	Eye-level	Shaky camera effect
Hue	Low-angle	Aspect Ratio
Saturation	High-angle	Compression
Brightness	Camera drone	
Digital Intermediate (D.I.)	Panning shot	

NOTES

1 For more on how digital intermediate has changed coloring practices in modern music videos see Carol Vernallis, "Music Video's Second Aesthetic?" in *The Oxford Handbook of New Audiovisual Aesthetics*, edited by John Richardson, Claudia Gorbman, and Carol Vernallis, 437–465 (Oxford: Oxford University Press, 2013).

2 For more on this story see Tyler Anderson, "Drake surprises a Miami student with a $50k Scholarship," *BBC News* (February 6, 2018), <https://www.bbc.com/news/newsbeat-42959635>

3 For an extensive discussion of music video editing practices, see Emily Caston, "'The First Cut Is the Deepest' Excerpts from a Focus Group on Editing Music Videos, with Explanatory Historical and Theoretical Notes," *Music, Sound, and the Moving Image* 11, no. 1 (2017): 99–118.

4 This quote from Monae comes from Angelica Florio, "Janelle Monáe's New Video About Female Sexuality will Leave You Feeling Like a Goddess," *Bustle* (April 10, 2018), <https://www.bustle.com/p/janelle-monaes-pynk-video-about-female-sexuality-will-make-you-feel-like-a-goddess-8746306>

5 See Felicia Kelley's documentary clip "The Making Of Janelle Monáe's "PYNK" Video With Emma Westerberg," *Genius* (May 10, 2018), <https://www.youtube.com/watch?v=4ZNFfYccXLM>

6 Ken McLeod provides the historical framework for Afrofuturism in pop music in "Space Oddities: Aliens, Futurism and Meaning in Popular Music," *Popular Music* 23, no. 2 (2003): 337–355.

7 Both Thompson and Monae identify as pansexual, and Monae has adopted the gender-neutral pronoun "they."

CHAPTER 6 CLIP LIST

YEAR	ARTIST	VIDEO
1982	Michael Jackson	Thriller
1984	The Cars	You Might Think
1989	Madonna	Like a Prayer
1991	R.E.M.	Losing My Religion
1995	Nine Inch Nails	Hurt
1996	Tool	Aenema
1996	The Smashing Pumpkins	Tonight, Tonight
2000	NSYNC	Bye Bye Bye
2005	Fall Out Boy	Sugar We're Goin' Down
2007	Justice	D.A.N.C.E.
2010	The Arcade Fire	Sprawl II (Mountains Beyond Mountains)
2011	Gotye (ft. Kimbra)	Somebody that I Used to Know
2012	Fun (ft. Janelle Monae)	We Are Young
2015	Jack Ü (ft. Justin Bieber)	Where are Ü Now?
2015	Björk	Stonemilker
2016	The Chainsmokers (ft. Halsey)	Closer
2019	FKA Twigs	Cellophane
2019	Alicia Keys	Raise a Man
2019	2Chainz (ft. Ariana Grande)	Rule the World

EDITING AND SPECIAL EFFECTS

- Editing Basics
  - *Storyboards*
  - *Offline vs. Online Editing*
  - *Diegetic vs. Non-diegetic Sound*
- Editing to Rhythm and Form
  - *Setting and Form*
  - *Cutting Rhythm*
- Special Effects
  - *Analog Effects*
  - *Digital Effects*

- Deep Dive: Travis Scott "Sicko Mode" (2018)

CHAPTER 6

Editing and Special Effects

Travis Scott's 2018 video for "Sicko Mode" (ft. Drake) contains a number of special effects that delight the senses but may be difficult for a viewer to explain without at least a cursory understanding of how special effects work. Scott collaborated with the seasoned director Dave Meyers, who in turn employed a renowned special effects company called MOD.[1] While it is normally true that editing usually happens after the director is done shooting the footage, the particular types of special effects seen in "Sicko Mode" are fully integrated into the process of shooting itself. In other words, Meyers and MOD needed to collaborate from the onset, starting with carefully constructed shots, having the finished product in mind from the beginning.

"Sicko Mode" represents something of a quantum leap in digital effects and editing. It takes as its point of departure all the normal processes associated with making a video. In order to truly understand this visual achievement, one needs to understand the basics of how a music video is edited. This chapter will also address the difference between analog effects that are created with the camera and those that are added digitally at the post-production stage—even though it turns out that the genius in "Sicko Mode" comes from blending these two approaches. Finally, because this video's special effects are highly rhythmic in nature, I will discuss the relationship between musical rhythm and the rhythm of cutting from shot-to-shot in music video.

EDITING BASICS

Storyboards

No matter how a music video is eventually edited, it usually begins the same way that feature films or episodes of television begin: with a **storyboard**. A storyboard is a visual way of organizing the flow of visual events that will transpire over the course of a video. It's like a form chart for a video's scenes. Because this step occurs before any filming has taken place, storyboards are usually drawn by hand. Downloadable templates for music video storyboards abound on the internet. At a minimum, they usually include a space to sketch an image, the time stamp at which each scene should begin, and the duration of the scene.

Figure 6.1 uses screenshots from The Arcade Fire's "Sprawl II (Mountains Beyond Mountains) to reverse engineer what such a storyboard might look like. As part of a larger concept album called *The Suburbs*, this video tells a story of urban sprawl through its settings and visual imagery.

102 INTERPRETING VISUALS

Scene Start	Duration	Scene Start	Duration
0:01	52"	1:02	48"
Scene Start	Duration	Scene Start	Duration
1:52	48"	2:50	48"
Scene Start	Duration	Scene Start	Duration
3:48	12"	4:23	33"

Figure 6.1 Reverse-engineered storyboard for "Sprawl II"

"Sprawl II" begins with the protagonist (played by Arcade Fire singer Régine Chassagne) walking through a suburban neighborhood. That the people sitting in these yards are literally faceless, wearing masks, underscores the song's message about the lack of vitality in such places ("these days I feel my life it has no purpose"). At 1:02 the setting moves to a desolate suburban shopping mall in an area completely devoid of trees ("dead shopping malls rise/like mountains beyond mountains").

A change of scenery to the wooded park area at night (1:52) underscores an optimistic change in the lyrics ("sat under the swings and kissed in the dark"). This also begins a series of settings in which dance is the primary focus. At 2:50 the protagonist dances with dizzying time effects inside a suburban shopping mall. The logic of the scene falls apart slightly when we see the faceless people dancing at 3:48 in front of a brick wall, the location of which is difficult to place. Most joyous are the scenes at 4:23, in which Chassagne dances in a purple sequined dress.

Planning the visual flow of a music video helps a director make links such as these between the lyrics, setting, and costumes. Storyboards can be as detailed or as basic as a director likes. Figure 6.1, for example, ignores all the times that a certain scene recapitulates, such as when the opening neighborhood comes back from 1:24 to 1:28. Many, if not most music videos bring back earlier settings and costumes, especially near the end of the video where editors usually cycle through all the previously seen material with lightning speed.

EDITING AND SPECIAL EFFECTS   **103**

Such recapitulations help us to distinguish between the roles of a music video's director—largely in charge of storyboarding and shooting the video—and the video's editor, who, among other things works to cut this footage and put these shots into their final order. The work of a music video editor can be divided roughly into two distinct processes: offline editing and online editing.

Offline vs. Online Editing

Despite being given a storyboard to work from, the exact timing and length of the **cuts**—the changes between distinct shots—is almost entirely left in the hands of the music video editor. This first step, in which long reels of footage are cut, spliced, timed, and arranged, is known as **offline editing**.

Prior to the advent of digital tools in the 1990s, all offline editing was **linear**. Linear editing is also known as "destructive editing" because the cuts were literal; editors took scissors to the original film reel to cut out individual shots, then taped them together in a particular order. Machines such as the Sony BVE-910 (Figure 6.2) were then used to dub the cut-and-pasted order of shots onto a single roll of film. Linear editing is most familiar to home consumers through the process of making mixtapes. A dual-well audio cassette player essentially mimics a linear editing machine. Side II, which contains a blank tape, takes the clips played from Side I and arranges them linearly. This process works the same in a dual-well VHS video deck and is certainly "destructive" (as anyone who has accidentally taped over something important knows).

Historically, there is a rough parallel between the age of linear audio recording and linear music video editing. Prior to the early 1990s musicians were still recording to tape, which was spliced to allow for "punch-ins" whenever an artist needed to fix an error in the performance without re-recording the entire take. Both audio recording and music video editing became more forgiving with the advent of digital post-production tools. In these **non-linear** editing suites, which are usually software-based in a computer, recorded clips can simply be dragged-and-dropped into their proper location. Because any mistake can be immediately undone by a simple keystroke, non-linear editing is also known as "non-destructive" editing. Most computers these days come with a host of basic non-linear editing programs; for example, iMovie (film) and Garageband (music) on Apple computers.

Figure 6.2 Sony BVE-910 linear editing machine

Figure 6.3 Titles added in 2 Chainz "Rule the World" (0:16)

Once a music video editor has gotten each of the clips trimmed and in the order they like, the other major step is known as **online editing**. Whereas offline editing concerns the arrangement of time-based elements, online editing is the stage in which the video is made to look and sound a certain way. It is in this online editing phase that color grading and other adjustments to a video's HSB values (see Chapter 5) take place. One of the simplest steps in online editing concerns the addition of titles, credits, and other text to the film footage (since this was not caught in camera during the filming process). Figure 6.3 shows the added title in 2 Chainz "Rule the World."

Diegetic vs. Non-diegetic Sound

Since the music heard in music videos is also not captured on camera, online editing also involves merging the song's recorded audio track with its film to create a complete multimedia product. For most videos in the 1980s and 1990s, this meant merging a silent film (the video) with the audio from the album (the song). Increasingly, artists in the new millennium blend this album music, which is usually **non-diegetic**, with sound captured or added during the filming of the music video itself, which is considered **diegetic** sound.

The difference between diegetic and non-diegetic sounds is easier understood in feature films. If the film characters are looking at a car, and the viewer hears the car start, it's simple enough to presume that the characters in the film also heard the car start. That sound is part of the film's **diegesis**, its narrative or plot. By contrast, the average cut on a film soundtrack is non-diegetic. A viewer does not presume that the characters are hearing triumphant fanfares when they have their first kiss, or that they are hearing tense string music as they walk into a haunted house. Both are examples of non-diegetic sound. Dance sequences in films, or sequences in which characters are wearing headphones, can complicate matters. Though the hit song playing in the background is clearly part of the movie's soundtrack, if the character is lip-synching or dancing synchronistically it might also be part of that character's narrative world and thus within the diegesis of the film.

Broadly, diegetic sounds in music video include: all sounds which were captured in-camera during the filming of the video (footsteps, chatting, etc.); those added with sound effects or voice-overs in post-production; or any sound apart from the recorded album-version audio track that is perceived as part of the narrative action. For example, in a brief interlude before the song's final chorus NSync's "Bye Bye Bye" (Figure 6.4) takes a departure from the music in the album version. Instead of dance-pop music, the listener hears sounds of car tires squealing as it fishtails, some ambient wind noise after the car comes to a stop, then finally the resumption of the album track after the driver cleverly inserts a disc into the car's CD player.

EDITING AND SPECIAL EFFECTS   **105**

Figure 6.4 Diegetic interlude in NSync "Bye Bye Bye" (2:57)

Figure 6.5 Extended Diegesis in Alicia Keys "Raise a Man" (4:22)

An extreme example of diegetic sounds in music video can be heard at the end of Alicia Keys's "Raise a Man" (Figure 6.5), in which the camera pans slowly right to reveal that the music studio is filled with friends and family, who we now hear singing and chatting for the first time. Prior to this moment, the video editor has kept all such diegetic sounds mute, mixing them in gradually only at the end as the album-version track fades out. Video intros (see Chapter 1) also regularly begin with non-album-version sounds and thus also present extended diegetic moments.

By contrast, the actual music track, roughly identical to the album version of the song, is usually presumed to be non-diegetic in music videos. Of course, the viewer/listener perceives the song and the video as integrated and meaningful together, but the characters in the music video—at least in narrative music videos—are acting in a fictional world separate from this music. An extreme example entirely divorced from the world of performance videos illustrates this clearly. None of the music videos produced by the LA-based hard rock band Tool contain images of the band. Instead, they usually feature recurring animated characters such as the "Medicine Twins" (Figure 6.6) that are developed over the course of several music videos (the band's guitarist, Adam Jones, worked previously as an animator for Disney). Nothing in the video's diegesis suggests that these characters are hearing any music, certainly not the album version of the band's 1996 song "Aenema." Assuming so would require accounting for the number of times we see these particular characters in liquid-filled

106   INTERPRETING VISUALS

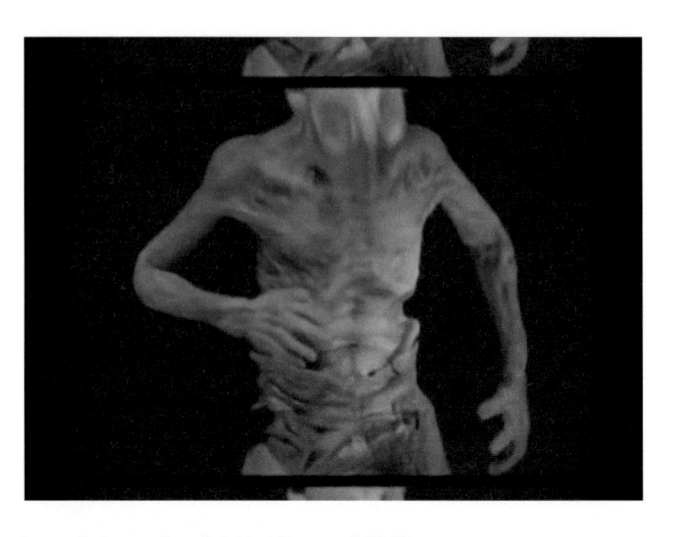

Figure 6.6 Album-version audio is non-diegetic in Tool "Aenema" (5:59)

jars or otherwise underwater, which *should* result in the viewer hearing a different audio quality since high frequencies are attenuated in these conditions.

Performance videos complicate the matter by offering a quasi-diegetic blend of these two extremes. It will be useful to return to several examples of such videos from Chapter 4 in order to illuminate this grey area. Certainly, the music in Pearl Jam's "Even Flow" (Figure 4.1) should be considered diegetic, since it was actually recorded live along with the video. But what about the music in Guns N Roses' "Paradise City" (Figure 4.2)? We hear the album version of the track along with footage of the band performing, but we don't hear the music of the actual live performance pictured, which necessarily sounds different than the album version due to the differences between studio and stadium acoustics. What about choreographed performance videos? We see Lizzo lip-synching to the album version of "Juice" (Figure 4.6) throughout the video, but where is the band playing the backing track? If no band, then where are the speakers playing the backing track in these various rooms that we see Lizzo lip-synching to?

Music videos regularly combine performance-type scenes with narrative scenes. Fall Out Boy's "Sugar We're Goin' Down" contains two radically different types of scenes. One recurring scene is basically a soundstage-performance (Figure 6.7b) type, in which the band plays in a rustic room. Again, such acoustics would not match the recorded audio. But these performance scenes are interspersed with a video-length narrative arc concerning a sordid love story between a beautiful woman and a young man with deer antlers (Figure 6.7a). Accordingly, the video promotes two radically different levels of diegesis relative to the album version of the song. In the performance scenes the viewer may be convinced that the four pictured band members hear something like the album-version audio, but the narrative scenes bear no relation to either the album-version audio or the song lyrics since such scenes are of the "extra-narrative" type.

In summary, while it may be easy enough to point to specific instances of diegetic sound in music videos (e.g. the car squealing in "Bye Bye Bye"), music videos more often than not present less of a clear-cut distinction between diegetic and non-diegetic sounds than feature films. Part of this has to do with the very nature of music videos—they blend music and visuals more seamlessly than film or television—and part of it has to do with our propensity as humans to interpret simultaneously occurring stimuli together, rather than separately.

EDITING AND SPECIAL EFFECTS **107**

Figures 6.7 (a) and (b) Varying diegesis in Fall Out Boy "Sugar We're Goin' Down" (1:12, 1:52)

EDITING TO RHYTHM AND FORM

Having already explored some of the basic "how" and "why" of music video editing, it is still necessary to examine *when* exactly editors make cuts between scenes, and how long these cuts last. The answers to both of these questions have to do with musical time, on both a small and large scale. In short, editors tend to change between distinct settings along with changes in a song's formal sections, and tend to cut between individual shots in those scenes in sync with a song's beat. "Closer," the 2016 music video by The Chainsmokers (featuring Halsey), showcases both techniques. The video was directed by Dano Cerny, and was edited by Jen Kennedy, both of whom have worked on other videos by The Chainsmokers and/or Halsey.

Setting and Form

As noted in Whitney Houston and Taylor Swift videos examined in Chapter 1, changes in music video settings tend to align with major changes in formal sections. Table 6.1 is a parametric form chart that graphs the song's formal structure alongside changes in setting. Distinct settings help to advance the story of the main couple (played by Halsey and Chainsmokers singer Jeremy Taggart) meeting, falling in love, and eventually falling apart. Since this song is a duet sung by these same two actors, Table 6.1 also notes who is singing each section.

The song's intro is actually set visually to the narrative ending, with the now estranged couple in a hotel bar. Considering the song's lyrics "now you're lookin' pretty in a hotel bar" gives this video an explicit narrative quality (see Chapter 4). Verse one then takes the

108 INTERPRETING VISUALS

Table 6.1 Parametric form chart (setting and formal section) in The Chainsmokers (ft. Halsey) "Closer"

TIME	SECTION	SINGER	SETTING(S)
0:01	Intro	n/a	Hotel bar
0:11	Verse 1	Taggart	Bedroom 1, party
0:50	Riserchorus 1		Bedroom 1, kitchen
1:12	Drop		
1:32	Verse 2	Halsey	Bedroom 1, pool
2:12	Riserchorus 2	Both	
2:33	Drop		Underwater, bedroom 2
2:52	Riserchorus 3	Taggart	Hotel Bar, bedroom 3
3:33	Drop	Both	Hotel rooftop

Figure 6.8 Party setting in "Closer" (0:52)

Figure 6.9 Pool setting in "Closer" (1:54)

viewer back in time to the place the couple first met: a house party with abundant white light (Figure 6.8). These shots are interspersed with a bedroom scene throughout the first verse/riserchorus/drop rotation that shows the couple being intimate. Note that the change away from the hotel to these new settings happens immediately on the downbeat of the verse.

The next big setting change happens on the downbeat of verse two, which shows the now-established couple at a pool. However, all is not well. The couple begins to quarrel, after which they literally drift apart as Taggart floats away on a raft (Figure 6.9). Interestingly, these shots are interspersed with the same darkly lit bedroom shots as before. But now, with the change in mood, the dark blue hues of the room connote less intimacy/sexiness and instead underscore the sadness visible in their faces as they begin to have fights in this same bedroom.

EDITING AND SPECIAL EFFECTS   **109**

Figure 6.10 Empty bedroom setting in "Closer" (2:56)

At the downbeat of the third prechorus the video cuts forward in narrative time to the hotel setting, where the couple is separated. Once again, the bedroom setting morphs to reflect this change in their relationship. Halsey now sits alone on the floor of the bedroom with the sheets pulled off the mattress (another explicit lyrical reference, see Figure 6.10). At 3:33 the video shifts and returns one final time to the hotel setting with the couple now alone on the rooftop but ends without explicitly revealing whether the couple will ever get back together again.

Cutting Rhythm

"Closer" also exemplifies a basic truth about the rhythm of cuts in music videos: they are notably faster than the cuts in classic films.[2] Such fast cuts, also known as **jump cuts**, feature individual shots that usually last only one to three seconds. Furthermore, the exact rhythm of these cuts—where editors switch from one to another—tends to align with recognizable subdivisions in the song's beat.[3]

Table 6.2 shows the entire four-measure intro that begins "Closer." The constantly moving eighth-notes in the highest synthesizer line (the one with the filter sweep) that subdivide the beat are moving at 180 BPM, or roughly one-third of a second each. Each of the eight cuts aligns precisely with an eighth-note in this meter—there are no slippery cuts that fall between beats. The longest shot (#2, of Taggart gazing at Halsey) lasts just 2.66 seconds. Most shots are just under or over one second.

Table 6.2 also reveals that editor Jen Kennedy is not only cutting to the *tempo* of the track, she's cutting the exact *rhythm* of the synthesizer. The most common cuts occur on beat 1 of each measure, as well as the "and" of 3. This is no coincidence; the lowest voice of the synthesizer changes on precisely these beats.

Kennedy's cuts to the rhythm of the synthesizer become even more explicit once the verse begins when she copies the "and-4-and-1" motif of the synth-horns heard in every other measure (e.g. 0:15, 0:20, 0:25). Just like the horns play four eighth-notes, lasting 1/3 of a second each, Kennedy creates a visual rhythm that does exactly the same thing. This makes the ending of the intro surprising. (Warning: what I say next is one of those things that, once you see, you cannot unsee). If you watch closely at 0:10, you'll see Kennedy squeeze in *four* shots of different colored eyes where *three* 8th-notes sound, creating a fleeting dissonance between the rhythm of the visuals and the rhythm of the synth. She elides this difference between visual and musical rhythm in order to reinforce the even number of eyes in the protagonist couple.

Table 6.2 Cutting to the beat in "Closer"; eighth-note = 0.33 seconds

MEASURE 1	1	+	2	+	3	+	4	+

MEASURE 2	1	+	2	+	3	+	4	+

MEASURE 3	1	+	2	+	3	+	4	+

MEASURE 4	1	+	2	+	3	+	4	+

To summarize, "Closer" demonstrates two truths about editing a music video: that cuts are relatively short, lasting between one and three seconds each; and that cuts tend to align with a song's prominent beats and/or the rhythm of specific musical figures.[4] This is such a standard for music video that longer, unbroken shots, such as those in Alicia Keys's "Raise a Man" (Figure 6.5), Feist's "1, 2, 3, 4" (Figure 5.14), and Sia's "Chandelier" (Figure 3.13–3.15), stand out as notable. Though rare in music video, this style of **continuity editing**, which promotes scrutiny and deeper assessment of subjects and settings through longer shots, is the classic mode of editing for feature films.

SPECIAL EFFECTS

The final step in online editing discussed in this chapter involves adding special effects to the footage, which is probably now already cut, has sound synched up, and has all of the necessary titles added. It would be impossible to discuss *all* of the special effects used in music video in a chapter of reasonable length, so I will proceed by presenting certain families of visual phenomena, each of which can be tweaked by a video's special effects editor to create the desired effect. Special effects fall into two broad families: analog and digital.

Analog Effects

Analog effects are all of those that are captured in real-time by the camera operator, whether they happen on the set itself, or result from physically manipulating the camera. All analog effects were thus technologically possible before the advent of digital post-production using computers, which started in the 1980s and 1990s. They can be found in some of the earliest films, even as far back as silent films from the early twentieth century.

"Tonight, Tonight" by the 1990s alternative rock band Smashing Pumpkins, pays homage to some of the earliest analog effects by parodying Georges Méliès's 1902 silent film *Le Voyage Dans la Lun* ("voyage to the moon"). Both the film and music video are full of a number of **mechanical effects**, including wind machines, pyrotechnics, and evocative makeup/costumes, all of which are performed by highly skilled stagehands who avoid appearing on-camera. "Tonight, Tonight" also pays homage to the film by adding time and motion distortion, which simulates the imperfections in camera speed and steadiness that were unavoidable in the early twentieth century.

The story of "Tonight, Tonight" parallels that of *Voyage* in depicting a couple who travels to the moon, only to find it overrun with violent space aliens. When the woman swings her umbrella at the alien (Figure 6.11), it appears to vaporize into thin air, symbolizing its death. This is done by quickly cutting between two shots. In the first, the woman's umbrella strikes (or comes close to striking) the alien on the head. (cut). In the second shot, a technical effects specialist, crouched so as to be behind a prop and thus out of the scene, sets off a liquid carbon dioxide (dry ice) bomb, which produces the cloud of vapor.

Another class of mechanical effects concerns the manipulation of light. In R.E.M.'s "Losing my Religion" a lens flare effect—a distortion that occurs when external light floods the camera lens—is used to animate the lyrics. When vocalist Michael Stipe sings "that's me in the spotlight" an actual spotlight is pointed toward the camera, resulting in a lens flare (Figure 6.12). This effect is particularly effective for two reasons. First, the spotlight operators themselves are dramatized on screen, so the viewer perceives this spotlight-effect as part of the narrative action. Second, the halo-like aura around Stipe created by this lens flare is particularly effective in amplifying the video's religious themes.

112 INTERPRETING VISUALS

Effects created by manipulating the camera itself are known as **in-camera effects**. Many in-camera effects work by manipulating a viewer's sense of time and/or visual perspective. Effects that manipulate a viewer's sense of time are known as **speed effects**. The most common in-camera speed effects are **time-lapse** (time is sped up) and **slow-motion** (time is slowed down). A famous opening scene from Madonna's "Like a Prayer" (Figure 6.13) dramatizes a burning cross by slowing down the footage considerably.

Nine Inch Nails' "Hurt" begins by using the opposite time-lapse effect to make visible the imperceptibly slow decay of a fox. The video ends by *reversing* this footage (reverse could be considered another speed effect) to bring the fox back to life, or at least simulate its recomposition (Figure 6.14).

Stop-motion effects, perhaps most famous through claymation series such as *Wallace & Gromit* or *Gumby*, are the result of a painstaking process wherein hundreds or even

Figure 6.11 Mechanical effects in Smashing Pumpkins "Tonight, Tonight" (2:12)

Figure 6.12 Lens flare effect in R.E.M. "Losing My Religion" (0:22)

EDITING AND SPECIAL EFFECTS   **113**

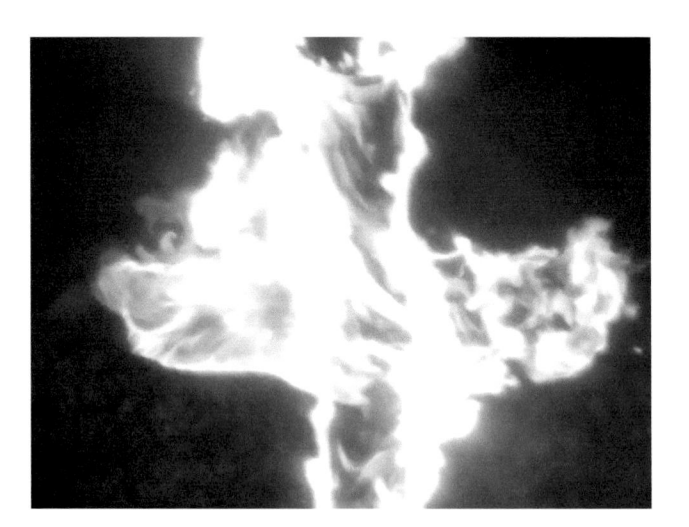

Figure 6.13 Slow-motion effect in Madonna "Like a Prayer" (0:10)

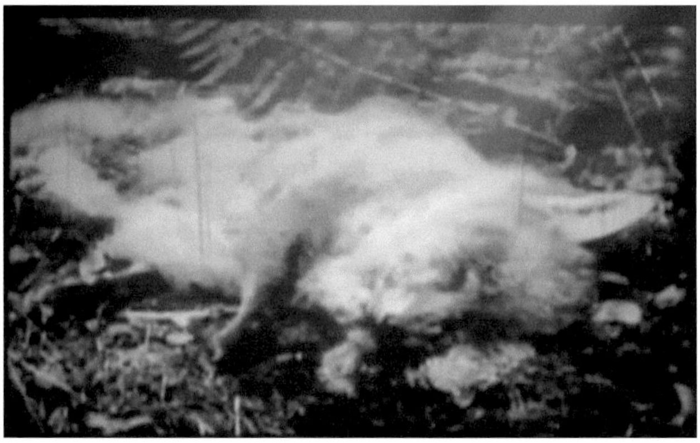

Figure 6.14 Time-lapse effect in Nine Inch Nails "Hurt" (4:48)

thousands of still images are captured, then shown in rapid succession. Doing stop-motion with clay figures is difficult enough, but stop-motion using human subjects presents the added challenge of getting them to stay as still as possible during these photo shoots. Peter Gabriel's 1986 "Sledgehammer" reportedly required Gabriel to lie as still as possible under a pane of glass for up to 16 hours at a time. A more recent video, Gotye's "Somebody that I used to Know" (ft. Kimbra), uses stop-motion footage of paint slowly being erased from Kimbra's body stroke-by-stroke (Figure 6.15). Erasing the geometric patterns that embed Kimbra and Gotye into the same painted wall acts as a metaphor for the breakup theme of the lyrics.

In-camera zoom techniques are usually not considered special effects, since they are primarily used to draw a viewer's focus toward or away from a subject. But one particularly celebrated use of the zoom known as a **dolly zoom** creates an unnatural special effect. By moving the camera on a mechanical dolly (see Chapter 5) at the same that they manipulate the camera zoom, a videographer can create the illusion of moving paradoxically at two different speeds, or even two different directions. In classic films such as *Vertigo* and *Jaws*, this effect is achieved by moving the camera dolly physically toward the subject (a staircase and

114   INTERPRETING VISUALS

Figure 6.15 Stop-motion effect in Gotye (ft. Kimbra) "Somebody that I Used to Know" (3:48)

Figure 6.16 Dolly zoom in Michael Jackson "Thriller" (8:27)

sheriff, respectively) while simultaneously zooming out. A slightly less unsettling dolly zoom happens just as Michael Jackson turns into a zombie in "Thriller" (Figure 6.16). The camera slowly inches toward the subject to show the horror on her face while simultaneously zooming in at a much faster rate.

Digital Effects

Many digital effects are just digitally enhanced versions of analog effects that were used in previous decades. Unlike the in-camera versions of these effects, digital effects are added in post-production using computer software such as Adobe Premiere or Apple's Final Cut Pro.

Digital speed effects (e.g. extreme slow-motion and extreme time-lapse), for example, simply take the in-camera version of these effects to extreme ends.

"We Are Young," by the American rock band Fun, unfolds the action of a bar riot—perhaps a flash mob—in extreme slow-motion using digital speed effects. This makes it possible to see incredible details, such as droplets of milk spewing out of someone's mouth as they are slapped (Figure 6.17).

EDITING AND SPECIAL EFFECTS **115**

A digital speed effect set in the opposite direction, extreme time-lapse, makes possible the dizzying visual excess seen throughout "Where are Ü Now?" By EDM duo Jack Ü (Skrillex and Diplo) featuring Justin Bieber. This special effect is used to particularly emotional ends. Fans were invited to hand-draw annotations onto portraits of Bieber (Figure 6.18b)—some flattering and some not—with the process shown in extreme time-lapse. These annotations are then projected onto filmed footage of Bieber's own body (Figure 6.18a) at roughly the

Figure 6.17 Digital speed effects (slow) in Fun "We Are Young" (1:32)

Figures 6.18 (a) and (b) Digital speed effects (time-lapse) in Jack Ü "Where are Ü Now?" (1:17, 1:25)

116 INTERPRETING VISUALS

Figure 6.19 Virtual reality in Björk "Stonemilker" (4:38)

same speed as the time-lapse, creating an overall effect that mimics people drawing hateful messages and pictures all over his vulnerable body with relentless speed.

Some digital effects mimic changes in perspective—including zooming, tracking, and panning shots—by manipulating *time* to create the illusion of changing perspective. For example, by transitioning quickly from an image in the foreground to an image in the background, an editor can create the illusion that the "camera" zoomed-in impossibly quickly. Recent virtual reality (VR) music videos lie at the cutting edge of these perspectival-shifting digital effects. By giving the user virtual control over manipulation of 3D camera footage, VR videos like Björk's "Stonemilker" (Figure 6.19, n.b. the perspective-control toggle in the upper left corner) provide the viewer with the illusion that they are choosing their own music video adventure.

Unlike digital speed and perspectival effects, which amplified existing technology, the advent of CGI in the early 1980s made it possible to create visual images previously impossible to capture in real life. Further innovations in post-production that began in the 1990s gave directors and editors increased control over speed and perspective that amplified in-camera effects seen previously in music video. State-of-the-art special effects techniques used in videos today combine these two approaches, integrating live-action footage with CGI, then further enhancing and manipulating this footage through extensive post-production.

One of the earliest videos to make extensive use of CGI was "You Might Think" by American New Wave band The Cars (Figure 6.20). Despite looking quite campy by today's standards, this was a monumental achievement in the early 1980s. In fact, in 1984, "You Might Think" was the most expensive video ever created. Soundgarden's CGI facial deformations in "Black Hole Sun" (see Chapter 3) represent, by comparison, a quantum leap into the mid-1990s, as does Linkin Park's entirely computer-generated setting in 2002's "In the End" (see Chapter 4).

But even the post-millennial technology in Linkin Park's video doesn't really enable the actors to *interact* with CGI elements—they are just surrounded by them. Later, the technology of that decade did advance to the point where it was possible to have near-seamless integration of live-action actors with CGI. Justice's EDM hit "D.A.N.C.E." is a choreographed performance video that features two actors walking around a venue interacting with the constantly evolving CGI cartoons on their shirts. Actors in such videos face the added challenge of having to pantomime actions with no physical stimulus, including "unzipping" a zipperless shirt to reveal cartoon-muscles underneath (Figure 6.21).

"Cellophane" by FKA Twigs is one of the most visually stunning CGI music videos to date, representing the state-of-the-art late in the second decade of the millennium. Chapter 5 discussed the intertextual uses of the video's extensive bronze hues.

EDITING AND SPECIAL EFFECTS   **117**

Figure 6.20 Primitive CGI in The Cars "You Might Think" (2:43)

Figure 6.21 Seamless integration of live actors with CGI in Justice "D.A.N.C.E." (1:26)

Director Andrew Thomas Huang began by hand-drawing the storyboard to present to Twigs (Figure 6.22), but also used CGI to render a digital mockup of the set to give her a more realistic picture of the final images.[5] He then collaborated with the UK visual effects team Analog Studio to produce the final product. As Figures 5.8a and 5.8b show, the result is not only a stunning achievement in terms of technical mastery of CGI but a truly artistic achievement that preserves FKA Twigs's musical and physical performance as the centerpiece of it all.

DEEP DIVE: TRAVIS SCOTT "SICKO MODE" (2018)

The cutting-edge special effects techniques seen throughout Travis Scott's 2018 video "Sicko Mode" draw from both analog and digital effects practices. Throughout this discussion, I rely heavily on two informational videos created by the website Cinecom,[6] in which seasoned cinematographers painstakingly recreate visual effects in hit music videos and feature films.

118 INTERPRETING VISUALS

Figure 6.22 Pre-visualization of FKA Twigs "Cellophane" by Andrew Thomas Huang

Figure 6.23 Rhythmic kaleidoscope effect in "Sicko Mode" (2:23)

"Sicko Mode" opens with a kaleidoscopic background effect done entirely in post-production (Figure 6.23). A tedious effect to create, it begins by taking several different vertical slices of stock background footage, cutting them to exactly the same width, and making them translucent (so the video's filmed footage shows through them). Next, the editor painstakingly copies and pastes each slice moving outward from the center of the frame. As each slice moves outward, a new one fills its previous position. This creates a rhythmic effect in the video's opening that helps fill a void since the beat layer has not yet dropped. When the effect recurs at 2:23 it is roughly synchronous with the trap beat, though the alignment of the visual movement with the sixteenth-notes in the hi-hats is less than exact.

Another effect created entirely in post-production is known as data moshing. Data moshing involves transitioning between two images while adding a level of visual distortion that makes the images appear to "melt" into one another. This visual effect acts as a clever solution to a musical problem. Since Scott's song actually opens with the "featured" singer, Drake, Scott's relatively late entrance in the track at 1:03 might go unnoticed if it weren't for the novel data moshing effect that transitions between their two faces (Figure 6.24). The horizontal distortion that eases this transition is timed exactly with the quarter-note pulse of the kick drum, creating a musical transition that introduces Scott's beat, which is different than Drake's.

EDITING AND SPECIAL EFFECTS   **119**

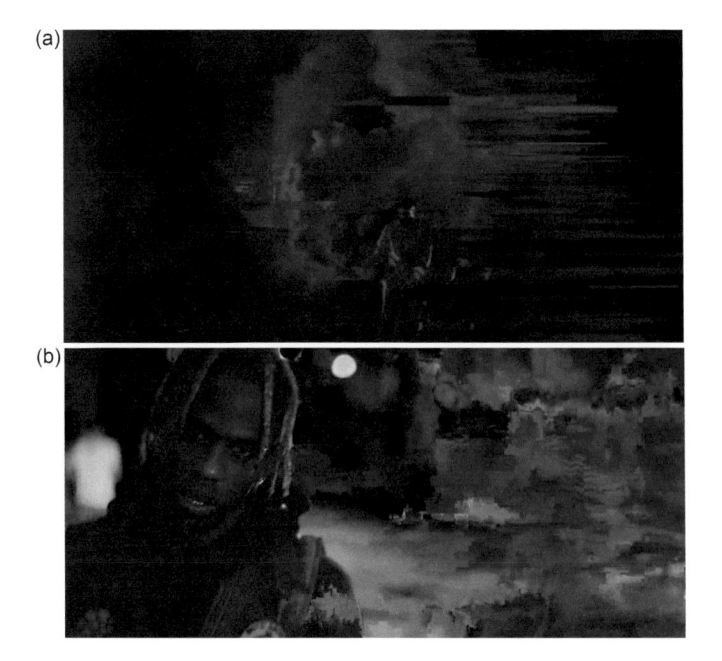

Figure 6.24 Data moshing between singers in "Sicko Mode" (1:02, 1:04)

Figure 6.25 Mechanical/digital slant effect in "Sicko Mode" (1:32)

While these two effects have very little to do with what Dave Meyers captured in-camera (one could imagine adding either effect to nearly any video after it was shot), most of the video's effects had to be visualized as an integral part of the filming process. One such effect, a mechanical slant effect, couples a simple mechanical effect captured in-camera with post-production perspectival shift. A viewer should perceive the entire setting as tilted, with objects rolling downhill from screen right to screen left while characters tilt in the opposite direction to remain upright.

The mechanical portion of the effect is simple enough. Objects that can roll (such as the shopping cart in Figure 6.25) are simply pushed and allowed to roll completely off the other side of the frame. If an object cannot roll (such as the plastic chair at 4:42), extremely thin wire that can later be edited out in post-production is used to pull the object. Meanwhile, the subject (Scott) actually tilts while wearing shoes that are either glued or nailed to the floor.

120 INTERPRETING VISUALS

Figure 6.26 Time-lapse dolly zoom in "Sicko Mode" (1:22)

In theory the post-production side of this trick is also relatively simple, though it is surely an exercise in timing. A perspectival shift rotates the entire frame diagonally but does so only to a degree of believability with regards to the speed of the objects sliding across the frame and the tilt of the subject. Too much rotation and the objects appear to fall unnaturally slow; too little rotation and the objects appear to move artificially fast.

Another completely integrated in-camera/digital effect is probably the video's signature achievement: a suite of effects in which Scott appears to alternately grow and shrink relative to the record store and cars behind him (Figure 6.26). This one shot combines time-lapse, stop-motion, and dolly zoom techniques in interesting ways.

Whereas a fully in-camera dolly zoom (such as that in "Thriller") moves the camera at one speed while zooming out at another, this version of the effect separates the in-camera portion of the effect from the digital portion. The in-camera portion is actually done using hundreds of individual photographs that inch ever closer, then ever away from Scott, which makes him appear to get taller, then shorter, and also gives his movements a jerky stop-motion quality. The relative zooming in and out onto the background image is done later, digitally, in post-production. These background shots are also shown in time-lapse, with participants appearing to have even jerkier movements than Scott's. Each of these interlocking yet independent effects combines to create an effect that is further heightened by showing it in both forward and reverse motion.

A final effect using perspectival shift also begins with delicate in-camera work. Several times in the video, portraits of small groups of individuals appear to be presented, somehow, in 3D (e.g. 1:28, 1:39, 4:37). By asking a subject to remain relatively still, then executing a painstakingly slow panning motion in a single direction, the viewer gets the illusion that they are seeing the subject(s) from two different angles. The sleight of hand comes from speed manipulation. If you presented this footage in real-time, a viewer would understand exactly what was happening. By speeding up the footage considerably in post-production, the angle appears to "snap" from one perspective to the other. Like the dolly zoom effect, this effect is heightened by playing the effect quickly back and forth in both forward and reverse motion.

Learning the technical details of these special effects is interesting on its own, but an *analysis* of "Sicko Mode" ought to move from observation of these details toward an interpretation of them. One possible interpretation is that, by carefully curating these shots of Houston, Scott's hometown, he is also sculpting a carefully curated presentation of that town for the public. Long overshadowed by more prominent East- and West-Coast scenes in the 1990s and 2000s, and then by Atlanta, the dominant Southern rap epicenter from the 2000s to the present, Houston is still perhaps not the first city mainstream audiences think of for hip-hop.

Scott in fact draws attention to Houston not only through the title of this video's corresponding album (*Astroworld*, named after the defunct Houston theme park), but

EDITING AND SPECIAL EFFECTS **121**

Figures 6.27 (a) and (b) Intersection of Elder and Kessler, Houston (1:09)

also immediately upon his visual entrance following the data-mosh dissolve from Drake. Figure 6.27a shows this entrance, with Scott riding a horse north on Elder street past its intersection with Kessler. Figure 6.27b shows a street-level view of this intersection.

Note the difference in the two images. In the street-level shot the bustling capitalism of Houston's skyscrapers is clearly framed by the southeast-facing alley. In Scott's video, by contrast, a hologram in the likeness of his face clouds this view. I interpret this as Scott showing us a different side of Houston which may not always appear on postcards or guided tours. Throughout the video Scott shows the viewer *his* community, with its record stores, cars, people, and places, all of which are highlighted further by brilliant special effects.

Table 6.3 Lingo you should know

Storyboard	Jump cut	Time-lapse
Cuts	Continuity editing	Stop-motion
Offline editing	Mechanical effects	Digital speed effects
Linear (destructive) editing	In-camera effects	Digital zoom
Non-linear (non-destructive) editing	Speed effects	Computer-generated imagery (CGI)
Online editing	Slow-motion	

NOTES

1 This story appears in a feature by the industry magazine *Shoot* on November 5, 2018 (uncredited author); https://www.shootonline.com/spw/mod-shifts-sicko-mode

2 Caston's interviews with seasoned professionals reveal this and other facets of music video editing practice; see Emily Caston, "'The First Cut is the Deepest' Excerpts from a Focus Group on Editing Music Videos, with Explanatory Historical and Theoretical Notes," *Music, Sound, and the Moving Image* 11 (2017): 99–118.

3 Carol Vernallis makes this point in "The Kindest Cut: Functions and Meanings of Music Video Editing," *Screen* 42, no. 1 (2001): 21–48.

4 As a cautionary tale (*pace* Vernallis 2001) it should be noted that, if a viewer chooses to entrain metrically to the fastest subdivisions in a song—for example, the faster sixteenth notes, which here would last only 0.166 seconds—their perceptual ability to sense whether or not a particular visual event happens precisely on that sixteenth note, just before it, or just after it, becomes more and more suspect.

5 See Linda Codega, "Music Video of the Year: FKA Twigs, Cellophane," *Shots* (January 27, 2020), <https://shots.net/news/view/music-video-of-the-year-fka-twigs-cellophane>

6 Access these Cinecom tutorials here: part One: <https://www.cinecom.net/after-effects-tutorials/sicko-effects-travis-scott-ft-drake/>, and part Two: <https://www.cinecom.net/premiere-pro-tutorials/sicko-effects-travis-scott-ft-drake-part-2/>.

UNIT 3

Interpreting Sociology

CHAPTER 7 CLIP LIST

YEAR	ARTIST	VIDEO
1993	The Breeders	Cannonball
1996	Tracy Bonham	Mother, Mother
1996	Fiona Apple	Shadowboxer
2008	Adele	Make You Feel My Love
2009	Beyoncé	Green Light
2009	Girls Generation	Gee
2012	Dani Shay	Girl or Boy (YouTube video)
2013	Miley Cyrus	Wrecking Ball
2014	St. Vincent	Birth in Reverse
2015	Rihanna	Bitch Better Have My Money
2015	Peaches	Rub
2015	Hayley Kiyoko	Girls Like Girls
2016	The Weeknd	False Alarm
2018	Lenny Kravitz	Low
2018	Ariana Grande	God is a Woman
2018	Big Freedia	Rent
2018	Troye Sivan	Bloom
2018	Janelle Monae	Make me Feel
2019	100 Gecs	Money Machine
2019	HER	Hard Place
2020	HAIM	The Steps

SEXUALITY AND GENDER DIVERSITY

- Sexuality and Gender in Music Video
  - *Persona*
  - *Gender and Sexuality*
- Women in Music Video
  - *Resisting the Male Gaze*
  - *Women as Instrumentalists and Composers*
- Deep Dive: Avicii (ft. Salem al Fakir) "Silhouettes" (2012)

CHAPTER 7

Sexuality and Gender Diversity

"Silhouettes," a collaboration between Swedish EDM producer Avicii and singer Salem al Fakir, was ahead of its time in 2012 in featuring issues facing the trans community, including gender dysphoria and sex reassignment surgery (SRS) as the cornerstone of its narrative action (Figure 7.1). Since then, many parts of the world have witnessed a greater awareness of sexuality and gender diversity than ever in modern history. And still, misunderstandings surrounding what sexuality is and is not, what gender is and is not, and how these two concepts differ from one another, abound.

Music videos—particularly those of the last decade—provide a fertile ground for the analysis of sexuality and gender diversity. This chapter picks up the discussion of narrative, artist, and actor personas from earlier in the book in order to see just how complex this issue gets when considering the sexualities and genders of different personas. Analyzing "Silhouettes" at the end of this chapter will provide the chance to apply most if not all of these concepts to a single video.

The second half of the chapter provides an annotated history of the ways women have been depicted in music videos. After applying what Laura Mulvey (1975) and others have described as the male gaze to music video, a survey of recent videos by women and LGBTQ+ artists will show how women are resisting this gaze. The chapter will also highlight women's contributions to instrumental performance and composition, and how those contributions are depicted in music video.

Figure 7.1 Trans visibility in Avicii "Silhouettes" (4:17)

SEXUALITY AND GENDER IN MUSIC VIDEO

Persona

In Chapter 3 I defined the four most common personas present in a music video: the narrator persona (who is telling the story); the human persona (the human we are hearing making the sound); the artist persona (any number of public roles that human plays as a recording artist); and the actor persona (a character in a music video, acted by either a human and/or artist). That chapter's analysis of Adele's video "Make You Feel My Love" already began assessing some aspects of gender and sexuality. The narrator's gender identity is never expressed in the lyrics since the first-person pronoun "I" is gender-neutral. Neither was the gender identity of the narrator's love interest, since "you" is also gender-neutral.

Any attempts to project what a listener may perceive about the gender identity of the narrator persona, or the sexuality of either the artist persona Adele or the human persona Adele Laurie Blue Adkins MBE onto these lyrics causes a number of problems. Since Adkins presents as **cisgendered**—that is, her gender identity matches the sex she was assigned at birth—a listener might assume that the narratorial "I" was the voice of a woman (Figure 7.2). Likewise, if one projects their assumptions about Adele's or Adkins's heterosexuality onto the lyrics, they would assume that the "you" was referring to a man.

Critics writing record reviews make these cis-normative and heteronormative assumptions regularly. Not only is this disrespectful to the human making the music, who may or may not want their private matters conflated with fictional songwriting, but it also short-changes the creative power of storytelling itself. Surely a skilled storyteller like Adkins is capable of telling a story from the narrative perspective of a life she has not directly lived. And, to restate the obvious, since many singers perform songs that they did not write the lyrics for, the author(s) of those lyrics (in this case, Bob Dylan) might have different gender identities and sexualities than the singer performing them.

And yet some artists, like South African/Australian pop singer Troye Sivan, publicly embrace their LGBTQ+ identities, sing about LGBTQ+ culture, and explicitly link these separate personas in interviews.[1] In cases like these, it is hard to resist conflating some or all of the four personas present in the video (Figure 7.3). About Sivan's video "Bloom"—a celebratory anthem that uses flowers as a metaphor for gay sex—Sivan says "[w]ithout getting into like any sort of details whatsoever, that was a song I wrote about a particular experience...."[2]

Figure 7.2 Gender-neutral narrator persona, cisgendered actor persona in Adele "Make You Feel My Love" (0:58)

Figure 7.3 LGBTQ+ artist, narrator, and actor identities in Troye Sivan "Bloom" (2:36)

Figure 7.4 Pansexuality in Janelle Monae "Make Me Feel" (1:03)

Gender and Sexuality

Of course, not every artist is gay or straight. Janelle Monae, for example, identifies as **pansexual**, meaning that they (Monae uses gender-neutral pronouns) are attracted to people from all across the gender spectrum.[3] Monae's video "Make Me Feel" features lyrics that never specify the gender of the narrator's desire. In the video we see Monae casting hungry stares across an arcade at a number of potential lovers, including a number of people who present with fluid gender expressions (Figure 7.4).

Trans artists—musicians whose artist and/or human persona exceed the normative range of presentations matching the sex they were assigned at birth—complicate simple identification of songs as either "gay" or "heteronormative." "Rent," by Big Freedia, a New Orleans-based bounce artist who uses feminine pronouns (she/her/hers), identifies the narrator's former lover as "boy." The video shows Freedia outside her crowded house where she is throwing out all of this "boy's" belongings for inability to pay his half of the rent (Figure 7.5). While the narrator's ("I") gender identity is never specified, the artist Big Freedia sings in a baritone range. Thus, a listener hearing the song alone (sans video) might conflate the artist and narrator into a gay song. Conversely, a viewer who does not know who Big Freedia is might interpret the song as straight, since Freedia presents as a woman.

Many singers, regardless of gender identity, sing in ranges that are between baritone and alto and therefore resist binary gender interpretations even more so than Big Freedia. Some artists who sing in this register also identify as **non-binary**, that is, they do not identify as a man or a woman, or use gender-neutral pronouns such as they/their/theirs or ze/zir/zirs.

Figure 7.5 Trans artist persona in Big Freedia "Rent" (2:33)

Figure 7.6 Gender-neutral vocal range in Dani Shay "Girl or Boy" (1:46)

Dani Shay's homemade YouTube video "Girl or Boy" (Figure 7.6) openly questions what it means to be a "girl" or a "boy," drawing from their own personal experience in fielding viewers' questions in the comments section of their videos. A number of artists who do not necessarily identify as trans, including Sam Smith and Grimes, have recently embraced gender-neutral pronouns and/or fluid gender identities.[4]

Interpreting what Victoria Malawey has called an artist's "trans vocality" gets even more interesting when considering how electronic vocal manipulation affects the perception of gender identity.[5] Laura Les, the singer of the American experimental electronic duo 100 Gecs, sings and speaks throughout "Money Machine" with a host of effects that manipulate the formants in her voice. Formants have a powerful effect on a listener's perception of a vocalist's biological sex.[6] Both Les, a transwoman, and Dylan Brady, a cisgendered man, use this effect throughout the band's output. For Brady, the effect makes him sound a bit more "emo" or perhaps "nasly." But for Les, who does not present as traditionally feminine (Figure 7.7), but who sings in a much higher range than Brady, the effect gives her voice a more feminine resonance.

WOMEN IN MUSIC VIDEO

Showcasing the audiovisual efforts of LGBTQ+ and non-binary artists, as well as lyrics that celebrate these identities, helps rewrite hegemonic music histories that focus on the contributions of straight, cisgendered, and largely white men. To extend this disruption of the musical patriarchy, the second half of this chapter highlights the contributions of women

SEXUALITY AND GENDER DIVERSITY **129**

Figure 7.7 Trans vocality in 100 Gecs "Money Machine" (0:02)

Figure 7.8 Hypersexualization in Miley Cyrus "Wrecking Ball" (1:15)

to music video. This section begins by looking at ways in which women have asserted their freedom from the male gaze and then specifically focuses on the musical contributions by women as instrumentalists and composers.

Resisting the Male Gaze

The **male gaze** is a term developed in 1975 by the celebrated film theorist Laura Mulvey,[7] which has received significant attention from later scholars as it applies to music video. Mulvey argues that women in film (and music video) are depicted as passive objects, ripe for the active, subjectifying gaze of the male. In music video specifically, there are at least four ways in which women are treated as passive subjects: hypersexualization, infantilization, objectification, and the victim trope.

Figure 7.8 shows American pop singer Miley Cyrus's hypersexualized body in "Wrecking Ball." Note the camera's unrelenting focus on her buttocks and breasts. Hypersexualization distracts a viewer's attention from women's musical contributions, including singing, instrumental performance, and composition. Instead, it presents the artist's body as a passive object to be gazed at.

130   INTERPRETING SOCIOLOGY

Figure 7.9 Infantilization and objectification in Girls Generation "Gee" (0:05)

Figure 7.10 The victim trope in The Weeknd "False Alarm" (0:41)

"Gee," a video by the Korean pop ensemble Girls' Generation, exemplifies two further aspects of the male gaze. The first concerns **infantilization**, the tendency to depict women as "clueless children who must depend on older men to teach them about love."[8] But the visual narrative in "Gee" also **objectifies** the women, treating them as stationary mannequins to be moved around by a store clerk rather than as independent musical artists (Figure 7.9).

"False Alarm," by the Canadian R&B singer The Weeknd, is interesting for its novel use of the first-person POV (see Chapter 5). Its narrative action, which focuses on the abduction of a young woman who is depicted as helpless and fearful (Figure 7.10), is an example of the **victim trope**, a cornerstone of Hollywood film practices dating back at least as early as the "damsel in distress" tied to the train tracks from the silent film era.

Many recent music videos, especially those by women and/or LGBTQ+ artists, resist these dominant narratives connected to the male gaze. "Girls Like Girls," written and directed by Japanese-American songwriter and LGBTQ+ activist Hayley Kiyoko, resists the kinds of hypersexualization and victimization regularly seen in music videos. While still calling attention to the physical and verbal abuse experienced by many women, the video ends with a catharsis in which a woman fights back against her male aggressor to defend her lover. Second, the video depicts their relationship as realistic love between two women, rather than

SEXUALITY AND GENDER DIVERSITY   **131**

Figure 7.11 Resisting hypersexualization in "Girls Like Girls" (4:04)

Figure 7.12 Resisting the victim trope in Rihanna "Bitch Better Have My Money" (5:16)

the hypersexualized norms seen in mainstream television programs about women such as *The L Word* and *Orange is the New Black* (Figure 7.11).

Rihanna's "Bitch Better Have My Money" takes resistance to the victim trope to extreme ends. The video shows Rihanna kidnapping the wife of a wealthy businessman for ransom. Ultimately, Rihanna tortures and kills this man, presumably with the knife she's seen brandishing just before (Figure 7.12). The ending scene shows Rihanna luxuriating, naked, in a chest of cash, covered in the man's blood. Her resistance to the victim gaze is not only depicted through the video's visual narrative but also through a pushed, aggressive vocal delivery throughout.

If the male gaze is aligned with the broader institutional power structures of patriarchy, then music videos that rely on **yonic imagery** (rather than phallic) act as sites of resistance. Chapter 5 discussed the extensive use of yonic imagery, including hot pink vagina pants, in Janelle Monae's "PYNK" (see Chapter 5). Ariana Grande's "God is a Woman" reimagines Michaelangelo's *The Creation of Adam* as a matriarchal icon, with God as a woman of color, and Grande, playing the role of Eve, reaching out from her womb-like enclosure, surrounded by a choir of Angels (Figure 7.13a). Another example of yonic imagery happens in Peaches' "Rub," a video written and directed entirely by a team of women. The video opens with a woman bowing to a monumental yoni in the desert (Figure 7.13b) before becoming a bold celebration of LGBTQ+ group sex featuring women of all body types who resist cisgendered heteronormative patriarchy.

These are just a few of the many visual techniques musicians use to resist the male gaze in music videos. The next section examines resistance in the musical domain by highlighting women's musical performance in music videos.

132   INTERPRETING SOCIOLOGY

Figure 7.13 Yonic imagery in (a) Ariana Grande "God is a Woman" (3:47) and **(b)** Peaches "Rub" (0:11)

Figure 7.14 The Sugamamas in Beyoncé "Green Light" (2:52)

Women as Instrumentalists and Composers

Beyoncé's "Green Light" features prominently her backing band the Sugamamas (Figure 7.14). The Sugamamas, a band made entirely of women, are the exception that proves the following rule: men are shown playing musical instruments in music videos far more often than women.

Unlike vocal performance, which leaves audible traces of the performer's sex and/or gender, it is impossible to hear gender in instrumental performance. Because one cannot *hear* that the iconic drumbeat of The White Stripes' hit "Seven Nation Army" is played by Meg White, music videos play an important role in making women's instrumental performance *visible*. These performances have often been marginalized in the Canon formation of popular music. For example, when mainstream sources rehearse the greatest rock guitarists of all time, it's nearly always American and European men: Jimi Hendrix, Jimmy Page, Eric Clapton, etc. Groundbreaking guitarists such as Sister Rosetta Tharpe, Joan Jett, and Orianthi paved the

SEXUALITY AND GENDER DIVERSITY   **133**

Figure 7.15 Virtuosic instrumental performance in (a) St. Vincent "Birth in Reverse" (1:21) and H.E.R. "Hard Place" (3:55)

Figure 7.16 Kim and Kelley Deal in The Breeders "Cannonball" (3:21)

way for some of the best guitarists of today, including H.E.R. and St. Vincent. Their music videos, which focus on instrumental virtuosity, draw the viewer's attention away from the sexualized/objectified body (Figure 7.15a and 7.15b).

In the early 1990s it became more common to see videos on MTV by bands composed mostly or entirely of women. "Cannonball," the 1993 hit single from The Breeders—a super-group formed by members of Throwing Muses and The Pixies—spends nearly all of its camera time focused on the instrumental performances of Kim and Kelley Deal (guitars), Josephine Wiggs (bass), and Jim Macpherson (drums). None of the women are shown in revealing clothing. Kim Deal, for example, is shown wearing a three-piece suit buttoned entirely to the throat (Figure 7.16).

134   INTERPRETING SOCIOLOGY

Figure 7.17 Studio footage in Fiona Apple "Shadowboxer" (1:48)

Soon after "Cannonball," MTV highlighted women's musical performance in videos by rock bands such as Veruca Salt, Hole, and others. The apex of this celebration of women's instrumental performance and songwriting came in 1997, when Sarah McLachlan and a host of other organizers started The Lilith Fair Festival; Lilith Fair, which showcased music created and performed by women, was the highest-grossing touring festival of 1997.

Two women featured prominently at the Lilith Fair, Fiona Apple and Tracy Bonham, showcase their classical training in several music videos. Fiona Apple's "Shadowboxer" (Figure 7.17) shows an artist playing the piano and singing in a recording studio. Shaky/hand-held shots and low-key black and white footage lends an air of authenticity to the video, putting the viewer in the position of watching Apple work in the studio.

Tracy Bonham plays both acoustic guitar and violin throughout her video "Mother, Mother" (Figure 7.18). But soon, her instrumental contributions to the track are thrown into question when the camera trains on a man playing an electric guitar while we hear Bonham playing an acoustic guitar. This is an example of **timbral mismatch**, a somewhat common facet of music videos in which the seen instrument does not match the heard one. When women are the ones heard making those instrument contributions and men are the ones *shown* making them (despite being on the wrong instrument), women's contributions to music are undervalued.

For whatever reason, the drum set has lagged behind the guitar, bass, and piano in terms of regularly showcasing women's instrumental performance. Notable pioneers behind the kit include Latin percussionist and composer Sheila E., Lori Barbero of Babes in Toyland, and of course Meg White of the White Stripes. Two more recent music videos that show women pounding the skins include HAIM's "The Steps" (Danielle Haim, Figure 7.19a) and Lenny Kravitz's "Low" (Jazmine Graham, Figure 7.19b).

While these instrumental performances are valuable in shifting the focus away from women as objectified bodies, it's important to bear in mind that many musically brilliant performances by women either do not involve external musical instruments, or they choose not to showcase these facets of performance in music videos. Virtuosic vocal performance, for example, takes a lifetime to master.[9] Composition (of both music and lyrics) is a similarly highly skilled art form that leaves no visible traces. Videos such as Missy Elliott's "Lose

SEXUALITY AND GENDER DIVERSITY　**135**

Figure 7.18 Tracy Bonham playing violin in "Mother, Mother" (1:38)

Figure 7.19 (a) Danielle Haim playing drums in HAIM "The Steps" (3:58) and (b) Jazmine Graham playing drums in Lenny Kravitz
"Low" (3:15)

Control," Erykah Badu's "Window Seat," and Grimes's "Kill V. Maim" feature music composed, recorded, and engineered entirely by these women. And yet their vision for these
music videos includes visually dazzling performances that center on the creation of complex
narrative worlds, rather than a "behind-the-scenes" view of the musician at work in her studio tirelessly adjusting parameters on a laptop computer.

　　Such behind-the-scenes work is often marginalized precisely because of its lack of visibility in music videos. Too often viewers assume that when a woman is shown "only" singing
that a man was behind the songwriting and/or production of the track. As the Canadian
musician/composer/engineer Grimes puts it:

136 INTERPRETING SOCIOLOGY

I'm tired of men who aren't professional or even accomplished musicians continually offering to 'help me out' (without being asked), as if I did this by accident and I'm gonna flounder without them. Or as if the fact that I'm a woman makes me incapable of using technology. I have never seen this kind of thing happen to any of my male peers.[10]

And yet valorizing the production prowess of these individual women risks overshadowing the musical collaborations of countless other women. Collaboration, rather than individual expression, is the new norm in popular music. Most music made today is not put together by individual, multi-talented women working alone in a studio but as part of a creative team. In celebrating women's instrumental performance, composition, and production, one should not forget the unseen women who write the lyrics, mix the audio, and edit the music videos to the hit tracks of today.

DEEP DIVE: AVICII (FT. SALEM AL FAKIR) "SILHOUETTES" (2012)

"Silhouettes" is a collaboration between Swedish EDM producer Avicii (Tim Bergling) and singer Salem Al Fakir. The track peaked at #4 on the Billboard U.S. Dance Club chart, and was certified platinum in Sweden. Visually, the video's narrative centers on gender dysphoria that leads to SRS. The protagonist's dysphoria is conveyed not only through scenes involving alcohol abuse but also through dark, undersaturated blueish hues (Figure 7.20); the protagonist is literally feeling "blue" throughout the first part of the video.

Talking about this complex narrative requires intentionality regarding gender pronouns. As the video begins, the protagonist presents as a cisgendered man, and, by the end, as a transwoman. Note that I am not using "transwoman" specifically because the protagonist has undergone SRS—one can adopt any gender identity they want regardless of surgery—but rather in the subjective sense of how this fictional character presents on-screen (makeup, wig, etc.).

The lyrics also help to advance this narrative, but in a complementary rather than explicit manner. Though the lyrics include themes of self-positivity and overcoming obstacles, they are never explicitly about sex or gender. One could imagine an entirely different video about a diminutive young girl who is bullied at school, who nevertheless joins the high school basketball team, works out incessantly (possibly hitting a growth spurt), and ends up joining the WNBA. With any complementary video, it is only natural to process the lyrical narrative and visual narrative together in a holistic way, and the song's formal design helps us appreciate such a narrative arc.

Figure 7.20 Dark hues as dysphoric in "Silhouettes" (1:21)

SEXUALITY AND GENDER DIVERSITY **137**

"Silhouettes" is cast in a relatively standard EDM form consisting of three main sections: verse, riserchorus, and drop. Table 7.1 charts the form of the video version, which is substantially different from the album version of the song. Such radical reconfigurations of formal designs are commonplace in EDM music. Known as "remixes," they can either be done by the original artist (in this case) or by others. Since EDM composers put together mixes by simply cutting and pasting samples in a digital audio workstation, Avicii's form is more flexible than, say, a record executive or disc jockey trying to make a radio edit of an acoustic rock song, a process which is usually limited to either doubling or removing an entire section for the purposes of duration.

As with most EDM forms, the verse advances a narrative, the riserchorus reflects on that narrative using the song title, and the drop section is a celebratory, wordless dance in which the beat returns. Verse one's lyrics are all about self-propulsion, moving forward without looking back. Alongside the word "newborn" the protagonist is depicted finally taking action, driving away from his dimly lit apartment full of empty bottles to an appointment at the SRS clinic (Figure 7.21).

Table 7.1 Formal design of "Silhouettes"

TIME	SECTION	DESCRIPTION
0:01	Video intro	Misé-en-scène
0:11	Intro	Bass sample
0:18	Verse 1	Vocals enter
0:47	Riserchorus	Beat removed; song title present
1:02	Drop	Beat returns
1:32	Transition	Beat drops out momentarily
1:41	Video insert	Doctor adjusts radio
2:02	Verse 2	Vocals re-enter
2:32	Riserchorus	Gentle trip-hop beat present under song title
3:02	Drop	Four-on-the-floor beat returns
3:40	Transition	Beat drops out momentarily
3:48	Video insert	Reflexivity: song announced on car radio
4:16	Drop	Beat returns
4:31	Video outro	Reflexivity: doctor sings riserchorus

Figure 7.21 Protagonist takes action, verse one of "Silhouettes" (0:44)

138 INTERPRETING SOCIOLOGY

The riserchorus takes a narrative leap forward in the visual domain, showing the protagonist in the future as a transwoman. This coincides with a change from dark/cool blue hues to warm, bright, saturated reds and oranges (Figure 7.22). The lyrics "we've come a long way" complement this visual narrative perfectly. Yet the arrival of the title lyric ("never look back at the faded silhouette") coincides with an old photograph of the protagonist as a cisgendered man hanging on the refrigerator. Technically, this moment would be an example of a conflicting narrative (see Chapter 4), but it's easy enough to imagine the protagonist moving forward with their life while still wanting to remember where they came from.

The drop section presents a visual montage of sorts, snapping back and forth between the blue/cisgendered shots of the verse and warm/transwoman shots of the riserchorus. Verse two advances the narrative, pairing lines about change coming soon with shots of the protagonist being wheeled into surgery (Figure 7.23). But this verse also engages in the same sort of back-and-forth montage as the riserchorus, showing future shots of the transwoman-protagonist. Cleverly the director recasts the blue, depressing alcohol of the opening as a happy object, now bathed in the bright warm colors of a party surrounded by friends.

The second riserchorus and drop sections continue to juxtapose shots from the surgical process with celebratory party scenes that occur in the future. As the drop progresses (it's twice as long as drop one) the video shows clearer shots of the protagonist as a transwoman, then the protagonist making out with a cisgendered man in the back of a taxi, and finally, the protagonist waking up in bed with this man (Figure 7.24). This ultimate satisfaction is

Figure 7.22 Warm hues illustrating self-actualization, "Silhouettes" (0:58)

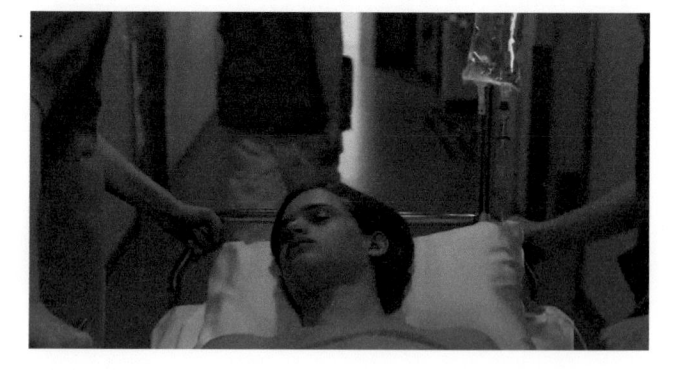

Figure 7.23 Advancing narrative in verse two of "Silhouettes" (2:15)

treated in warm golden hues. In a satisfying audiovisual parallel, the protagonist's journey toward this level of self-actualization is complete at precisely the same time that the song's EDM form—two verses, two risers, two drops—is also completed.

At this point (3:44) the video still has another minute to go. The album version of the song, with a total duration of 3'31," would have already ended because it doesn't contain the video insert before verse two. So why does the video, having already concluded its musical and visual narrative journey, continue for another minute? Following yet another video insert (this time announcing the song on the radio), Avicii adds a third drop section, which merely shows more of the same kinds of footage already heard in the previous minute. Generally, I avoid being critical of artistic choices in this book, but I think this extended version of the video misses the mark. A stronger remix would have ended the video like the album version of the song, after the second drop, showing the protagonist waking up happy in bed with a partner.

In summary, "Silhouettes" uses two opposing color and light palettes to help advance the story told through its visuals, which are only complementary to the lyrical narrative. The video version's extended formal design includes a video intro, two video inserts, and a third drop section not heard in the album version. With only two color palettes and four scenes, such a visual treatment would be better served by two sets of verse-riser-chorus-drop sections. Nevertheless, "Silhouettes" is a powerful video for its vivid depictions of both gender dysphoria and SRS, especially given its 2012 premiere.

Figure 7.24 Protagonist's ultimate satisfaction after drop two in "Silhouettes" (3:44)

Table 7.2 Lingo you should know

Cisgendered	The victim trope
Pansexual	Yonic imagery
Trans	Timbral Mismatch
Non-binary	
Hypersexualization	
Infantilization	
Objectification	

NOTES

1 See a telling interview with Sivan in Davey Davis, "Troye Sivan Talks Being a Queer Icon—And Being Labeled a Bottom," *Them* (August 28, 2018), <https://www.them.us/story/troye-sivan-bloom-interview>. Sivan states:

> I live in this very particular, surreal world where I hang out almost exclusively with queer people. I live 10 minutes from West Hollywood, which is like one of the gayest places in the world. You know, for me, this is really real life, being able to celebrate these things, being able to talk about these things, and just being as open and honest as you want, and I didn't want to come to this album writing for anyone but me and my friends.

2 See David Mack, "Troye Sivan Put an Interviewer On Blast after They Asked Him Whether He's a Top or Bottom," *Buzzfeed* (August 28, 2019), <https://www.buzzfeednews.com/article/davidmack/troye-sivan-interviewer-top-bottom>

3 For a detailed examination of masculinity in this context, especially in a video by Tyler the Creator, see Maeve Sterbenz, "Movement, Music, Feminism: An Analysis of Movement-Music Interactions and the Articulation of Masculinity in Tyler, the Creator's 'Yonkers' Music Video," *Music Theory Online* 23, no. 2 (2017).

4 See Stefania Sarrubba, "21 Non-Binary Artists who are Helping Redefine the Idea of Gender," *Gay Star News* (June 13, 2019), <https://www.gaystarnews.com/article/nonbinary-gender-neutral-artists-list/>

5 See Victoria Malawey, *A Blaze of Light in Every Word: Analyzing the Popular Singing Voice* (New York and Oxford: Oxford University Press, 2020).

6 For more on formants as they relate to gender, see Valentina Cartei and David Reby, "Effect of Formant Frequency Spacing on Perceived Gender in Pre-Pubertal Children's Voices," *PLOS One* (December 3, 2013), <https://journals.plos.org/plosone/article?id=10.1371/journal.pone.0081022>

7 See Laura Mulvey, "Visual Pleasure and Narrative Cinema," *Screen* 16, no. 3 (1975): 57–68.

8 This quote comes from Souyoung Kim, "Female Empowerment or Exploitation?" *The Crimson* (October 8, 2013), <https://www.thecrimson.com/column/k-pop-generation/article/2013/10/8/Female_Empowerment_Exploitation_Kpop/>

9 Kate Heidemann provides a thorough analysis of the embodied skills needed to produce common vocal timbres in "A System for Describing Vocal Timbre in Popular Song," *Music Theory Online* 22, no. 1 (2016), <http://www.mtosmt.org/issues/mto.16.22.1/mto. 16.22.1.heidemann.html>

10 See Grimes's interview in R.J. Cubarrubia, "Grimes Rails against Sexism: 'I'm Done With Being Passive.'" *Rolling Stone* (April 24, 2013).

CHAPTER 8 CLIP LIST

YEAR	ARTIST	VIDEO
1982	Michael Jackson	Billie Jean
1983	Herbie Hancock	Rockit
1986	Salt N Pepa	Push It
1989	N.W.A.	Straight Outta Compton
1991	Cypress Hill	How I Could Just Kill a Man
2000	D'Angelo	Untitled (How Does it Feel?)
2002	Christina Aguilera (ft. Lil' Kim)	Can't Hold Us Down
2017	K'Naan, Snow Tha Product, MC Riz, and Residente	Immigrants (We Get the Job Done)
2017	Luis Fonzi and DaddyYankee	Despacito
2017	Asma Lamnawar	Andou Zine
2017	Oumou Sangaré	Kamelemba
2018	Supaman (ft. Acosia Red Elk)	Why?
2019	BTS	Boy with Luv
2019	21 Savage (ft. J. Cole)	A Lot
2019	Lil' Nas X (ft. Billy Ray Cyrus)	Old Town Road

REPRESENTING RACE AND ETHNICITY

- Race and Ethnicity in Music Videos
- A History of BIPOC Musicians on MTV
  - *1980s Pop*
  - *The Golden Age of Hip-Hop*
  - *MTV Español and Other Cable Channels*
- BIPOC Musicians after MTV
- Deep Dive: Kendrick Lamar "Alright" (2015)

CHAPTER 8

Representing Race and Ethnicity

Since 1943 the Pulitzer Prize in Music has been awarded to an American composer each year for the finest piece of music composed, recorded, or performed. George Walker became the first Black composer to win the award for his 1996 piece *Lilacs* for soprano voice and orchestra. In 2017 the Chinese composer Du Yun became the first woman of color to win the award for her opera *Angel's Bone*. The next year the award went for the first time to a non-classical work: Kendrick Lamar's 2017 hip-hop album *DAMN*.

But it was Lamar's previous album, 2015's *To Pimp A Butterfly*, that really put him on the map. One video in particular from that album, "Alright," addresses the core issue of this chapter head-on: issues of race and ethnicity in music video, including racism and police brutality (Figure 8.1).

In order to fully appreciate these issues, however, they need to be put into context. Clearly issues of race and racism have prevented **BIPOC (Black, Indigenous, and People of Color)** musicians from being recognized by white supremacist critical institutions such as the Pulitzer Prize Award for Music. But BIPOC musicians had had a difficult time trying to penetrate popular institutions as well, especially MTV in the early 1980s.

While Black musicians saw more of themselves on MTV by the late 1980s, it would not be until a decade later that Latinx musicians received the same airplay. This chapter takes a closer look at the history of BIPOC musicians in music video since the premiere of MTV in the early 1980s. This representation changes for a number of ethnic groups after MTV gives way to a number of different cable channels playing specialty programming to targeted demographics. Ultimately, YouTube and other internet video platforms have made visible a

Figure 8.1 Police brutality in Kendrick Lamar "Alright" (5:54)

144   INTERPRETING SOCIOLOGY

much greater plurality of race and ethnicity in music video. Before addressing this history, it's necessary to understand how race and ethnicity are represented in music videos.

RACE AND ETHNICITY IN MUSIC VIDEOS

"Immigrants (We Get the Job Done)" is a music video from *The Hamilton Mixtape*, a collection of songs from Puerto Rican-American composer Lin-Manuel Miranda's hit Broadway musical *Hamilton,* reworked by hip-hop and pop artists. While *Hamilton* addressed issues of race as central to the founding of America, "Immigrants" recasts the struggle in terms of issues faced by present-day BIPOC populations, especially in light of the United States' increasingly racist immigration policies.

"Immigrants" presents the opportunity to understand how race and ethnicity are depicted in music video. Most obviously, this and other music videos present **visible minorities**, people who present as non-white, non-European, or Indigenous. The term visible minority comes from the Canadian census, where it is used to designate 1 of 12 different ethnic groups: Chinese, West Asian, Latin American, Southeast Asian, Arab, Filipino, Black, Korean, Japanese, South Asian, Other, or Multiple.[1] Though finer-grained than the United States' 2010 five-part system (Hispanic, Black or African-American, American Indian or Alaska Native, Asian, Pacific Islander), it is, like all classification systems, not without its faults. However, the term itself is useful for the analysis of music videos, since music videos present BIPOC musicians largely as *visible* phenomena.

"Immigrants" is a four-verse song separated by a chorus featuring the song title. Each verse is rapped by a different visible minority. Verse one features K'Naan. How does the video depict K'Naan as a visible minority, and how does the viewer decide which ethnic group(s) he belongs to? To most viewers, K'Naan presents as Black (Figure 8.2). However, it's important to be clear about exactly what that term means. If using Black to describe K'Naan's **race**, then it means he is part of a group of "people who share certain inherited physical characteristics, such as skin color, facial features, and stature."[2]

And yet such biological descriptions of race have little bearing on our modern world. All humans living on the planet today share ~99.9% of our DNA with one another. It is true that early on in human evolution certain biological traits were selected based on region. For example, K'Naan's dark skin was advantageous for living near the equator, where it helped protect against skin cancer, while the white police officer's pigment shown in Figure. 8.1 was advantageous for living in northern climates since it was more efficient at processing vitamin D in areas with less abundant sunlight. However, current scholarship in genetics, evolution, and sociology all critique the idea that there ever was such thing as a "pure" 100% race of any kind, and instead consider race to be a **social construction**: a concept that bears little objective reality and is instead driven by human preconceptions.

Figure 8.2 K'Naan in "Immigrants (We Get the Job Done)" (1:26)

REPRESENTING RACE AND ETHNICITY   **145**

For this reason, one might prefer the terms **ethnicity** and **ethnic group**. These terms avoid the biological determinism of "race," and instead connote "shared social, cultural, and historical experiences, stemming from common national or regional backgrounds, that make subgroups of a population different from one another."[3] Verse two is rapped by Snow Tha Product. While it's less clear that she presents as a *visible* minority (Figure 8.3), her Spanish-language rapping places her in an ethnic group that can be described as either Latin American or Hispanic. In this way music videos can also present *audible* minorities.

With its two primary media (visuals and audio), a music video provides opportunities to examine the difference between depictions of race and ethnicity. Take, for example, the third verse of this video, rapped by Riz MC. Figure 8.4 shows our first close up of Riz. Riz presents, visually, as a South Asian visible minority. So, when he starts rapping shortly after, listeners may be surprised to hear a rather posh London accent. This is, of course, an example of racial **stereotyping**, a set of judgments about whole categories of people. While the visual assessment was based on Riz's "inherited physical characteristics," his rap is a reminder that people who share such physical characteristics may belong to a number of distinct ethnic groups, and may have grown up all over the planet, resulting in vastly different spoken languages and accents.

Thus far the discussion has focused on these artists' visual and aural presentation, but not the lexical content of their raps. All four rap about the imbalance between the valuable contributions immigrants have made to American society and the hazardous conditions they continue to face despite these contributions. The fourth and final verse is rapped by Residente (Figure 8.5). While Snow raps in two different languages, Residente's is the only verse to be presented entirely *sin inglés*, forcing the non-Spanish-speaking viewer to either turn on captions or look up a translation. By starting in English, then gradually introducing more Spanish, the video parallels the United States' gradual increase in Spanish speakers over the past century (of course, much of U.S. territory was taken from people who were already speaking Spanish).

Figure 8.3 Snow Tha Product in "Immigrants (We Get the Job Done)" (2:01)

Figure 8.4 Riz MC in "Immigrants (We Get the Job Done)" (3:41)

Figure 8.5 Residente in "Immigrants (We Get the Job Done)" (4:08)

These four rappers present as minority, both visually and aurally, wholly within the universe of the music video itself. Many viewers, however, will take an extra step to look up information about these celebrities on the internet. Perhaps they already know this information prior to viewing. This encyclopedic pursuit of a musician's race or ethnicity (for example, via Wikipedia or Google) is a separate step in our understanding of music video. That K'Naan is Somali-Canadian, or that Riz MC is Pakistani-British are more matters of fact than perception. With similar pigments, and accents that are likely only discernible to a select few listeners, the aural distinction between Snow Tha Product (Mexican-American, born in California) and Residente (Puerto Rican)—both of whom are American citizens—is likely lost to most.

Such foregrounding of race and ethnicity as seen in "Immigrants..." was not always the case in music video. Musicians who were not white had a difficult time getting their videos played in the early days of MTV. The next section examines the history of representation of BIPOC musicians on MTV and, briefly, other cable music video networks.

A HISTORY OF BIPOC MUSICIANS ON MTV

1980s Pop

When MTV premiered in 1981 there was a palpable divide in the music industry between, on the one hand, rock music made by mostly white musicians, and, on the other hand, disco-influenced pop music made by mostly Black musicians. MTV favored the former. Former director of programming Buzz Brindle explained that "MTV was originally designed to be a rock music channel...It was difficult for MTV to find African-American artists whose music fit the channel's format that leaned toward rock at the outset."[4]

A number of prominent people called out MTV for this blatant racism. Disco musician Rick James and Art Rocker David Bowie were among the first celebrities to do so. But the nail in the coffin for MTV's stance came from direct economic pressures. Walter Yetnikoff, who was president of CBS Records, threatened to pull all of the company's videos from MTV if the network didn't play a particular video by one of their star artists: "Billie Jean," by Michael Jackson.

Of course, MTV relented, and in so doing aired one of the most iconic music videos of all time. The video was also important for making a Black performer highly visible on a cable television channel largely marketed to white audiences. *Soul Train*, a dance-and-music-focused show produced by and for Black audiences had been doing this for years, but it only reached mainstream television in 1976. Aside from showcasing the disco music that is so important to Black culture (not to mention Jackson's exquisite dancing), the video also has a lot to say about racism in early 1980s America.

"Billie Jean" exhibits a complementary relationship between its lyrical and visual narratives. In the video, the woman we presume to be Billie Jean is a white woman. But something untoward has happened to her. A gumshoe attempts to track down the character played by Jackson, but it's not only Jackson's dancing that's magical—he seems to have the ability to

REPRESENTING RACE AND ETHNICITY **147**

disappear as well as morph into a tiger. Once the white police officers are on his trail, they stop to ask a white woman for clues on the way up to Billie Jean's apartment (Figure 8.6). She points up to the scene of the supposed illicit activity.

The assumption that the presence of a Black man in the apartment of a white woman constitutes a crime is an example of racism. This plays into a longer history of portraying Black men as threatening and/or hypersexualized to white women in all kinds of media. At the end of the video, Jackson escapes capture by supernatural means, successfully framing the gumshoe instead. The shape-shifting supernatural occurs as a regular trope in several of Jackson's videos, most famously "Thriller" and "Black or White."

Jackson's mainstream success paved the way for other breakthrough videos by Black artists in the early 1980s. Shortly afterward jazz legend Herbie Hancock tried his hand at pop commercial success with "Rockit" (also on CBS Records). The mostly electronic track was ahead of its time technologically, making use of sequencers, vocoders, and an early drum machine. Visually speaking most of the screen time is dominated by robots and other automated paraphernalia that complement the music, with comparatively few shots of Hancock himself performing the vocoder (Figure 8.7).

Figure 8.6 Racism in Michael Jackson "Billie Jean" (4:13)

Figure 8.7 Technology in Herbie Hancock "Rockit" (2:02)

148   INTERPRETING SOCIOLOGY

In short order several other prominent Black musicians scored hit videos on MTV, including Prince's anthem "When Doves Cry" (1984), as well as two of the first by Black women: Whitney Houston's ballad "Saving All My Love For You" (1985) and Janet Jackson's dance-pop anthem "What Have You Done For Me Lately?" (1986).

The Golden Age of Hip-Hop

In 2017, after steadily gaining greater proportions of the market share, hip-hop finally outsold rock to become the highest-grossing music genre. Hip-hop began in The Bronx in the late 1970s when vocalists (called MCs) began toasting and rhyming over DJs spinning drum breaks on repeat from old funk records. These vocalizations would eventually coalesce into what we now know as rapping. What began as a regional art form, with specific styles based in specific neighborhoods, would find a way into mainstream music videos in a period known as the Golden Age of Hip-Hop from the late 1980s into the early 1990s.

MTV realized the popular and commercial appeal of hip-hop around 1986. One of the first hip-hop videos to air was "Push It" by the rap trio Salt N Pepa. Sandra Denton (Pepa) immigrated to Queens from Jamaica, then later met the other two musicians in Brooklyn. The lyrics, like many hip-hop lyrics, are about sex and desire. Yet the "Push It" video represents these three musicians as highly skilled performers, engineers, rappers, and dancers in a simulated live performance setting (Figure 8.8).

MTV realized quickly that they could further monetize hip-hop by creating a specialty show called *Yo! MTV Raps* where most of these videos would be played. Because Nielsen (the ad-tracking agency) was only reporting viewer data for periods lasting at least 30 minutes, MTV would only be able to attract potential advertisers selling to a majority-Black audience if they could reap this kind of sustained viewing. (Jay-Z references this phenomenon obliquely in "99 Problems": "so advertisers can give 'em more cash for ads"). *Yo! MTV Raps* aired from 1988 until 1995. A year later a similar show called *Rap City* ran on the cable channel BET (Black Entertainment Television).

This explosion in commercial attention to hip-hop arrived just in time for one of its most lucrative subgenres, gangsta rap, which was most popular between 1988 and 1993. Gangsta rap tended to focus specifically on the hardships and hard-earned successes faced

Figure 8.8 Rap group Salt N Pepa (0:41)

REPRESENTING RACE AND ETHNICITY   **149**

by inner-city minorities. One of the first gangsta rap videos was N.W.A.'s "Straight Outta Compton." Both the video and the lyrics depict discrimination and police brutality (Figure 8.9), a topic as relevant to BIPOC urban youth in 2020 as it was in 1989.

Black musicians were not the only minority group to achieve fame in gangsta rap. Latinx musicians such as Senen Reyes and Louis Freese rose to fame as the two frontmen of the rap group Cypress Hill. Reyes (aka Sen-Dog) is a Cuban immigrant, while Freese (aka B-Real) was born in California to Cuban and Mexican parents. Their video "How I Could Just Kill a Man" was one of the first to be censored on MTV for gun violence (Figure 8.10).

MTV replaced *Yo! MTV Raps* with another specialty program called *MTV Jams* in 1996. This was largely to accommodate the waning of gangsta rap relative to the growing market share of R&B, another majority-Black genre. At the genre's apex, around 80% of hits on Billboard's R&B chart were also appearing on Billboard's *Hot 100* chart—the top 100 songs in any genre. Chapter 3 examined one of the first R&B mega-hits: TLC's "Waterfalls." Usher, Aaliyah, and Toni Braxton all scored hit R&B videos in this period as well.

Figure 8.9 Police brutality in N.W.A. "Straight Outta Compton" (2:18)

Figure 8.10 Latinx representation in Cypress Hill "How I Could Just Kill a Man" (0:28)

150   INTERPRETING SOCIOLOGY

According to music video scholar Murali Balaji, R&B videos often objectify the bodies of visible minorities.[5] Balaji provides an extensive analysis of the intersection between race and gender in Christina Aguilera's video "Can't Hold Us Down" (featuring Lil' Kim). The song's lyrics are about double standards for women relative to men. But in the video there is also a double-standard between Lil' Kim (a Black woman) and Aguilera (who Balaji analyzes as presenting as white, despite her half-Ecuadorian parentage). At the beginning of the video Aguilera's character walks into a neighborhood that is clearly not her own. When she is sexually assaulted by a Black man, all of the neighborhood's Black women step in to defend her. At the end of the video, Aguilera is able to walk away from this sexual violence and harassment, while the Black women who defended her are presumably left to endure it on a daily basis. In addition, the video traffics in stereotypes of highly sexualized Black women, which, as Balaji further notes, Aguilera adopts as a sort of "primitive sexuality" throughout the video (Figure 8.11).

Theories of the male gaze (see Chapter 7) could certainly be applied to this video, but sexual objectification of Black bodies affects men as well. Compare D'Angelo's "Untitled (How Does It Feel?)" to a video that features remarkably similar eye-level shots, Sinead O'Connor's "Nothing Compares 2 U" (see Chapter 5). Whereas the focus of the latter remains from the chin up, the camera slowly pans down throughout D'Angelo's video to reveal frontal nudity that stops well below his waistline (Figure 8.12). The camera's gaze highlights the artist's athletic torso and sexually suggestive pelvic bones rather than his masterful singing voice.

MTV Español and Other Cable Channels

MTV placed a much higher premium on highlighting majority-Black genres such as hip-hop and R&B throughout the late 1980s and most of the 1990s. Only in the last few years of the millennium did the network turn its attention to the so-called "Latin Invasion" that was taking over American airwaves. Musically, these genres were characterized by mixing rhythms from a number of distinct Afro-Cuban traditions (e.g. Samba) with those imported from EDM. Chapter 2 showed how vast arrays of auxiliary percussion help to define the instrumentation of these genres as well.

Two videos that made Latinx musicians visible on MTV have already been examined in earlier chapters (Marc Anthony in Chapter 2 and Jennifer Lopez in Chapter 5). Shortly

Figure 8.11 Racial/sexual stereotypes in Christina Aguilera "Can't Hold Us Down" (2:43)

REPRESENTING RACE AND ETHNICITY   **151**

Figure 8.12 Sexual objectification in D'Angelo "Untitled (How Does It Feel?)" (4:01)

afterward, MTV essentially stopped playing music videos of any kind in favor of reality televi-sion programs. One can trace this evolution all the way back to the network's 1994 premiere of *The Real World*. Just like they consolidated all hip-hop videos into *Yo! MTV Raps* around that time, MTV now created a separate cable network called "MTV Tr3s" to consolidate inter-est in Latin music.

MTV Tr3s, Along with MTV2, a 24-hour music video cable network, were now the places consumers would have to go to see music videos, freeing up MTV's main cable channel for more lucrative dramas and reality programs. At the very moment that Latinx musicians were gaining visibility on Americans' televisions, those programs was stripped away from all but the select few who could afford premium cable packages with channels numbering in the hundreds. Despite the rise in BET's viewership for specialty shows such as *106 & Park* and *Rap City*, the larger consequence of this move was that, for the majority of viewers, music videos lost the cultural relevance they had enjoyed for nearly two decades.

BIPOC MUSICIANS AFTER MTV

Fast-forward momentarily to August of 2017, when a music video sung entirely in Spanish—"Despacito" by Luis Fonzi and Daddy Yankee—became the most widely accessed video file (of any kind, not just music) in the history of the internet video platform YouTube (Figure 8.13). The song's catchy melody and infectious reggaeton beat (reflecting the art-ists' Puerto Rican heritage) shattered all kinds of Billboard chart records as well, and paved the way for a second wave Latin music in the United States—what has been dubbed the "Despacito effect." With hip-hop records outselling rock for the first time that same year, 2017 saw a paradigm shift in the popularity of BIPOC musicians in music video. MTV was a network created for white rock music that was slow to embrace music by minorities, a vacuum filled by YouTube.

YouTube began rather modestly in 2005, but most users didn't have the home internet bandwidth to stream a music video until years later. Around 2009 more and more record companies and independent artists took advantage of this increased bandwidth. Once net-works like MTV and BET were no longer in control of which videos got played when, there

152 INTERPRETING SOCIOLOGY

was no longer a sense that the world was in the middle of a "golden age" or "invasion" for any certain minority group. Nor was it the case that videos by a certain minority group had to be played together. Users searched for whichever videos they wanted to see, by performers of any and all ethnicities, and controlled when, where, and for how long they watched them.

This represented a sea change for any number of distinct minority groups. East Asian musicians, for example, were never able to penetrate MTV like Black or even Latinx musicians. This all changed for Korean pop musicians following the viral K-Pop hit "Gangnam Style" by Psy, which in 2012 became the first music video to reach a billion views on You-Tube. Whereas "Gangnam Style" irreverently mocked the newfound vanity of a once derelict district of Seoul, "Boy With Luv," by BTS, addresses homosexuality in Korean culture, still a taboo topic (Figure 8.14). The video, which features the American singer Halsey, broke another YouTube record, becoming the most-viewed music video within 24 hours of its release (74.6 million views).

Even in the YouTube era, the success of East Asian artists in America is often constrained by their willingness to perform in one of a few acceptable styles. The Korean-American singer Eric Nam, for example, has lamented how his particular brand of earnest, confessional, singer-songwriter music doesn't fit the dominant mold for Korean popular music in the Western world: all K-Pop all the time.[6] Western audiences often acquire a taste for a small, highly curated subset of a particular genre, making it difficult for other musicians from that culture to penetrate that market without changing their music.

Back in the United States, the increased market share enjoyed by hip-hop musicians after 2017 also allowed room for a greater diversity of musical styles and representations in music video. Unlike traditional gangsta rap videos, which often depict Black families (especially Black men) living in poverty and spending time on the streets, "A Lot," by the Atlanta-based British-American rapper 21 Savage, shows a large multi-generational Black family living in a classically appointed house (Figure 8.15). While American audiences are used to seeing white families depicted this way—such as in the HBO series *Succession*—Black families have historically not been able to accrue comparable generational wealth due to systemic racism.

Nowhere is this range of expression more apparent than in the genre-bending, record-shattering hit that was "Old Town Road." The country-rap anthem gained popularity on the social media platform Tik-Tok in 2018. It was remixed in 2019 as a major-label collaboration with the country singer Billy Ray Cyrus, resulting in 19 consecutive weeks at #1 on the Billboard *Hot 100*, a record previous shared by the likes of Mariah Carey and Boyz II Men. The track pushes genre boundaries by mixing a hip-hop drum machine with country-style

Figure 8.13 Latinx representation in Luis Fonzi and Daddy Yankee "Despacito" (1:03)

REPRESENTING RACE AND ETHNICITY **153**

singing and a banjo.[7] It also pushes social boundaries in both the hip-hop and country communities. Lil' Nas X the artist is openly gay, as is the character-persona he presents in the video (Figure 8.16). While artists such as Tyler the Creator and Frank Ocean helped clear a path for LGBTQ+ artists in the hip-hop community, with "Old Town Road" Lil' Nas X became the first openly LGBTQ+ musician to win a CMA (Country Music Association) award.

These chart-toppers are all high-budget music videos backed by record labels. Perhaps the biggest change to music videos in the YouTube era comes from the ability for independent artists all over the world to upload videos of any production value and reach millions—possibly billions—of viewers. For many, these music videos streaming from parts of the world they will never visit and rarely see on television will be the closest experience they get to that culture's sights and sounds.

With 60 million views, "Andou Zine," by the Moroccan singer Asma Lamnawar, was one of the most watched music videos of 2017. The video is both sung and spoken (there is a lengthy video intro) in Arabic, with English subtitles provided. While there are familiar synths and drum machines—this is a pop song after all—those sounds are paired with more traditional percussion and string instruments from the region. The video's visual narrative begins with Lamnawar driving in the remote desert, where she comes upon a traditional

Figure 8.14 Korean representation in BTS "Boy With Love" (2:17)

Figure 8.15 Generational wealth in 21 Savage "A Lot" (0:43)

154 INTERPRETING SOCIOLOGY

Figure 8.16 Genre crossover in Lil' Nas X "Old Town Road" (3:18)

Figure 8.17 Moroccan wedding in Asma Lamnawar "Andou Zine" (4:22)

Moroccan band whose bus has broken down on the way to play a wedding. After some reluctance, she agrees to drive them to the wedding, at which point, of course, she then becomes the charismatic lead singer of the band (Figure 8.17). Once the ceremony is underway audiences are treated to a visual feast of what it is like to be at a lively Moroccan wedding, surrounded by dancing, music, family, food, and laughter.

Another view into a world few will ever visit comes from the hip-hop musician Supaman in his video "Why?" Supaman is an Indigenous rapper from the Apsáalooke people (aka Crow Nation) of the North American continent who specializes in creating loops that blend electronic and traditional sounds. One of these loops is a sample taken from the dancing body of Acosia Red Elk, of the Umatilla people, who is adorned with percussion instruments (Figure 8.18). The video shows the vast plains where these people live, and treats us to the sights and sounds of their culture's dress and music. But all is not celebratory. Supaman's lyrics, which are rapped in English, teach us about the struggles faced by Indigenous people, including racism, colonialism, alcoholism, depression, and other health issues.

"Kamelemba" is a remarkable music video by the singer Oumou Sangaré, who comes from the Wassoulou region of West Africa. Watching the video with the sound off, one would not get the same sense of transportation to a foreign land. Visually, it depicts the reality of a diaspora, in which people from a certain traditional background have now been driven to live in drab urban areas. But sonically the video, sung entirely in the Wassoulou language, allows the viewer to hear singing in a language spoken by less than 200,000 people in the world. Like "Andou Zine" the track features a mix of electronic instruments and the traditional string and percussion instruments of the Wassoulou people. The lyrics, subtitled in English (Figure 8.19), provide a rather universal social critique of the way women are treated in her

REPRESENTING RACE AND ETHNICITY **155**

Figure 8.18 Traditional dress in Supaman "Why" (0:29)

Figure 8.19 Wassoulou culture in Oumou Sangaré "Kamelemba" (0:39)

society, a protest accentuated visually by Sangaré and her accompanying dancers performing dances, rituals, and social behaviors traditionally only carried out by Wassoulou men.

In summary, the representation of BIPOC musicians in the MTV era was constrained by business practices and marketing pressures. While these and other social forces still constrain the artistic expression of minorities, music videos that would never have been given airtime on cable television have thrived in the user-generated universe of YouTube and other online media hubs. One can now easily access videos by musicians from almost any ethnic group in the world with just a few clicks.

DEEP DIVE: KENDRICK LAMAR "ALRIGHT" (2015)

One of the most memorable scenes from Kendrick Lamar's music video "Alright" is shown in Figure 8.20a and 8.20b. After a long video intro, Figure 8.20a appears just as the beat drops and the music begins. Seeing Lamar and his fellow Black Hippy bandmates in a classic car recalls classic gangsta rap videos all the way back to the late 1980s. But this isn't the standard gangsta rap trope; a few seconds later the camera zooms out to show us that Lamar's car is not traveling freely down the road. It has in fact been hoisted onto the shoulders of LAPD officers who are, symbolically, acting as pallbearers for the many Black men they've killed.

156 INTERPRETING SOCIOLOGY

Figure 8.20 (a) and (b) Police as pallbearers in "Alright" (2:30, 2:35)

One way to interpret this intentional pairing of a classic hip-hop trope with the reality of racist power structures in America (specifically in Compton and the greater LA area) is through the lens of what the celebrated African-American intellectual W.E.B. Du Bois called the **double consciousness** of Black Americans.[8] A number of scholars have written about double-consciousness in hip-hop. For example, Imani Perry's 2004 book *Prophets of the Hood: Politics and Poetics in Hip Hop* explains hip-hop as a primarily African-American art form that nevertheless must embrace the values of the ruling (white) class.[9] Drawing on Perry's work, Jim Bungert applies double-consciousness theory directly to Lamar's 2015 *To Pimp a Butterfly* to highlight the album's themes of "systemic racism, the war on drugs, white privilege, police brutality, prison reform, and so forth.[10]

These themes have made "Alright" something of a rallying cry at **Black Lives Matter** demonstrations, a movement originating in the United States in 2013 in direct response to the acquittal of Trayvon Martin's murderer. Noriko Manabe has argued that, despite the use of "Alright" as a protest anthem, we should listen carefully to that hook (sung by Pharrell) so as not to lose sight of the ambiguity in the original.[11] Just as spoken English uses a rising pitch at the end of a sentence to indicate a question, Pharrell ends the chorus hook with a rising pitch at the end of his last syllable (al-RIGHT). This is yet another example of Du Boisian double-consciousness in which one can hear a difference between the meaning of that phrase as a declaration [we ARE going to be alright], and the possibility that Pharrell himself doesn't believe it [ARE we going to be alright?].

The ambiguity in that declaration is somewhat flattened by the video's visuals. In each of the three choruses the video complements the title lyric with scenes of partying and success. Such scenes usually feature breakdancing, attractive women, and money flying out of classic cars (Figure 8.21). Lamar celebrates the final line of the final chorus atop a light pole, his

REPRESENTING RACE AND ETHNICITY   **157**

increased elevation representing a culmination of sorts (Figure 8.24). However, immediately after the final chorus is finished, a police car rolls up to quash Lamar's celebration.

Another way to read Lamar flying over the city is as yet another expression of this double consciousness. In the video intro he describes his life living in hotel rooms, apart from the war being fought back in the city. This war in the city is shown to us in the video's opening, as experienced by community members other than Lamar himself. Figure 8.22 shows an example of this, with an unnamed Black man being taken down, violently, by the police.

Lamar's success has brought him into the world of multinational capitalism, which presents its own challenges for Lamar, who is now battling depression and anger. This is symbolized by Lamar floating above the problems in the city wearing white (Figure 8.23a). Even when he's part of a celebration on the ground, he's still crowd-surfing in white atop the black-clad revelers (Figure 8.23b).

Ultimately Lamar floats higher and higher above the city until he reaches his apex atop a light pole (Figure 8.24). It is only upon reaching this highest point that he is shot by the white police officer. Symbolically this represents the fact that, even as one of the most successful Black artists on the planet, Lamar is still subject to the war based on Apartheid and discrimination he describes in the video intro.

Of course, Lamar's venerated artistic expression does not take place in a bubble. The Black Lives Matter movement began just before the video was filmed. Since the murder of Eric Garner in 2014 it has been directed more particularly toward the killing of Black

Figure 8.21 Signs of success in "Alright" (3:01)

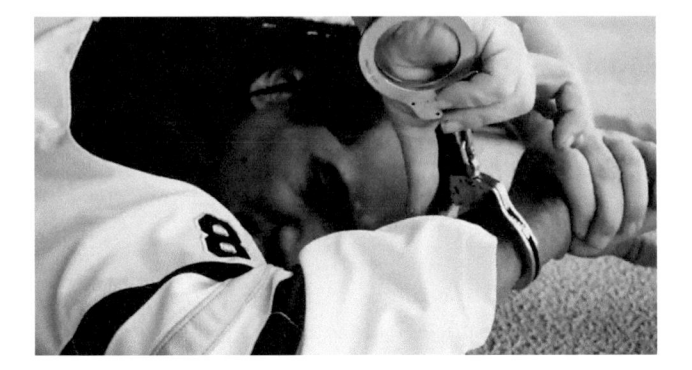

Figure 8.22 Violent police takedown in "Alright" (1:35)

158   INTERPRETING SOCIOLOGY

Figure 8.23 (a) and (b) Lamar floating above the city in "Alright" (3:11, 5:21)

Figure 8.24 Lamar's final perch in "Alright" (5:59)

people at the hands of the police. Black people are killed by the police more than twice as often as white people.[12] The murders of Michael Lorenzo Dean, Breonna Taylor, and George Floyd in 2020 have drawn a more intersectional focus to this issue. One now regularly sees LGBTQ+ and Indigenous activists acting in concert with BLM protesters at marches across the United States. Chapter 9 broadens the examination of music video and protest to include all manner of causes that music has put its weight behind in the service of political movements.

Table 8.1 Lingo you should know

BIPOC (Black, Indigenous, people of color)	Social construction	Double consciousness
Visible minority	Ethnicity	Black Lives Matter (BLM)
Race	Stereotype	

NOTES

1 Note that Indigenous, Aboriginal, Native, or First Nations people are not considered a visible minority in Canada, since they are considered members of Sovereign nations.

2 Definitions of race and ethnicity in this chapter are drawn from *Sociology: Understanding and Changing the Social World,* an open textbook published under a Creative Commons License (CC BY-NC-SA) by the University of Minnesota Press in which the original author explicitly does not receive attribution; See Chapters 10.2 and 10.3 specifically: http://open.lib.umn.edu/sociology/front-matter/publisher-information/

3 See *Sociology: Understanding and Changing the Social World.*

4 This quote is reproduced in Nadra Kareem Nittle, "How MTV Handled Accusations of Racism and Became More Inclusive," *Thoughtco* (February 27, 2018), <https://www.thoughtco.com/when-mtv-first-aired-black-videos-2834657>

5 See Murali Balaji, "Vixen Resistin': Redefining Black Womanhood in Hip-Hop Music Videos," *Journal of Black Studies* 41, no. 1 (2010): 5–20.

6 The podcast *Song Exploder* devotes an entire episode to the music of Eric Nam, which includes an interview in which Nam discusses these pressures <https://songexploder.net/eric-nam>

7 Interestingly, the banjo is sampled from a distinctly *un*-country source: The Nine Inch Nails album *Ghosts I–IV.*

8 See W.E.B. Du Bois, *The Souls of Black Folk* (Chicago: A.C. McClurg, 1903).

9 See Imani Perry, *Prophets of the Hood: Politics and Poetics in Hip Hop* (Durham, NC: Duke University Press, 2004).

10 See Jim Bungert, "'I Got a Bone to Pick': Formal Ambivalence and Double Consciousness in Kendrick Lamar's 'King Kunta,'" *Music Theory Online* 25, no. 1 (2019): 5.4.

11 See Noriko Manabe, "We Gon' Be Alright? The Ambiguities of Kendrick Lamar's Protest Anthem," *Music Theory Online* 25, no. 1 (2019).

12 This statistic comes from the podcast *Code Switch* episode "A Decade of Watching Black People Die," (May 31, 2020), <https://www.npr.org/2020/05/29/865261916/a-decade-of-watching-black-people-die>

CHAPTER 9 CLIP LIST

YEAR	ARTIST	VIDEO
1989	Billy Joel	We Didn't Start the Fire
1990	Jesus Jones	Right Here, Right Now
1990	Madonna	Justify my Love
1992	Dr. Dre (ft. Snoop Doggy Dogg)	Nuthin But a G Thang
1994	Nine Inch Nails	Closer
1996	The Roots	What They Do
1997	Björk	Pagan Poetry
1998	Motörhead	Killed By Death
1998	The Cardigans	My Favourite Game
2004	Jay-Z	99 Problems
2004	M.I.A.	Sunshowers
2005	Panic! at the Disco	I Write Sins, Not Tragedies
2010	M.I.A.	Born Free
2011	Kanye West	All of the Lights
2012	M.I.A.	Bad Girls
2012	Pussy Riot	Mother of God, Drive Putin Away
2014	Katy Perry	Birthday (lyric video)
2015	Darkstar	Pin Secure
2016	Beyoncé (ft. James Blake)	Forward
2017	Kesha	Prayin'
2018	Cardi B	Money
2018	Childish Gambino	This is America
2018	Childish Gambino	Feels Like Summer
2018	DJ Khaled	No Brainer
2018	Janelle Monae (ft. Grimes)	PYNK
2018	Delta Rae	Hands Dirty
2019	John Legend	Preach

MUSIC VIDEO AND POLITICS

- Censorship
  - *Lyrical Censorship*
  - *Visual Censorship*
- Political Music Videos
  - *#MeToo, #TimesUp*
  - *Black Lives Matter*
  - *Other Political Videos*
- Deep Dive: The 1975 "Love It If We Made It" (2018)
  - *Visual Analysis*
  - *Lyrical and Musical Analysis*

CHAPTER 9

Music Video and Politics

It could be said that most, if not all music videos are "political." In light of the last two chapters, even the act of seeing a single performer in music video raises questions about the ways that a performer's gender, sexuality, and ethnicity are represented. Railton and Watson claim that these types of representation in music video have a direct effect on viewers in that they "both constrain and make possible ways of thinking about ourselves as individuals within contemporary society."[1]

And yet it's also fair to say that some music videos are more political than others. This chapter ends with deep dive into British rock band The 1975's "Love It If We Made It," a video by white male performers that expresses pessimism through quick cuts between cataclysmic geopolitical events. Just like two political videos by white men of the previous generation—Billy Joel's "We Didn't Start the Fire" (1989) and Jesus Jones' "Right Here, Right Now" (1990)—the musician stands apart from these cataclysms, watches them from a distance, and ultimately claims no responsibility for their causes.

In other videos artists position themselves directly at the forefront of the struggles they sing about. Some cannot help it—they've been personally oppressed by the very forces they're opposing. The majority of this chapter addresses such videos, focusing on those that engage with two global protest movements—BlackLivesMatter and #MeToo/#TimesUp—as well as those aimed at climate change, corporate greed, and other issues.

But first, this chapter will examine ways in which larger political machinations, particularly those in the United States, have worked against free expression in music video through censorship. Censorship standards for both lyrical and visual content in music videos are subjective. Most importantly, they change drastically over time, and depend uniquely on the channel, be it MTV, BET, CMT, YouTube, etc.

CENSORSHIP

After MTV discovered that gangsta rap from two different coasts—Compton and Long Beach in the west, Brooklyn and Queens in the east—had huge commercial potential, they soon realized an inherent problem. While both of these styles reflected the way that certain cultures talked, that way of speaking was different from the manner allowed on mainstream television. Mainstream television is a culture. It carries certain norms and expectations of its speakers. Those norms and expectations are driven largely by white, straight, cisgendered, temporarily abled executives and shareholders. Though norms have changed over the past 30 years or so, in the early 1990s when gangsta rap was at its apex its norms clashed violently with the hegemonic values of mainstream culture.

162   INTERPRETING SOCIOLOGY

This battle must be put into the context of a broader struggle between liberal and conservative values in the early 1990s known as the **culture wars**, a term coined in 1991 by the sociologist James Davison Hunter.[2] Hunter was particularly concerned with the rise of the religious right in America. His most vocal counterpart in this war was the white, Holocaust-denying presidential candidate, Pat Buchanan. In his 1992 bid for the presidency Buchanan used the term "culture war" to describe what he saw as an assault on so-called traditional American values—by which he meant those rooted in white supremacist, patriarchal, homophobic appropriations of Evangelical Christianity.

Lyrical Censorship

Nowhere was the religious right more active in the censorship of music and music video than when it came to gangsta rap. The censorship of gangsta rap fits Michael Eric Dyson's definition of censorship to a tee, in that it "seeks to prevent the sale of vulgar music that offends mainstream moral sensibilities by suppressing the First Amendment."[3] Parent and church groups on one side of the culture wars gained significant media attention by using donations to purchase all extant copies of offending CDs from the shelves of record stores and bulldozing them on television.

One way that gangsta rap artists got around lyrical censorship on MTV was to record and release two different versions of tracks destined to become music videos. Such **clean versions** essentially replace all words that the artist suspected MTV would censor with alternative lyrics that meant roughly the same thing and worked within the rhyme scheme. This had curious ramifications for music video. The audio for Dr. Dre's clean version of "Nuthin But a G Thang" (one of the first tracks to feature Snoop Doggy Dogg) replaces the original couplet containing the words "motherfucker" and "lynching" with "dog pound" and "bow-wow-wow." However, since filming two different versions of the video would be cost-prohibitive, Snoop mouthed the words "bow-wow-wow" (Figure 9.1) in both the MTV-version of the video and the copy released by the record company. The uncensored version, which was available on VHS and later on YouTube, combines this same video footage with the album-version audio and, therefore, amounts to moments of inaccurate lip-synching. Notice also in Figure 9.1 that the stylized marijuana leaf on Snoop's hat has been blurred for the MTV-version.

When an artist either fails to (or chooses not to) record a clean version of a track MTV and radio had no other choice than to play a **bleeped version** of the audio, in which the offending word or words is replaced by an added noise. Some artists will, however, anticipate

Figure 9.1 Clean version of Dr. Dre (ft. Snoop Doggy Dogg) "Nuthin But a G Thang" (3:27)

MUSIC VIDEO AND POLITICS   **163**

Figure 9.2 Bleeped version of Panic! at the Disco "I Write Sins Not Tragedies" (1:46)

this, and make available a pre-mixed version in which only the vocal track (i.e. not the bass or other instruments) is altered. Such seems to be the case with Panic! at the Disco's "I Write Sins Not Tragedies," in which the taking the Lord's name in vain was simply muted, allowing the other instruments to sound throughout the vocal interruption. Lead singer Brendan Urie cleverly avoids the lip-synching problem seen/heard in "Nuthin But a G Thang" by covering his mouth during the bleep (Figure 9.2).

In extreme cases when an artist makes no concessions, producing neither clean nor bleeped versions, MTV may opt to play an **edited version** that simply removes an entire offending section of the video. An early example of this was the edited version of Dire Straits's video "Money For Nuthin." The third verse of the song contained a homophobic slur. MTV's edit cut directly from Verse 2 to Chorus 3, omitting the entire offending verse (and a chorus, so as not to have two consecutive choruses). A viewer who had never heard the album version of the track would never suspect that anything had happened.

Visual Censorship

Just as lyrical censorship is subject to conventions of a certain time—what can and cannot be said on the air changes drastically—what can or cannot be broadcast in a music video's visuals is highly subjective. Some visual censorship is purely for legal and/or copyright reasons. Rap videos used to be awash in blurred hats and clothing because the artists didn't have the rights to display the logos of those companies. This is one of the many satirized elements in The Roots "What They Do" (Figure 9.3a). However, nowadays, companies pay good money to have their products featured in music videos. DJ Khaled's "No Brainer" features more paid product placements—fashion brands Fashion Nova and Dolce & Gabbana; alcoholic beverages Belaire Rosé, Bumbu Rum, and Cîroc vodka; Kandypens vapes (Figure 9.3b)—than it does artists (Justin Bieber, Quavo, Chance the Rapper).

Artists in the MTV era were subject to the whims of executives who were interested in attracting advertising dollars from companies marketing to conservative suburban viewers while still playing content from the day's edgiest artists. While many artists succeeded in creating videos that toed this subjective line, MTV banned a number of videos for various reasons.

164   INTERPRETING SOCIOLOGY

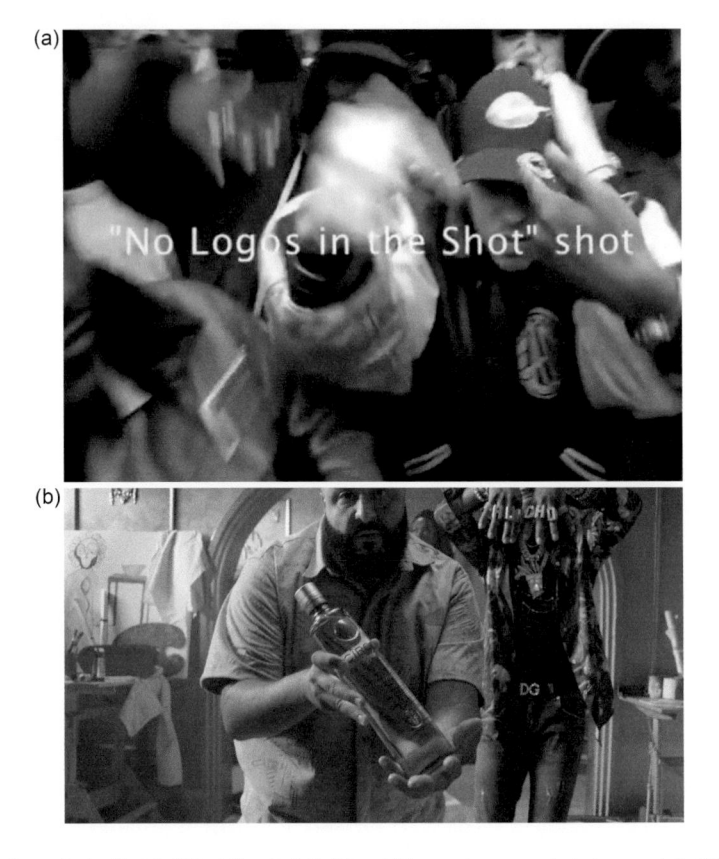

Figure 9.3 (a) No Logos in the Shot in "What They Do" (2:47) and (b) conspicuous product placements in "No Brainer" (1:32)

Only a highly edited version of Nine Inch Nails' video "Closer" was seen on MTV. Director Mark Romanek keenly anticipated which scenes wouldn't make the cut with MTV, including mutilated animal corpses, female nudity, a live monkey bound to a cross, lead singer Trent Reznor in bondage, and images of Reznor's face as he mouthed the word "fuck" in the chorus hook (which was of course aurally bleeped as well). Instead of shooting two videos, Romanek simply inserted a faux-documentary style "Scene Missing" slide whenever such a scene occurred. As was the case for a number of these videos, the original version was only available for purchase on VHS and, years later, was shown late at night on the separate cable channel MTV2.

Other artists didn't bother creating a clean version of their visual content, and their videos were banned outright by MTV. One of the earliest was Madonna's "Justify My Love." Like "Closer" the video traffics in sadomasochism but further transgresses the social norms of the early 1990s by depicting gender-nonconforming individuals engaging in non-heteronormative sex acts (Figure 9.4).[4] Even though the video actually shows no nudity per se, it was still banned from MTV—a clear example of Dyson's definition of censorship as that which "offends mainstream moral sensibilities."

Several videos were banned from MTV in the 1990s and even MTV2 in the early 2000s for graphic or dangerous depictions of violence. Hard rock group Motörhead's 1998 "Killed By Death" was banned for glorifying death by electric chair.[5] Jay-Z's "99 Problems"—another Mark Romanek-directed video full of borderline content, including gun violence and animal

MUSIC VIDEO AND POLITICS · **165**

Figure 9.4 Non-heteronormative sex in Madonna "Justify My Love" (2:47)

Figure 9.5 Violence in The Cardigans "My Favourite Game" (4:02)

harm—was only aired on MTV and BET in 2004 preceded by a long video disclaimer. For his video "My Favourite Game" by the Swedish pop group The Cardigans director Jonas Åkerlund shot no fewer than five different endings in an attempt to meet various countries' censorship standards. Throughout the video lead singer Nina Persson plays chicken with a number of drivers, causing them to crash their vehicles. In some endings, such as the one shown in Figure 9.5, she dies after putting a stone on the gas pedal and running headlong into a van full of men. Ultimately, it wasn't the ending that mattered. Several international music video outlets removed some (even all, in the case of MTV-UK) joyriding scenes *throughout* the video for fear that they encouraged reckless driving.

Even after the move to MTV2 in the 2000s, in which many of the above videos were finally aired, the network still had lines it was not willing to cross. In one such case the motive was purely political. Though "Sunshowers," by the British-Sri Lankan pop star M.I.A., features no visual support for the Palestinian Liberation Organization, the video's

166   INTERPRETING SOCIOLOGY

Figure 9.6 Nudity as a statement in Cardi B "Money" (0:12)

lyrics briefly mention it. MTV asked M.I.A. to either submit a bleeped version or to release a statement disavowing the PLO. She did neither, and MTV never played the video. MTV's motive was clear: it could not afford to be seen supporting a political organization largely antithetical to Zionist Americans, who make up a much larger portion of its viewership than Palestinians.

Music video's move to YouTube and other online platforms has loosened the censorship restrictions in music video immensely. In 1997, for example, Icelandic singer Bjork's "Pagan Poetry" was banned from MTV for showing her bare breasts. Cardi B's 2018 video "Money," on the other hand, shows women's bare breasts throughout. In both cases the women are merely singing, posing, and dancing without a shirt, not engaging in sex acts. In other words, MTV was simply censoring Björk's body for existing. The situation is akin to most cities in America banning women being topless in public, whereas this is perfectly acceptable and legal in other cities and cultures (especially in Europe). The difference may be that Cardi B, as an American, is making a *statement* by having dancers in suits with their nipples barely exposed (Figure 9.6), since the nipple seems to be the tipping point for American censorship (recall, for example, the infamous "nip-slip" during the 2004 Super Bowl).

And yet even YouTube has its limits. The sorts of non-heteronormative sex acts shown in Madonna's 1990 video "Justify My Love" pale in comparison to those in the 2015 video "Rub" by the Canadian electronic musician Peaches. Mathias Korsgaard describes "Rub" as an example of an "NSFW" (Not Safe for Work) video, adding that the video is in "keeping with Peaches' tendency to aesthetically assault heteronormative values."[6] "Rub" was banned from YouTube for a number of these assaults, which Kat George summarizes as "plus-sized bodies, hairy vaginas, sweaty orgies, same-sex cunnilingus, and all manner of other sex acts as well as hints of BDSM. There's nothing sanitized about "Rub" and it challenges the notion that the only legitimate female sexuality is the one sanctioned by male desire."[7]

Another M.I.A. video, "Born Free," was banned from YouTube in 2010 for depicting the mass incarceration and murder of redheads (Figure 9.7). While fictional, in keeping with the political nature of most of her work, M.I.A.'s video is clearly meant to remind the viewer of times when such events have happened to real groups of marginalized people.

Standards for censorship change even on YouTube. Rihanna's "S&M" was banned from YouTube in several countries when it was released in 2011 for far fewer transgressions than "Rub." At the time of this writing, I was able to access all three of these videos on the platform so long as my settings were adjusted to allow maximum freedom in "age-restricted content." Ultimately, YouTube and other internet video platforms give each user more control of what they consider appropriate levels of censorship—something previously impossible on twentieth-century cable networks such as CMT, BET, and MTV.

MUSIC VIDEO AND POLITICS   **167**

Figure 9.7 Mass murder of redheads in M.I.A. "Born Free" (3:34)

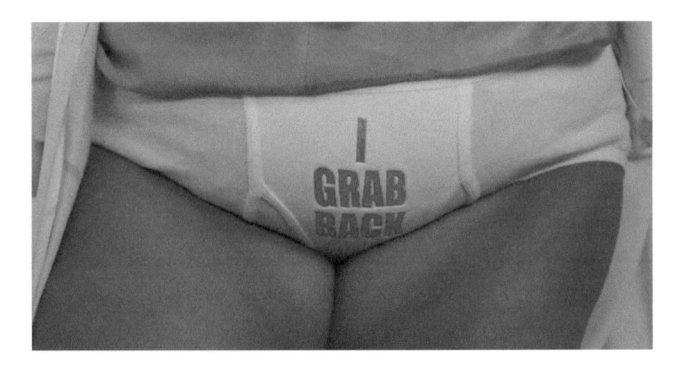

Figure 9.8 "I Grab Back" anti-Trump statement in Janelle Monae "PYNK" (2:27)

POLITICAL MUSIC VIDEOS

#MeToo, #TimesUp

Two related movements largely known by their social media tags—#MeToo and #TimesUp—aim to raise greater awareness of sexual assault and discrimination and to bring their perpetrators to justice. Jillian Mapes notes that, while we have seen a recent increase in music videos that resonate with these movements in the years since late 2017 (when allegations about Harvey Weinstein came to light), music and music video have always been vehicles for women to share these painful stories.[8] And yet some are unmistakably current. Janelle Monae's "PYNK," a video addressed extensively in Chapter 5, shows a woman wearing "I Grab Back" underwear (Figure 9.8), a direct response to Donald Trump bragging about grabbing women by their genitals.

Country singer Brittany Hölljes of the band Delta Rae sits in the middle of a room surrounded by newsprint stories about notable perpetrators of sexual assault in their video "Hands Dirty." With the help of her bandmates she painstakingly cuts out the lyrics to the song from these stories. Her final lyrics of the bridge are in fact "me too" (Figure 9.9). Upon seeing and hearing these words the camera cuts away from the room to show a number of women mouthing "me too." Delta Rae's video is notable for its intersectionality, highlighting the struggles of BIPOC and trans women throughout.

168 INTERPRETING SOCIOLOGY

Figure 9.9 #MeToo in Delta Rae "Hands Dirty" (2:37)

Figure 9.10 Kesha's struggles in "Prayin'" (3:51)

Many of Megan Trainor's videos have a political focus. "All About That Bass" helped change unhealthy Hollywood beauty standards. Trainor famously pulled "Me Too" from the VEVO platform after she discovered that the editor had airbrushed images of her to make her appear thinner. Her video "No" directly resonates with #TimesUp, instructing women how to simply say "no" to the next person who gives them unwanted sexual advances. Some videos that resonate with these movements are more personal than political. Perhaps none is more powerful than Kesha's "Prayin,'" which details her years of abuse at the hands of producer Lukasz "Dr. Luke" Gottswald. Both the images and lyrics paint this song as a quasi-religious confessional. As she sings about fighting off years of self-doubt and finally getting the courage to move forward, she fights off pigs in men's suits (Figure 9.10). Like Christine Blasey Ford and so many other women whose struggles against abusive men were ultimately dismissed by the court, so were Kesha's suits against Gottswald.

Black Lives Matter

Black artists have been singing and rapping about police brutality in music videos since the late 1980s, with N.W.A.'s "Straight Outta Compton" (1989) and Public Enemy's "Fight The Power" (1989) representing distinct struggles on the west and east coasts, respectively. Kendrick Lamar's "Alright" is just one of a number of recent videos that directly engages with the Black Lives Matter movement, a modern response to police brutality against Black people that has changed very little since the time of N.W.A. and Public Enemy.

MUSIC VIDEO AND POLITICS   **169**

Beyoncé's "Forward" (ft. James Blake) is a double entendre. Not only does it act as a *fore-word* to "Freedom," the next track on Beyoncé's visual album *Lemonade*, it is also a testament to moving forward, to making lemonade from the lemons in Beyoncé's personal life. The video presents an extra, more political narrative on this meaning. One woman who is having a particularly difficult time moving forward, Lezley McSpadden, mother of Michael Brown who was murdered by Ferguson police officer Darren Wilson, is shown holding a picture of her son in the video (Figure 9.11). Reactions to Brown's murder and Wilson's eventual acquittal led to a wave of influential protests in Ferguson and elsewhere including the rallying cry "hands up/don't shoot."

John Legend's "Preach" examines the broader social cost of racist law enforcement practices and policies. Throughout the video police officers are busy killing a young Black man at a traffic stop and separating a migrant family at the border (Figure 9.12). So busy, in fact, that they are unable to stop the school shooting we watch unfold over the course of the video while the officers are distracted. At the time of this writing, Legend has attached a fundraiser to the YouTube video that allows viewers to donate to FREE AMERICA, which aims to "end mass incarceration and invest in just, equitable, and thriving communities."

Childish Gambino's "This is America" is one of the most overtly political (if cryptic) music videos of the past decade. Its heavily coded symbolism has been the topic of countless interpretations on the web. A few of these images are unmistakable in their relationship to

Figure 9.11 Michael Brown's mother in Beyoncé "Forward" (44:58)

Figure 9.12 Border Patrol separating a family in John Legend "Preach" (2:52)

170 INTERPRETING SOCIOLOGY

Figure 9.13 Gun control in Childish Gambino "This is America" (1:56)

the Black Lives Matter movement. First, the video is full of costumes and poses associated with racist Jim Crow artwork.[9] Another comes when Gambino opens fire on a choir with a fully automatic assault rifle (Figure 9.13), a clear reference to the 2015 slaughter of nine African-Americans in a South Carolina church. That the shooter, a 21-year old white supremacist named Dylann Roof, was allowed to purchase the gun legally speaks to just what kind of America "this" is.

Other Political Videos

Another of Gambino's videos, "Feels Like Summer," addresses climate change. Despite being a seemingly universal problem for all of earth's inhabitants, climate change, like sexual violence against women, disproportionately affects earth's BIPOC inhabitants. In this entirely animated video, Gambino's avatar walks quietly down the street observing people's interactions. The song's lyrics, the constant sunshine, and the overwhelming red-orange hues in the video suggest that it is quite hot outside (Figure 9.14). Yet nobody is inside in the air conditioning. This may be an intentional irony: while many real-life families, living on streets that look like this and in houses that look like this, may not be able to afford air conditioning (and thus will suffer the most as climate change continues), most of the people Gambino sees playing in their yards on this street are in fact caricatures of wealthy hip-hop artists (Chance the Rapper, Nicki Minaj, etc.) who will have the resources to keep themselves cool as temperatures rise.

Up until 2018 it was illegal for women to drive cars in Saudi Arabia. Despite being filmed on location in Morocco (where it is legal for women to drive), the message in M.I.A.'s video for "Bad Girls" is unmistakable. Driving with their defiant fists held proudly out the window—all while wearing ornate niqabs (Figure 9.15)—these women defy legal and cultural norms throughout the video, including dancing provocatively and brandishing assault rifles. All of this occurs while men in white robes, checkered *keffiyeh*, and sunglasses stand rank-and-file as they look on disapprovingly.

It is difficult for a mainstream music video, which is often backed by a major record label, to make a convincing stand against corporate greed. Nevertheless, a few have tried. Australian pop band Midnight Oil's 1990 "King of the Mountain" is a live performance video (with a mix of live and studio audio) shot as part of a demonstration in front of the World Trade Center. The band sings of "liquid tarmac wastelands" while a flag bearing the ExxonMobil logo waves. More recently, these anti-corporate sentiments have gained traction under the broader Occupy Movement (formerly known as "Occupy Wall Street" in the United States).

MUSIC VIDEO AND POLITICS **171**

Formed as a response to the 2008 world financial crisis, "Occupy" aims to highlight the exaggerated class differences between C.E.O.s (the "1%") and the average worker (the "99%"). British electronic duo Darkstar's video "Pin Secure" amplifies this class difference as a difference in *species*. Workers on the graveyard shift at a drugstore are human, while everyone who shops at the store is a non-human animal like their Koala-boss (Figure 9.16). All the while the workers are kept in their place by sensational news headlines that warn of immigrants taking over "skilled" British jobs.

Figure 9.14 Climate change in Childish Gambino "Feels Like Summer" (0:41)

Figure 9.15 Women transcending cultural norms in M.I.A. "Bad Girls" (0:38)

Figure 9.16 Corporate greed in Darkstar "Pin Secure" (0:50)

172   INTERPRETING SOCIOLOGY

Figure 9.17 Music as protest in Pussy Riot "Mother of God Drive Putin Away" (0:24)

No band has made more of a political splash in recent years than the Moscow-based feminist punk collective known as Pussy Riot. Its members regularly make international headlines for engaging in protests that challenge Vladimir Putin, The Russian Orthodox Church, restrictions on women and the LGBTQ+ community in Russia, and other political causes. Pussy Riot gained international attention in 2012 when three of its members were arrested for "hooliganism" connected with a guerrilla performance in Moscow's Cathedral of Christ the Saviour. One member was released within the same year, but two of the women served over a year and a half in prison before pressure from the international community mounted and the women were freed. A music video for their song "Mother of God Drive Putin Away" features live footage from the protest (Figure 9.17). Pussy Riot's song is notable for blending choral singing (the melody parodies Russian composer Sergei Rachmaninoff's *Ave Maria*) with punk rock shouting, both of which are in Russian.

DEEP DIVE: THE 1975 "LOVE IT IF WE MADE IT" (2018)

The following analysis will dive deeper into the political impact of The 1975's "Love It If We Made It" through a detailed assessment of its visual design, then its musical/lyrical design. Separating the two is difficult in this thoroughly multimedia video, which often links heard lyrics with corresponding visual images, or with the actual text of those lyrics appearing onscreen. Rather than merely cataloging all the political references in the lyrics and visuals, this deep dive will consider the highly subjective act of a single viewer attempting to perceive and identify these references. Throughout the analysis I will also make intertextual connections between The 1975's video and two remarkably similar videos by white artists of a different generation: Billy Joel's "We Didn't Start the Fire" (1989) and Jesus Jones' "Right Here, Right Now" (1990). Each of these three videos traces the same basic visual narrative, with the artist guiding the viewer through a highlight reel of the day's most tragic geopolitical catastrophes.

Visual Analysis

The visual design of "Love It If We Made It" owes a significant debt to a genre known as **lyric videos**. Lyric videos are produced by a fan with no permission given by the artist or record company. They have been uploaded to YouTube since people have had the bandwidth to do so. The earliest lyric videos were essentially karaoke monitors scrolling through a song's

MUSIC VIDEO AND POLITICS   **173**

lyrics in real time over a static background. As soon as amateur lyric videos began to include newly filmed footage, lavish set designs, gorgeous location shoots, and professional editing, they sometimes became so popular as to rival the "official" videos released by an artist. Predictably, record companies finally got wise and started making their own lyric videos. For her song "Birthday" Katy Perry did both. As of the time of this writing, the "standard" music video has received around 75 million views while the lyric video (Figure 9.18) has received nearly four times as many (~272 million).

Performance shots in "Love It If We Made It" are limited to simulated soundstage footage. In light of Pussy Riot's willingness to risk—and, for three of them, ultimately suffer—arrest and prosecution as they performed in a restricted space for their video, what are we to make of The 1975—a white, cisgendered male band—only shown singing or playing their instruments as multihued shadow-musicians (Figure 9.19)? Though they differ in depth and fidelity, the dancing silhouettes over bright tropical colors evoke the iconic Apple iPod ads of the early 2000s. Handheld technology is also referenced as the lyrics "INFORMATION" and "APPLICATION" flash on the screen, which are accompanied by the square application icons seen on most mobile devices.

Probably the most distinctive visual feature of "Love It If We Made It" is the blinding parade of short video clips that depict some sort of political catastrophe. Understanding these political references is necessarily a subjective affair. With so many presented in quick succession, it's doubtful that any one listener/viewer will be able to place each reference to a

Figure 9.18 Lyric video visual design in Katy Perry "Birthday" (0:45)

Figure 9.19 Shadow performances in The 1975 "Love It If We Made It" (0:24)

174 INTERPRETING SOCIOLOGY

specific event. It seems more likely that each will perceive some of these references as specific and the rest as general.

For instance, like most people in the United States, I recognize Donald Trump (2:55) but was unable to recognize a different white man at 0:30. For many (if not most) viewers of music video—as well as people who listen to music by itself—there is always the temptation to "look up" on the internet something we don't understand or recognize. For listeners of the audio alone, this most often involves pulling up the lyrics. And for viewers of some music videos—this one included—it may involve looking up where some of these shots are taken from and therefore what they "mean." Indeed, searching Google for "Love It If We Made It video meaning" returns a number of hits, including "every reference in The 1975's powerful 'Love It If We Made It' video."[10] This is, in fact, where I learned that the white man pictured alongside the "SAYING CONTROVERSIAL THINGS" lyric at 0:30 is a right-wing conspiracy theorist, influencer, and former editor of Breitbart News named Milo Yiannopoulos (0:30).

Another image at 1:51, which shows tanks blowing stuff up somewhere, brings to mind not a specific political event for me but rather a remarkably similar video that shows political events unfolding. "Right Here, Right Now" is a hit video from 1990 by another British band, Jesus Jones, that alternates shots of the band performing with images of conflicts happening on the European continent at the end of the 1980s. Along with the soundstage performance footage, the video features lead singer Mike Edwards watching these events on television. For many viewers of my generation, shots of George H.W. Bush and Mikael Gorbachev will help to place many of these events within the context of the Cold War's end, including the fall of the Berlin Wall just one year prior. A shot of the changing map of central Europe, including Czechoslovakia, brings to mind the Velvet Revolution.

But as sad as it may be to say, images of tanks—in both videos—are just too prevalent to be specific. Few viewers (at least outside of central Europe around the early 1990s) will be able to place the most violent images in "Right Here, Right Now" within the context of the bloody Romanian Revolution (Figure 9.20), in which just over 1,000 people died overthrowing communism. But the song's celebratory hook about the world "waking up" from history was all too soon. Had Jesus Jones's video been created just a year later, it would have likely featured images of U.S. tanks and air strikes slaughtering thousands of Iraqis in the Persian Gulf.

Just as "Right Here, Right Now" features images that are specific to the early 1990s, the most recognizable images in "Love It If We Made It" all resonate with a few specific political currents of its time. As a British band, The 1975 draws attention to missteps by their own government (Grenfell Tower Fire, London Riots), but is also critical of atrocities in the

Figure 9.20 Non-specific tank imagery in Jesus Jones "Right Here, Right Now" (0:18)

MUSIC VIDEO AND POLITICS **175**

Figure 9.21 Specific imagery of Guantanamo Bay Detention Facility in "Love It If We Made It" (0:44)

United States, including images of Justice Brett Kavanaugh's confirmation hearing just after charges of sexual assault were brought against him, and the United States detention facility at Guantanamo Bay (Figure 9.21).

Lyrical and Musical Analysis

Just as the difference in performance space (restricted church, simulated soundstage) reflects a difference in the level of engagement between Pussy Riot and The 1975, the difference is also revealed in the 1975's conditionals in the title hook: "would" and "if." Pussy Riot is willing to actively "drive" Putin away, but the 1975 seems content to watch and hope. This disconnected stance is only slightly more engaged than a political song by another white artist a decade earlier, Billy Joel's "We Didn't Start the Fire," in which the artist not only distances himself from the atrocities, but claims they were not his (generation's) fault.

"We Didn't Start the Fire" seems to serve as a lyrical template for The 1975's coded approach to lyrics. Like the visuals, both songs feature lyrics that will be specific to some listeners but completely lost on others. Billy Joel's song takes the sheer number of references to the extreme by including *only* proper nouns. Eschewing complete sentence structure, he simply rattles off a ticker tape of 118 people, places, and events, most of which are politically controversial in some way. Remarkably, the references proceed in chronological order, meaning that it's likely an individual listener will recognize a subset of those references based on when they were born.

Joel's video is similar to "Love It If We Made It" in that the artist stands apart from any of this, reading a newspaper in the kitchen, air-drumming on a table, and posing for shots in front of the world burning (Figure 9.22). But unlike The 1975's video, Billy Joel's does not help the viewer understand the myriad political references by featuring text or even visual images of the political events described in the lyrics. Joel's website in fact hosts a fan-made video called a "Historically Accurate Almanac" that pairs each of the 118 lyrical references with corresponding visual footage.[11]

Unlike Billy Joel's video, which features no on-screen text, the lyrical-political references in "Love It If We Made It" are easier to understand while watching the video than when listening to the lyrics alone. This is because of two "value-added" features in the visuals. First, many of the song's lyrics are printed on screen at the moment they're heard. The specific manner in which most lyrics are presented on-screen in flashing text recalls Kanye West's

176   INTERPRETING SOCIOLOGY

Figure 9.22 Politically neutral footage in Billy Joel "We Didn't Start the Fire" (3:44)

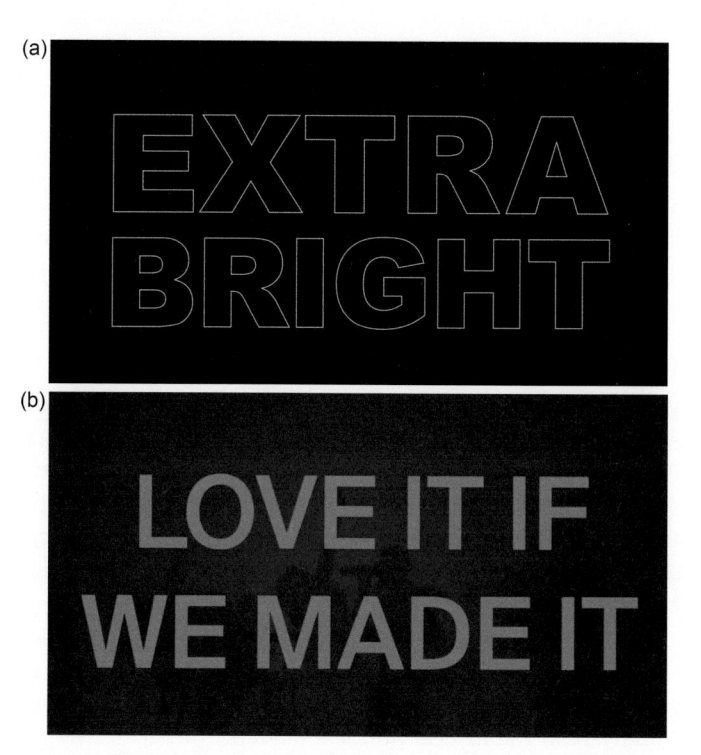

Figure 9.23 (a) and (b) Flashing text in Kanye West "All of the Lights" (1:25) and The 1975 "Love It If We Made It" (1:08)

"All of the Lights" (Figure 9.23a and 9.23b). Both videos are presented with disclaimers at their openings warning that they may cause seizures in photosensitive viewers.

This flashing text helps viewers understand coded lyrical references. One of Donald Trump's most misogynistic quotes "I MOVED ON HER LIKE A BITCH" flashes in all caps directly following a shot of his face at the same time that we hear those lyrics. Such shots also transform lyrics that could be perceived as general into more specific references within the

MUSIC VIDEO AND POLITICS   **177**

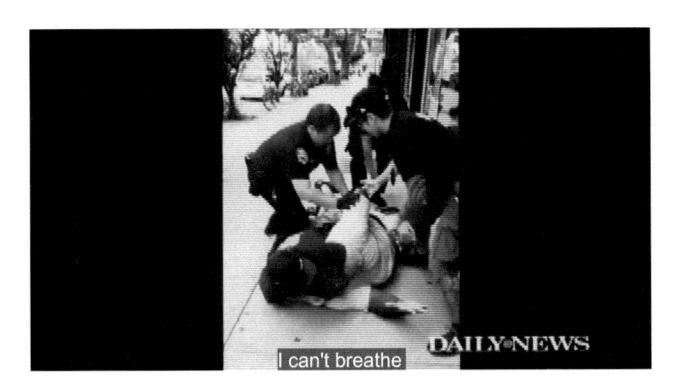

Figure 9.24 Eric Garner's murder with closed captioning in "Love It If We Made It" (0:37)

Figure 9.25 European refugee crisis in "Love It If We Made It" (un-captioned, 1:38)

context of the video. For example, "suffocate the Black man" is linked directly to the murder of Eric Garner by an image that shows his plea with closed captioning (Figure 9.24).

Even those lyrics that do not appear printed on-screen are usually illustrated by a descriptive shot. Such corresponding images usually track the lyrical progression quite closely. Three quick images at the beginning of verse one (sex, car exploding, man overdosing) describe three of the opening seven words. "Beach of drowning three-year olds" is cut to the now infamous image in Figure 9.25 of a drowned refugee child in the Mediterranean.

Still other connections between heard text and seen images are tenuous and/or subjective. These images are at best complementary to the heard lyrics. For example, while "the war has been incited" could have been cut to any number of armed conflicts in the past 20 years the specific shot used is of the World Trade Center. Finally, some coded and unexplained lyrical references are presented without a visual explanation. Listeners who know what melanin is, for example, might still be unaware of the controversies surrounding monetizing it.

I remember when "We Didn't Start The Fire" came out. My cousin and I were on a road trip and we wanted to be able to sing along. Since there was no "looking it up," we just traded turns with the headphones and a pad of paper writing down all of the lyrics we could. Being all of eight years old, almost none of the political references registered. I shudder to think what I wrote down for "Panmunjom," having never heard the word let alone its political significance. "Love It If We Made It," by contrast, seems like a video for the information age, when looking things up on the internet has become our hair-trigger response to uncertainty.

Table 9.1 Lingo you should know

Culture wars	Bleeped version	Edited version
Clean version		

NOTES

1 See Diane Railton and Paul Watson, *Music Video and the Politics of Representation* (Edinburgh: Edinburgh University Press, 2011): 10.

2 See James Davison Hunter, *Culture Wars: The Struggle to Define America* (New York: Basic Books, 1991).

3 This definition comes from Michael Eric Dyson, "Gangsta Rap and American Culture," in *The Hip Hop Reader*, edited by Timothy Francis Strode and Tim Wood, vol. 49, 172–181 (London: Pearson, 1995/2008).

4 For a more thorough analysis of Madonna's video, see Camille Paglia, *Sex, Art, and American Culture* (New York: Viking Books, 1992).

5 A more extensive list of videos censored by MTV for violence and other reasons is provided by Laura Finley in "Music Videos," in *Violence in Popular Culture: American and Global Perspectives*, edited by Laura Finley, 205–208 (Westport, CT: Greenwood, 2019).

6 See Mathias Bonde Korsgaard, "Changing Dynamics and Diversity in Music Video Production and Distribution," in *The Bloomsbury Handbook of Popular Music Video Analysis*, edited by Lori Burns and Stan Hawkins, 13–26 (London: Bloomsbury, 2019).

7 See Kat George, "How Music Videos Challenged the Male Gaze in 2015," *Dazed* (December 21, 2015), <https://www.dazeddigital.com/music/article/28899/1/how-music-videos-challenged-the-male-gaze-in-2015>

8 See Jillian Mapes, "The Chorus of #MeToo, and the Women Who Turned Trauma into Songs," *Pitchfork* (October 23, 2019), <https://pitchfork.com/features/article/2010s-on-women-singing-openly-about-abuse/>

9 Julia Craven points out the myriad visual connections between the video and Jim Crow era artwork in "Donald Glover's 'This Is America,' Through the Eyes of a Jim Crow Historian," *The Huffington Post* (May 9, 2018), <https://www.huffpost.com/entry/donald-glover-this-is-america-jim-crow-history_n_5af31588e4b00a3224efcc40>

10 See Tom Connick, "A State-Of-The-Planet Address: Every Reference in the 1975's Powerful 'Love It If We Made It' Video," *New Music Express* (October 16, 2018), <https://www.nme.com/blogs/nme-blogs/1975-love-it-if-we-made-it-video-explained-2390473>

11 https://www.billyjoel.com/news/watch-literal-fan-made-video-billy-joels-didnt-start-fire/

Index

Note: **Bold** page numbers refer to tables, *Italic* page numbers refer to figures and page numbers followed by 'n' refers to end notes.

AABA form 18
acoustic guitar 34, *34*
acoustic instruments 32–35, **37**
actor persona 53
Adele 52, 53, *53*, 126, *126*
Aenema (Tool) 105, *106*
Afro-Futurism 96, *96*, 98
Aguilera, Christina 150, *150*
album version 20
Alejandro (Gaga) 77, *78*
All of the Lights (West) 175–176, *176*
All the Stars (SZA and Lamar) 73, *73*
Alright (Lamar) 57, *58*, 143, *143*, 155–158, *156–158*
Alternative Nation 2
analog effects 111–114
Anderson, Laurie 43, *43*
Anderson.Paak 55, *55*
Andou Zine (Lamnawar) 153–154, *154*
Andress, Ingrid 35, *35*
Anthony, Marc 39, *40*, 150
Anuel AA 76, 77, *77*
Apple 134, *134*
Arcade Fire, The 101–102, *102*
arpeggio 47
artist persona 53
Asma Lamnawar 153–154, *154*
aspect ratios 96
auto-tune 41
auxiliary percussion 39
Avicii 125, *125*, 136–139, *136–139*, **137**

Bad Girls (M.I.A.) 170, *171*
Ballin (DJ Mustard and Rich) 56, *56*
Bandcamp 5
banjo 38
Barbie Dreams (Minaj) *20*, 20–21

Barna, Alyssa 28n8
Basket Case (Green Day) 85–86, *86*
bass layer 31
Beastie Boys 71, *71*
beat layer 31
Becky G 7, *8*
beginning-refrains 18
Beyoncé 11, 11n2, 69, *70*, 76, *76*, 98, 132, *132*, 155, 169, *169*
Big Boi 34
Big Freedia 127, *128*
Big Me (Foo Fighters) 70, *71*
Billboard 5, 39, 136, 149, 151, 152
Billie Jean (Jackson) 146–147, *147*
BIPOC (Black, Indigenous, and People of Color) musicians 143–144; hip-hop 148–150; MTV 150–155; 1980s Pop 146–148
bird's eye 92
Birthday (Perry) 173, *173*
Birth in Reverse (St. Vincent) 133, *133*
Bitch Better Have My Money (Rihanna) 131, *131*
Björk 116, *116*, 166
Black Hole Sun (Soundgarden) 58, *59*, 116
Black Is King (Beyoncé) 11n2, 98
Black Lives Matter 156–158, 168–170
Black Panther 73
Blake, David K. 48n5
Blanco, Benny 69, *70*
Blank Space (Swift) 18, *18*
bleeped version 162
Bloom (Sivan) 126, *127*
Bonham, Tracy 134, *135*
Born Free (M.I.A.) 166, *167*
bowed strings 39
Bowie, David 146
box notation 46, **46**
Boy With Luv (BTS) 152, *153*

breakup songs 55
Breeders, The *133*, 133–134
bridge 18
brightness 85
Bruno Mars 6, *7*, 66, *67*
BTS 152, *153*
Buchanan, Pat 162
buildup 16, 31
Bye Bye Bye (NSYNC) 94, *94*, 104, *105*

camera drones 92
Cannonball (The Breeders) *133*, 133–134
Can't Hold Us Down (Aguilera) 150, *150*
Cara, Alessia 55, *56*
Cardi B 6, *7*, 166, *166*
Cardigans, The 165, *165*
Cars, The 116, *117*
Cash, Johnny 89, *89*
Caston, Emily 122n2
cello 39
Cellophane (Twigs) 88, *88*, 90, 116, *118*
censorship 161–162; lyrical 162–163;
    visual 163–166
CGI setting 75, *75*
Chainsmokers, The 24, **25**, 107
Chandelier (Sia) 20, 51, *51*, **59**, 59–61, *60*, *61*, 111
Charli XCX 7
Chicks, The 79, *80*, 81n6
Childish Gambino 21, *21*, 22, 169–170, *170*, *171*
Chillin (Calderon) 3, *4*
chord layer 31
choreographed-performance videos 68
chorus 16
cinematography 16, *17*, 83; digital intermediate
    85–86, *86*; eye-level 90–91, *91*; handheld
    shots 93; HSB 84–90, *85*; low-angle/high-angle
    91–92; panning and tracking shots 92–93;
    point-of-view 90, *90*; PYNK (Monae) 94–98,
    95–98; shaky camera effect 93–94
cisgendered 126
clean versions 162
Closer (Chainsmokers) 24, 25, **25**, *25*, 107, **108**,
    108, 109, *109*, **110**, 111
club setting 75, *75*
CMA (Country Music Association) award 153
Cobain, Kurt 32, 44
coda 20, 21
color grading 85, *95*
color interpretation 86–90
Come On Eileen (Save Ferris) 40, *40*
complementary-narrative 69
compression 96–97
conflicting-narrative 69
continuity editing 111
Coolio 72, *73*

Cooper, Bradley 74, *74*
Cornell, Chris 58
Crash Test Dummies 68, *69*
Craven, Julia 178n9
Crombie, Fiona 88
cross-cutting 75
Cry Pretty (Underwood) 38, *38*
cultural moment 1, 7
culture wars 162
cuts 103
cutting rhythm 109, **110**, 111
Cypress Hill 149, *149*
Cyrus, Miley 129, *129*

Daddy Yankee 151, 152
Daft Punk 42, 53, *53*, 54
D.A.N.C.E. (Justice) 116, *117*
D'Angelo 150, *151*
Darkstar 171, *171*
Deal, Kim 33
delay 44
Delta Rae 167, *168*
dependent bridges 18
desire 56–57
Despacito (Fonzi and DaddyYankee) 151, *152*
destructive editing 103
diegesis 104
diegetic sound 104–106, *105*
digital effects 114–117, *115*
digital intermediate (D.I.) 85–86, *86*
digital speed effects 114, *115*
DJ Khaled 163, *164*
DJ Mustard 56, *56*
DJs 20, 21, 24, *24*, 54, 56, *56*, 148
Doja Cat 15, *15*, 26–28, **27**
dolly zoom 113, *114*, 120
double consciousness 156
Drake 6, *6*, 55, 87, 92, *92*, 101, 118, 121
Dr. Dre 72, *72*, 162, 162–163
drop 23
drum: break 21; machine 36, 39; sampling 36–37,
    37; set 35, 39
Du Bois, W. E. B. 156
Dyson, Michael Eric 162

Eastside (Halsey and Blanco) 69, *70*
edited version, MTV 163
editing: cutting rhythm 109, **110**, 111; diegetic
    vs. non-diegetic sound 104–106, *105–107*;
    offline *vs.* online 103–104; setting and form
    107–109, **108**; storyboard 101–103, *102*
effects, sounds 41
Eilish, Billie 5
electric bass 32, *33*
electric guitar 34

INDEX **181**

Electricity (Dua Lipa and Silk City) 87, *88*
electronic dance music (EDM) form 23–24, 37,
    41–44, 53, 76, 137
electronic instruments 36–38, **37**
Elicker, Martina 81n1
Elliott, Missy 6, 134–135
empowerment lyrics 55–56
end-refrain 18
En Vogue 21, 57
ethnic group 145
ethnicity 145
Even Flow (Pearl Jam) 65, *66*, 106
Everybody Dance Now3
explicit-narrative 68
extra-narrative 68
eye-level shots 90–91, *91*

fade-out 20
al Fakir, Salem 125, 136–139
Fall Out Boy 35, *35*, 41, 106, *107*
False Alarm (The Weeknd) 90, *90*, 130, *130*
Faraway Look (Yola) 89, 89–90
Feels Like Summer (Gambino) 170, *171*
Feist 92, *92*, 111
feminine pronouns 52
Ferguson, Brent 81n4, 169
filter sweep 44
Finesse (Cardi B and Bruno Mars) 7, *7*
first-person 52
FKA Twigs 88, *88*, 90, 116, *118*
Fonzi, Luis 151, *152*
Foo Fighters 32, 41, 53, 70, 71, *71*
form 15; chart 16, **17**; drum break, rap verse 21;
    EDM 23–24; *Juicy* (Doja Cat) 26–28; parametric
    form chart 24–26; postchorus 19–20; SSVC
    22–23; strophic 18–19; terminally climactic 22;
    verse/chorus 16–18; video intro, fade-out,
    coda 20–21
Formation (Beyoncé) 76, *76*
Forward (Beyoncé) 169, *169*
Frampton, Peter 41
Freedom (Rage Against the Machine) 78, *78*
Free Your Mind (Vogue) 21, 57
Fun 114, *115*

Gabriel, Peter 2, *2*, 113
Gaga, Lady 74, *74*, 77, *78*
Gangnam Style 4, *5*, 152
Gangsta's Paradise (Coolio) 72, *73*
Garageband 46, **46**, 103
Garner, Eric 157, 177, *177*
Gee (Girls Generation) 130, *130*
gels 84, *84*
gender and sexuality 127–128
gender-neutral 52

genre-parody 71
Gangsta's Paradise (Coolio) 72, *73*
Giant (Rag N Bone Man and Harris) 76, *76*
Gigantic (Pixies, The) 33, *33*
Girl or Boy (Shay) 128, *128*
Girls Generation 130, *130*
Girls Just Wanna Have Fun (Lauper) 18
Girls Like Girls (Kiyoko) 130, *131*
God is a Woman (Grande) 131, *132*
God's Plan (Drake) 92, *92*
Goodbye Earl (The Chicks) 79, *80*, 81
Got Money 41, *41*
Graham, Jazmine 134, *135*
Grande, Ariana 93, *93*, 131, *132*
Gray, Macy 87, *87*
Green Day 85–86, *86*
Green Light (Beyoncé) 132, *132*
Green Light (Lorde) 75, *75*
Grohl, Dave 32, 53
Guantanamo Bay 175, *175*
Guns N Roses 65, *66*, 84, 106

HAIM 67, *67*, 134, *135*
Haim, Danielle 134, *135*
Halsey 24, 25, **25**, *25*, 70, 107
Hancock, Herbie 36, 147, *147*
handheld shots 93, *93*
Hands Dirty (Delta Rae) 167, *168*
Hard Place (H.E.R.) 133, *133*
harmonizer effect 42, *42*
Harris, Calvin 67, *67*, 76, *76*
Heap, Imogen 42, 43
Heidemann, Kate 140n9
Heil Sound 41, *42*
H.E.R. 133, *133*
heteronormative 52
Hey Ya (Outkast) 23, **23**, 32, *33*, 34
Hide and Seek (Heap) 42, *42*
high-angle shot 92, *92*
hip-hop music 2, 3, 5, 15, 20–22, 33–37, 41, 57,
    68, 71, 120, 143, 144, 148–154, 156
Hips Don't Lie (Shakira) 56–57, *57*
Hölljes, Brittany 167
Hotline Bling (Drake) 55, 87
Houston, Whitney 16, *17*, 18, 84, *84*, 85,
    107, 148
Howard, Brittany 34, *34*, 37
How I Could Just Kill a Man (Cypress Hill) 149, *149*
Huang, Andrew Thomas 88, 117, *118*
hue 84–85
hue, saturation, brightness (HSB) 84–90, *85*
human persona 52
100 Gecs 128, *129*
Hunter, James Davison 162
Hurt (Cash) 89, *89*

Hurt (Nine Inch Nails) 112, *113*
hypersexualization 129, *129*, 130, *131*

If I Were a Boy (Beyoncé) 69, *70*
If You Had My Love (Lopez) 91, *91*
I Love Rock and Roll (Jett) 34, *34*, 40
imagery 77–78
Immigrants (We Get the Job Done) (K'Naan, Snow Tha Product, MC Riz, and Residente) 144–146, *144–146*
in-camera effects 112
in-camera zoom techniques 113–114
independent bridges 18
I Need To Know (Anthony) 39, 40, *40*
infantilization 130, *130*
In My Feelings (Drake) 6, *6*
instruments: acoustic 32–35, **37**; electronic 36–38, **37**; timbres and effects 40–45; *Umbrella* (Rihanna) 45–47; uncommon 38–40
intertextual videos 65, 70
In the End (Linkin Park) 75, *75*
intro 16
I Try (Gray) 87, *87*
I Wanna Dance With Somebody (Houston) 16, **17**, *17*, 18, 20, 84, *84*
I Write Sins, Not Tragedies (Panic! at the Disco) 163, *163*

Jackson, Michael 25, **26**, 114, *114*, 146–147, *147*
James, Rick 146
Jay-Z 3, *4*, 21, 31, 45–47, **46**, 77, *77*, 148, 164
Jean, Wyclef 56–57
Jepsen, Carly Rae 19, **20**
Jesus Jones 161, 172, *174*, 174–175
Jett, Joan 34, *34*, 41, 132
Joel, Billy 161, 172, 175, *176*, 177
Judah & The Lion 38, *38*
Juice (Lizzo) 68, *68*, 71
Juicy (Doja Cat) 15, *15*, 26–28, **27**
jump cuts 109
Jumpers (Sleater-Kinney) 67, *67*
Justice 116, *117*
Justify my Love (Madonna) 164, *165*, 166
Just Playing (Dreams) (Notorious B.I.G.) 20

Kahn, Joseph 18
Kamelemba (Sangaré) 154–155, *155*
Kaposi's Sarcoma 57
Karma Police (Radiohead) 22
KAROL G 76, *77*, 93
Keep Their Heads Ringin' (Dre) 72, *72*
Kennedy, Jen 109
Kesha 168, *168*
Keys, Alicia 39, *39*, 105, *105*, 111

Kiss (Prince) 18, 19, **19**
Kiyoko, Hayley 130, *131*
K'Naan 144, *144*, 146
Kravitz, Lenny 134, *135*

Lamar, Kendrick 57, *58*, 73, *73*, 143, *143*, 155–158
Latin Invasion 150
Lauper, Cyndi 18
Lavengood, Megan 48n3
lead guitar 32
Legend, John 169
Lemonade (Beyoncé) 155, 169
Les, Laura 128
LGBTQ+ 6, 9, 10, 98, 125, 126, *127*, 128, 130, 131, 153, 158, 172
Like a Prayer (Madonna) 77, 112, *113*
Lil' Nas X 5, *5*, 79, 153, *154*
Limp Bizkit 2, *3*
linear editing 103
Linkin Park 75, *75*
Lipa, Dua 87, *88*
live performance videos 65
Lizzo 68, *68*, 71, 106
Locked Out of Heaven (Mars) 66, *67*
Lopez, Jennifer 91, *91*
Lorde 75, *75*
Losing my Religion (R.E.M.) 111, *112*
A Lot (21 Savage) 152, *153*
love and sex 56–57
Love it if We Made it (The 1975) 161, 172–177, *173–177*
Low (Kravitz) 134, *135*
low-angle shot 91, *91*
lyrics 51; analysis 175–177; breakup songs 55; censorship 162–163; *Chandelier* **59**, 59–61, *60*, *61*; desire 56–57; persona 52–54; politics and social justice 57; pronouns 52; self-positive 55–56; surreal/nonsense 58; videos 172–173

McLeod, Ken 99n6
Madonna 77, 112, *113*, 164, *165*, 166
Make it Better (Anderson.Paak) 55, *55*
Make Me Feel (Monae) 127, *127*
Make You Feel My Love (Adele) 52–53, *53*, 126, *126*
Malawey, Victoria 128
male gaze 129–131
mandolin 38
Marshmello 23, **23**, 24, *24*, 54
masculine pronouns 52
mechanical effects 111
Méliès, Georges 111
melody layer 31
#MeToo 167–168, *168*
Meyers, Dave 101, 119

INDEX **183**

M.I.A. 166, *167*, 170, *171*
Minaj, Nicki *20*, 20–21
Miranda, Lin-Manuel 144
mise-en-scène 74–79, *79*
MK XYZ 6, *6*
Mmm Mmm Mmm Mmm (Crash Test Dummies) 68, *69*
Monae, Janelle 83, *83*, 94–98, *95–98*, 99n7, 127, *127*, 167, *167*
Monét, Victoria 93, *93*
Money (Cardi B) 166, *166*
Money Machine (100 Gecs) 128, *129*
Monopoly (Grande and Monét) 93, *93*
More Hearts than Mine (Andress) 35, *35*
Mother, Mother (Bonham) 134, *135*
Mother of God Drive Putin Away (Pussy Riot) 172, *172*
movie music videos (MMV) 72–74
MTV 1–3, 6, 9, 10, 39, 133, 134, 143, 146, 161–166; *see also* BIPOC (Black, Indigenous, and People of Color) musicians
MTV Jams 149
MTV Tr3s 151
Mulvey, Laura 125, 129
Murali Balaji 150
My Bloody Valentine 44, *44*
My Favourite Game (The Cardigans) 165, *165*
My Man (Becky G) 7, *8*

narratives 65; mise-en-scène 74–78; MMV 72–74; music video 68–70; parody and satire 70–71; performance video 65–68; *Ride Out in the Country* (Yola) 79–81
narrator persona 52
nature settings 76
Nine Inch Nails 112, *113*
1975, The 161, 172–177
99 Problems (Jay-Z) 3, *4*, 148, 164
Nirvana 31, **32**, 53
No Brainer (DJ Khaled) 163, *164*
non-binary 127
non-diegetic sound 104–106, *106*
non-linear editing 103
Nookie (Limp Bizkit) 2, *3*
Nothing Compares 2 U (O'Connor) 91, *91*
Notorious B.I.G. 20
Novoselic, Krist 32
NSFW (Not Safe for Work) video 166
NSYNC 94, *94*, 96, 104, *105*
Nuthin But a G Thang (Dr. Dre) *162*, 162–163
N.W.A. 149, *149*, 168

objectification 130, *130*, 150, *151*
Ocean, Frank 22, 153

O'Connor, Sinead 91, *91*
offline editing 103, 104
Old Town Road (Lil' Nas X) 5, 152, 153, *154*
1, 2, 3, 4 (Feist) 92, *92*, 111
120 Minutes 2
online editing 104
Only Shallow (My Bloody Valentine) 44, *44*
O Superman (Anderson) 43, *43*
Outkast 23, **23**, 33, *33*, 36
outro 18

Pagan Poetry (Björk) 166
Panic! at the Disco 163, *163*
panning shot 93
pansexuality 127, *127*
Paradise City (Guns N Roses) 65, *66*, 106
parametric form chart 24–26
parody 70–71
Party for One (Jepsen) 19, **20**
Pass It (MK XYZ) 6, *6*
Peaches 131, *132*, 166
Pearl Jam 65, *66*, 106
pedal steel guitar 38
performance video 65–68
Perry, Imani 156
Perry, Katy 173, *173*
personas 52–54, 126
piano 35
Pictures (Judah & The Lion) 38, *38*
Pin Secure (Darkstar) 171, *171*
Pixies, The 33, *33*
Pleasantville 85, *86*
plot twist 18, 79, 80, *80*, 81
point-of-view (POV) 90
pop music 1, 4, 6, 18, 26, 31, 37, 41, 44, 45, 146–148, 153
postchorus 19–20, 23
Prayin (Kesha) 168, *168*
Pray to God (HAIM and Harris) 67, *67*
Preach (Legend) 169, *169*
prechorus 16
Prince 18, 19, **19**, 91, 148
pronouns 52
Prophets of the Hood: Politics and Poetics in Hip Hop (Perry) 156
pump-up chorus 16
Pussy Riot 172, *172*
PYNK (Monae) 83, *83*, 94–98, *95–98*, 167, *167*

race and ethnicity 144–146; *see also* BIPOC (Black, Indigenous, and People of Color) musicians
Rage Against the Machine 78, *78*
Rag N Bone Man 76, *76*
Raise a Man (Keys) 39, *39*, 105, *105*, 111

Rap City 3, 148, 151
rap verse 21
Real World, The 3, 151
Red Hot Chili Peppers 22, **22**
reflexive settings 76
refrain 18
R.E.M. 111, *112*
Rent (Big Freedia) 127, *128*
Residente 145–146, *146*
reverb 44
Reznor, Trent 164
rhythm guitar 32
Rich, Roddy 56, *56*
Ride Out in the Country (Yola) 65, 79–81, *80*
Right Here, Right Now (Jesus Jones) 161, 172, *174*, 174–175
Rihanna 21, 31, 45, **46**, 47, 77, *77*, 131, *131*, 166
riserchorus 23
riserchorus-drop 24
Ritual (Marshmello) 23, **23**, *24*
Riz MC 145, *145*, 146
rock band 44, 53, 67, 68, 77, 105, 111, 114, 134, 161
Rockit (Hancock) 36, 147, *147*
rock music 1–2, 18, 22, 32–34, 37, 137, 146, 151
Roland 808 drum machine 34, 36, *36*
Romanek, Mark 87, 164
Roots, The 71, *72*, 91, 163
Rub (Peaches) 131, *132*, 166
Rule the World (2Chainz) 104, *104*

Sabotage (Beastie Boys) 71, *71*
Salt N Pepa 148, *148*
sample 36
sampling 20
Sangaré, Oumou 154–155, *155*
satire 70–71
saturation 85
Save Ferris 40, *40*
Scars to Your Beautiful (Cara) 55, *56*
Scott, Travis 101, 117–121
second-person 52
Secreto (Anuel AA and KAROL G) 76, *77*
Self-Control (Ocean) 22
self-positivity 55–56
setting and form 107–109, **108**
Seven Nation Army (The White Stripes) 132
sexuality and gender 127–128; persona 126; *see also* women
Shadowboxer (Apple) 134, *134*
Shakira 56–57, *57*
shaky camera effect 93–94, *94*
Shallow (Gaga and Cooper) 74, *74*
Shay, Dani 128, *128*
Sia 51, *51*, **59**, 59–61, **60**, *61*
Sia and David Guetta 44, *45*, 68, *69*

Sicko Mode (Scott) 101, 117–121, *118–120*
sidechaining 44
Silhouettes (Avicii) 125, *125*, 136–139, *136–139*, **137**
Silk City 87, *88*
simulated-performance videos 66
Sivan, Troye 7, 126, *127*
Sleater-Kinney 67, *67*
Sledgehammer (Gabriel) 2, *2*, 113
Slowdive 44, *45*
slow-motion 112
Smashing Pumpkins, The 39, *39*, 58, 111, *112*
Smells Like Teen Spirit (Nirvana) 31, 32, **32**, 44
Snow Tha Product 145, *145*, 146
social construction 144
social justice 57
Sony BVE-910 linear editing machine 103, *103*
Soul Train 146
Soundcloud 5
Soundgarden 58, *59*, 116
soundstage-performance videos 66
Speakerboxxx/The Love Below 34
special effects: analog effects 111–114; digital effects 114–117, *115*
specific-parody video 71
spectrogram 44
speed effects 112
Sprawl II (The Arcade Fire) 101–102, *102*
Star is Born, A 74
Stay High (Howard) 34, *34*, 37
Steps, The (HAIM) 134, *135*
Sterbenz, Maeve 62n5
stereotyping 145
stompbox effect *43*, 43–44
Stonemilker (Björk) 116, *116*
stop-motion effects 112–113, *114*
storyboard 101–103, *102*
Straight Outta Compton (N.W.A.) 149, *149*, 168
strophic form 18–19
St. Vincent 133, *133*
Suburbs, The 101
Sugamamas, The 132, *132*
Sugar For the Pill (Slowdive) 44, *45*
Sugar We're Goin' Down (Fall Out Boy) 35, *35*, 40, 106, *107*
Summach, Jay 28n3
Supaman 154, *155*
super-simple verse/chorus form (SSVC) 22–23, **23**
surreal lyrics 58, *59*
Swift, Taylor 18, *18*, 107
synth-bass 36
synthesizers 36
synth-lead 36
synth-pads 36
SZA 73, *73*

Taggart, Drew 24, 25
talk box 41, 42, *42*
Tego Calderón 3, 4
telecine machine 84
terminal climax 22
terminally climactic form 22
third-person 52
This is America (Gambino) 21, *21*, 22, 169–170, *170*
Thompson, Tessa 98, 99n7
Thriller (Jackson) 25, **26**, *26*, 114, *114*
TikTok 5, 93
timbral mismatch 134
timbre 40–41
time-lapse 112
#TimesUp 167–168, *168*
Titanium (Sia and David Guetta) 44, *45*, 68, *69*
TLC 57, *58*, 149
Tonight, Tonight (Smashing Pumpkins) 39, *39*, 111, *112*
Tool 105, *106*
To Pimp A Butterfly (Lamar) 143, 156
T-Pain effect 41, *41*
tracking shot 93
trans artists 127
travel settings 76
12-bar blues 19, **19**
21 Savage 152, *153*
2Chainz 104, *104*

Umbrella (Rihanna and Jay-Z) 45–47, 77, *77*
Under the Bridge (Red Hot Chili Peppers) 22, **22**
Underwood, Carrie 38, *38*
Untitled (How Does It Feel?) (D'Angelo) 150, *151*
upright bass 39

Vernallis, Carol 12n7, 62n4, 81n2, 122n3
verse 16, 23
verse/chorus form 16–18, 27
victim trope 130

video intro 20
Video Music Awards (VMA) 2, 9
Vintage Funk Kit 03 (VFK) 46, **46**
viola 39
violin 39
virtual reality (VR) 116, *116*
visible minorities 144
visual analysis 172–175
visual censorship 163–166
vocal manipulation 41
vocoder 43, *43*
Voyage to the Moon (Méliès) 111

Walker, George 143
Waterfalls (TLC) 57, *58*, 149
We Are Young (Fun) 114, *115*
We Didn't Start the Fire (Joel) 161, 172, 175, *176*, 177
Weeknd, The 90, *90*, 130, *130*
Westerberg, Emma 83, 94–97
West, Kanye 175–176, *176*
What They Do (The Roots) 71, *72*, 91, 163, *164*
White, Meg 132
White Stripes, The 132
Why? (Supaman) 154, *155*
wind instrument 40
women 128–129; instrumentalists and composers 132–136; male gaze 129–131
worm's eye shot 91
Wrecking Ball (Cyrus) 129, *129*

Yetnikoff, Walter 146
Yola 65, 79–81, *80*, 89, 89–90
Yo! MTV Raps 2, 148, 149, 151
yonic imagery 131
You Might Think (The Cars) 116, *117*
YouTube 1, 2, 4, 9, 12n7, 51, 61, 128, 143, 151–153, 155, 162, 166, 169, 172

Ziegler, Maddie 51, *51*, 60, 61

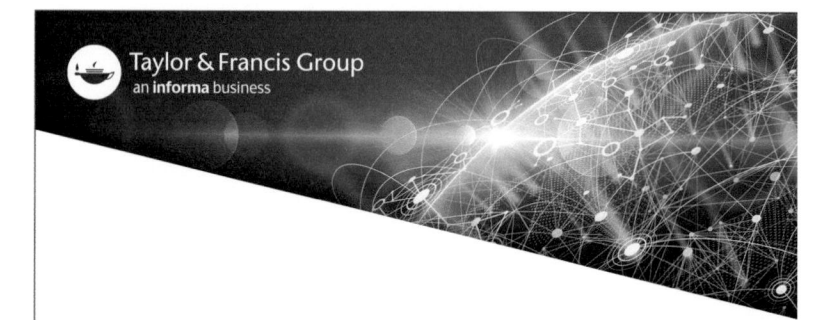

Taylor & Francis eBooks

www.taylorfrancis.com

A single destination for eBooks from Taylor & Francis
with increased functionality and an improved user
experience to meet the needs of our customers.

90,000+ eBooks of award-winning academic content in
Humanities, Social Science, Science, Technology, Engineering,
and Medical written by a global network of editors and authors.

TAYLOR & FRANCIS EBOOKS OFFERS:

A streamlined
experience for
our library
customers

A single point
of discovery
for all of our
eBook content

Improved
search and
discovery of
content at both
book and
chapter level

REQUEST A FREE TRIAL
support@taylorfrancis.com